HOLLAND HOUSE

Charles James Fox by K. A. Hickel

HOLLAND HOUSE

Leslie Mitchell

Duckworth

First published in 1980 by
Gerald Duckworth & Co. Ltd.
The Old Piano Factory
43 Gloucester Crescent, London NW1

ISBN 0 7156 1116 X

British Library Cataloguing in Publication Data

Mitchell, Leslie
    Holland House.
    1. Holland, Henry Richard Vassall Fox, *Baron*
    2. Holland, Elizabeth Fox, *Baroness*
    3. Politicians – Great Britain – Biography
    4. Politicians' wives – Great Britain – Biography
    I. Title
    941.07′092′2   DA522.H/

    ISBN 0-7156-1116-X

Photoset by
Specialised Offset Services Limited, Liverpool
and printed in Great Britain by
Redwood Burn Limited, Trowbridge & Esher

To M.

Contents

Illustrations

Preface

I would like to thank all the owners of manuscript collections cited in this book, in particular the Warden and Fellows of All Souls College, Oxford and George Howard Esq., of Castle Howard. I am also indebted to the librarians and archivists of the British Museum and County Record Officers, without whose assistance any work of scholarship would be a much more perilous undertaking. The same point applies with equal force to the Grants Committee of the British Academy, without whose generosity many types of research would prove to be impossible.

Many of my pupils and friends have helped with the transcription and translation of manuscripts, and I would like to express my sincere gratitude to Glenn Black, Adam Brett, Enrique Conill, Janet Day, Andrew Duncan, Brett Haran, John McDowell, David Morton, Christopher Pelling, Charles Powell and Jonathan Powell. I hope that they will not think their efforts have been wasted.

I am grateful to Lord Moyne and the Robert Dawson Studio for the picture of Lady Holland, and to the National Portrait Gallery for the others.

University College, Oxford   L.M.

1

Holland House and the Hollands

Holland House stood roughly two miles from Marble Arch on
the main road running out of London towards the west. When
Henry Fox, 1st Baron Holland, bought the property, in 1767,
the turnpike road to town made journeys uncomfortable and,
still passing through open countryside, gave scope for the
more enterprising kind of highwayman. When the 3rd Lord
Holland died, in 1840, the sprawl of London had engulfed the
House. It now stood alone in the centre of Holland Park,
surrounded by suburban villas and artisan terraces. This
development was not resented by the family. Indeed, they
tried hard to find profitable speculations within it. Above all,
it had always been Holland family policy that London should
come out to meet them and not vice versa.

Previous owners had already endowed the House with a
good history, even before the Fox family came to add to it.[1]
Begun in 1604, Holland House had bankrupted its builder, Sir
Walter Cope. Through marriage, it passed to the Rich Earls
of Holland, and later Warwick, who were Cavaliers in the
most romantic vein and rakes in the Restoration. Two
dissolute Earls in succession were enough to bring the Rich
family to ruin. The arrival of Henry Fox and his family did
nothing to raise the property's reputation. In 1744, Fox had
eloped with the eldest daughter of the Duke of Richmond. As
Paymaster General, he had secured the family fortunes by the

1. For a full discussion of the history of the House, see L. Sanders, *The Holland
House Circle* (London 1908), pp. 1-11.

adroit manipulation of public money. The line between corruption and what were regarded as the natural perquisites of office-holding was a thin one. Critics endlessly accused the Fox family of buying Holland House out of public funds. For three generations, the family would be stung into reply by such claims.

If Henry Fox was skilled in acquiring money, his sons were just as practised at losing it. Both his elder sons, Stephen Fox, 2nd Baron Holland, and Charles James Fox were addicted to gambling, the latter compulsively. At their father's death in 1774, the depredations from gambling losses were such that the family could never again feel financially secure. Throughout its greatest period, Holland House was always bedevilled by financial worries. It was almost providential that Stephen Fox only outlived his father by a matter of months, leaving a son and a daughter as minors. The children could be taken in by sympathetic relatives and the House itself could be let.

Henry Richard Fox, who became 3rd Baron Holland at the age of one in 1774, therefore inherited a very chequered family career. If Holland House was to become one of the great meeting points of the Whig party, the Fox family were barely Whigs at all at the time of his accession to the title. His grandfather had served governments of all complexions. His uncle Charles was a junior minister in Lord North's government. The Hollands could claim none of the ancestral Whig feelings of Cavendish Dukes of Devonshire or Russell Dukes of Bedford. In Whig terms, they were parvenus. In addition, their social position was always put at risk by memories of Henry Fox's peculation and Charles James Fox's mastery of vice. Even the Holland title was somewhat second-hand, being taken over from the Rich family. The individuality and independence of Holland House stemmed from these facts. At the outset, they were socially set apart from the mainstream, and this applies as much to mainstream Whiggery as to their opponents. In a party which claimed Demosthenes among its progenitors, the Hollands must have looked very new indeed.

The family's greatest asset was talent. Henry Fox, the 1st

Baron, was accused of corruption, but he knew more about the management of politics than any of his contemporaries. Charles James Fox was reckless, even debauched, but he was just too clever to ignore. The clan feeling was very strong.[2] It was based on the belief that the family was able, socially daring and intellectually adventurous. All these trends were confirmed in the new Lord Holland by the adoration he felt for his uncle, Charles James Fox, who was the dominant intellectual influence in his life. After his mother's death left him an orphan in 1778 Holland's official guardian was another uncle, the Earl of Upper Ossory, but it was Charles Fox whose creature he became. Under his influence, Eton and Oxford[3] were cast aside; 'I confess that considering Oxford in any way I cannot imagine to myself a worse place for the education of a Gentleman. There is pedantry without science, insolence without learning, and intolerance without firmness.'[4] As a remedy, Charles Fox sent him to Europe. From 1791 to 1796, Holland toured Europe, and came home knowing French, Spanish and Italian with passable German and Portuguese.[5] Thus magnificently equipped, he embarked on an involvement with European affairs that was to become one of the major themes of Holland House politics.

With this ancestry, there was never the slightest doubt that Holland would not ultimately find a career in politics. Unlike his uncle and grandfather, however, it could not be a career based on oratory. Holland's speeches in the Lords were startlingly infrequent, being plagued at first by a youthful stammer and then by excruciating attacks of gout. As late as 1835, the nervousness involved in public speaking had not worn off. Holland was relieved that 'friend and foe ... seemed

2. Add. MS. 51737, f 16; Holland to Caroline Fox, 9 March 1804.

3. Holland was an undergraduate at Christ Church as the contemporary of George Canning, Charles Jenkinson, Lord Morpeth and Bobus Smith. He and Canning established a reputation for radicalism, and sat at the feet of Dr Parr, who, much to the embarrassment of the College authorities, insisted on making periodic visitations to Christ Church. See W. Hinde, *George Canning* (London 1973), pp. 22-3.

4. Add. MS. 51733, f 116-7; Holland to Caroline Fox, 21 Nov. 1795.

5. In addition, Holland knew Latin and Greek of course. He was prepared to devote whole letters to correcting Brougham's attempts at Greek in terms of tense, metre and accents. Holland to Brougham, 10 Sept. 1830; Brougham MSS. 14957.

pleased to encourage an old and shattered Debater and
treated the somewhat fumbling efforts of an old performer of
62 with all the tenderness which a maiden speech generally
secures'.[6] There could, however, be no opting out. The name
of Fox demanded a public career, and the obligation was
vigorously passed on by Holland to his own son.[7] Even so, it
can hardly have been accident that, with these embarrassments, Holland should prefer to pursue politics in the salon-
dining of Holland House than in Westminster debates.

A family name and its tradition offers refuge as well as
imposing obligations. One of the most important debates
carried on among his contemporaries involved the question of
how far Holland depended on the Fox name as a means of
intellectual support. Many people took the view that his
frequent lapses of judgment stemmed from the fact that he
had never been accustomed to making decisions for himself.
Instead, he simply accepted political dictation from Charles
Fox, from his sister Caroline, and ultimately from his wife.
John Russell, 6th Duke of Bedford, one of Holland's oldest
friends, thought him 'entirely without judgment or discretion,
and this I have thought for the last 22 years'.[8] This important
problem must not be prejudged here, but it is readily under-
standable that nervousness and insecurity could avoid
responsibility and decision-making by simply applying to any
given situation a family tradition handed down and
interpreted by other people.

Certainly his strengths were those associated with the Fox
family. He was, by common consent, one of the most
aggreeable and amiable men of his generation.[9] He was
capable of unaffected friendship. As a companion, he had a
Pickwickian warmth and toleration that was irresistible. Like
Charles James Fox, he was the best dinner-table company in

6. Add. MS. 51871, f 905; Holland's Political Journal, 25 Aug. 1835.

7. Add. MS. 51748, f 84-5; Holland to Henry Fox, 8 March 1820.

8. Bedford to Lord William Russell, 19 Jan. 1829; G. Blakiston, *Lord William
Russell and his Wife* (London 1972), p.182.

9. R. Sheridan to Mrs Sheridan, Aug. 1815; ed. C. Price, *The Letters of Richard
Brinsley Sheridan* (Oxford 1966), iii 227-8. See also, Sébastiani to Mme. Adelaide, 6
Aug. 1838; Bibliothèque Nationale n.a.fr. 12220, f 70.

London, with a particular talent for bringing out the best in young people. His sense of humour and wit could keep pace with any of his guests. The news that the Prince Regent had decided to give up the wearing of corsets produced the notion that 'Royalty without support makes a bad figure – what would such a relaxation of all restraint produce ... what great bodies would it separate ... it would clearly subvert or rather overturn and demolish the form of our happy constitution'.[10] Like his Uncle Charles too, Holland 'was not extremely fond of sporting'.[11] Even the occasional game of cricket in which Charles Fox indulged[12] held no attraction for Holland. But he followed him so exactly in a total indifference to religion that honest churchwomen were alarmed as to what his future in eternity might be.[13] There was little that was heroic in his character and much that was wayward, but the Fox family gift for inspiring genuine affection was his in full measure.

Holland House then had no hero in the conventional sense. It may, however, have had a heroine. Elizabeth Vassall, the future Lady Holland, was born in Golden Square, Soho in 1771. Her family owned large estates in Cornwall County, Jamaica, and, when her father died, in 1795, she became an heiress. She grew up to be one of the most beautiful women of the last decades of the eighteenth century. These qualities, together with the West Indian fortune, made her a very attractive proposition in the London marriage market. In 1786, she was married to Sir Godfrey Webster, when she was fifteen and he forty-nine. As an epithalamium, a minor poet ventured the following:

> Imperial nymph, ill suited is thy name
> To speak the wonders of that radiant frame
> Wherever Thy sovereign form on Earth is seen
> All eyes are vassals; thou alone art Queen.[14]

10. Holland to Ebrington, 23 Dec. 1817; Fortescue MSS. 1262M/FC75.
11. *Parl. Deb.*, vol. 74 1074-5, 2 June 1818.
12. Perhaps characteristically, he was usually run out between the wickets.
13. Mrs G. Villiers to Clarendon, c. 25 Oct. 1840; Sir H. Maxwell, *Life and Letters of Lord Clarendon* (London 1913), i 213.
14. S. Keppel, *Sovereign Lady* (London 1974), p.3.

Three children were born to this marriage, but, perhaps predictably, all real affection between husband and wife was missing, whereupon the young Lady Webster began to cause difficulties. Rumours proliferated and her standing in London society was brought into question.

To ease the situation, Sir Godfrey took his wife abroad in January 1791, and, with a break of only four months, Lady Webster remained out of England until June 1796. Like Lord Holland, this long stay abroad was a determining experience in her life, and gave her a liking for foreign travel and a mastery of foreign languages that almost equalled his own. She heard Robespierre speak in the National Assembly, she met Mme de Staël for the first time in Switzerland, and went on to establish herself as one of the principal favourites at the Neapolitan Court. She developed what she called 'a determined love of being abroad'. In the English colonies in Italy, there was a lack of restraint in social attitudes that particularly appealed to her. Sir Godfrey found the pace of his wife's movements too much for him, and he returned home early in 1792 leaving Lady Webster to deal with the Continent on her own terms.[15]

These terms were exacting. She later boasted about her independent line,

> My principles were of my own finding, both religious and moral, for I never was instructed in abstract or practical religion, and as soon as I could think at all, chance directed my studies; for though my parents were as good and as virtuous people as ever breathed, and I was always an only child, yet I was entirely left, not from system, but from fondness and inactivity, to follow my bent.[16]

She sometimes joined other travellers like the Devonshires and Spencers, but more often took her own way. Her greatest confidante was Lady Bessborough, the mother of Lady Caroline Lamb, whom Byron characterised as 'the hack whore of the last century'.[17] Together, these ladies embarked

15. ibid., p.13 seq.
16. ibid., p.6.
17. Byron to J. Murray, 31 Aug. 1820; ed. L. Marchand, *Byron's Letters and Journals*, vii p.169.

on what almost amounted to hunting expeditions for young
Englishmen visiting Italy as part of the Grand Tour. In these
five years, Lady Webster had affairs with Viscount Morpeth,
Sir Gilbert Elliot, William Wyndham and, above all, with
Thomas Pelham.[18] If her husband had seen residence abroad
as the answer to embarrassment, the cure was worse than the
disease.

Lady Webster's only experience of England between 1791
and 1796 was a brief visit between September and December
1793. Although she was presented at Court,[19] she was already
a highly controversial woman, whose attitudes and manners
gave cause for gossip and concern. A visit from her was
already compromising, and Sussex neighbours of the
Websters were not impressed by her behaviour;

> Lady Webster (or the Diavo-lady) will be at Stanmer this week, and
> (hang her!) next week she will probably do us the honour of a visit ...
> I had rather see old Beelzebub a thousand times! ... Her Ladyship
> has entirely adopted foreign Manners and Customs, our family will, I
> suppose, never recover from the astonishment they were thrown into
> when they discovered André, the Italian, washing his Lady's feet
> when she went to Bed.[20]

Italian, Spanish or negro servants were to become a feature of
Holland House life, and they contributed to the foreignness of
that milieu, which was one of its major characteristics. Lady
Webster could only stand the constraints of England for three
months, and her departure abroad was greeted with relief;
'She says she means to go abroad ... Heaven grant she may
keep her Resolution.'[21] There was no doubt in Lady Webster's
mind that for anyone of spirit or intellect almost anywhere
was preferable to England.

Very early in life therefore, the future Lady Holland had
acquired the reputation that would be hers for the next fifty

18. Add. MSS. 51706, f 109; T. Pelham to Lady Webster, 21 Jan. 1794. ibid., f 180;
19 June 1794.

19. S. Keppel, *The Sovereign Lady*, pp. 44-5.

20. Maria Holroyd to Miss Firth, 12 Sept. 1793; ibid., p.43.

21. Maria Holroyd to Miss Firth, 22 Sept. 1793; J. Adeane, *The Girlhood of Maria
Josepha Holroyd* (London 1896), pp. 238-9.

years. Macaulay's description of her, written in 1831, could have been applied just as well in the 1790s:

> She is a bold looking woman, with the remains of a fine figure, and the air of Queen Elizabeth. A great lady, fanciful, hysterical and hypochondriacal, ill-natured and good natured, sceptical and superstitious, afraid of ghosts, and not of God – would not for the world begin a journey on a Friday morning and thought nothing of running away from her husband.[22]

Towards the end of her life, memoirs began to appear about events in the 1790s, which not surprisingly gave Lady Holland a great deal of pain. In the sober 1840s, the peccadillos of a different generation looked particularly black. Her self-defence was interesting. When accused of being 'flighty and coquettish' by the Malmesbury Diaries, Lady Holland pleaded simply that 'my weakness was a desire to be reckoned what I never was, clever'.[23] If she had claimed an untrained intelligence, she might have been nearer the mark.

The crucial point is, however, that when Lady Webster met Holland in Florence in January 1794, they already had much in common. Both had had difficult, even eccentric childhoods. Both were sceptics about religion. Both came from slurred moral backgrounds. Above all, both enjoyed all things European. Initially, the only difference between them concerned politics. Lady Webster had not as yet shown any great interest in the subject, and found Holland's views very extreme. She expressed her relief that, being out of England, he 'was out of the way of saying foolish, violent things'.[24] Apart from this one fact, they complemented each other almost perfectly. In March 1795, Holland sent her the first of his birthday odes which were to be forwarded annually until his death in 1840. In it he hailed a certain lady who was heard to pray:

22. J. Clive, *Thomas Babington Macaulay* (London 1973), p.210.

23. Lady Holland to Henry Fox, 25 March 1845; ed. Ilchester, *Elizabeth, Lady Holland to Her Son 1821-1845* (London 1946), pp. 225-6.

24. *Sovereign Lady*, p.48.

Give me, indulgent Genius, give
Midst learned cabinets to live,
Midst curiosities, collections,
Specimens, medals and dissections.
With books of every tongue and land
All difficult to understand.[25]

In a real sense, such a prayer was also, for Holland,
autobiographical.

The couple returned to England in June 1796. The
following July, Sir Godfrey[26] and Lady Webster were divorced
by Act of Parliament. Under the terms of the settlement,
Webster received £6,000 in damages and the promise of
£7,000 a year from the revenue of the West Indian estates.
When the Hollands finally married therefore, in July 1797,
they did so in straitened financial circumstances. Even so, it
was to be a remarkably successful marriage. Lady
Bessborough, who attended the ceremony, reported that she
had never seen 'creatures so happy. He flew down to meet me,
kiss'd me several times, ne vous déplaise, and can do nothing
but repeat her name. Such perfect happiness as theirs scarcely
ever was instanc'd before. Un tel hymen c'est le Ciel sur la
terre'.[27] The birthday ode for 1831 finished with the lines

One truth, which be it verse or prose
From my heart's heart sincerely flows
I loved you much at twenty-four
I love you better at threescore.[28]

The quality of Holland House life depended on its owners
complementing each other. The whole phenomenon came to
an end effectively with Lord Holland's death in 1840.[29]

25. ibid., p.58.

26. Sir Godfrey Webster committed suicide, in June 1800, and his death plunged
the Hollands into protracted legal wranglings over the extent to which Lady
Holland's Vassall family property should be divided between her three children by
Webster as well as by her Holland children.

27. Lady Bessborough to Lord G. Leveson Gower, 9 July 1797; ed. Lady Granville,
The Letters of Lord Granville Leveson Gower (London 1916), i 162-3.

28. Add. MSS. 51730, f 57; March 1831.

29. Add. MSS. 51747, f 180, Lady Holland to Caroline Fox, 15 May 1841.

The social price to be paid was heavy. When Holland House opened its doors, it did so in the shadow of opprobrium. The new Lady Holland's record was unenviable. The divorce had been the scandal of the year, and a son, Charles Richard, had been born to them nine months before they were married. For two or three years, Lady Holland could not attend any social function without causing confusion and embarrassment.[30] Her former husband hoped that

> Lady H. will descend to ordinary and practical Conduct in future – for another such Coup will render Her Situation not pleasant – I never could Convince Her of the necessity of Conformity to Established Rules. She always looked upon them as formed by Dull People, and Calculated for Des Esprits bornes – But as such Make up the Mass of Mankind they Must not be openly shocked, or ill treated.[31]

Worst of all, even the toleration of the Fox family had been tried beyond endurance. Charles James Fox refused to attend the wedding, and Holland's sister, Caroline Fox, said nothing. The estrangement of the Hollands, not only from London society, but also from their own family, was complete. Holland could only entreat his sister 'not to join in the common outcry' against his wife.[32] The burr of moral disapproval never quite escaped them. The painter Farington, on learning that Lady Holland's bed was made up by male servants, thought her 'altogether a sensualist'.[33] As late as 1838, the French ambassador had to reassure his Court that, when Lady Holland visited Paris, 'elle ne vous fera aucune demande de venir chez la Reine, ainsi vous serez à votre aise'.[34]

30. Lady Harriet to Lady Georgiana Cavendish, Nov. 1798; ed. Sir G. Leveson Gower, *The Letters of Lady Harriet Cavendish 1796-1809* (London 1940), p.7.

31. Sir G. Webster to J. Barham, 13 July 1799; Bodleian Library, Clarendon MSS., c 338. See also Maria Holroyd to Miss Firth, 10 June 1796, *The Girlhood of Maria Holroyd*, p.390.

32. Add. MSS. 51734, ff 3-5, Holland to Caroline Fox, July 1796.

33. Diary of Joseph Farington, 4 Sept. 1806; ed. J. Greig, *The Farington Diary* (London 1922-1924), iii 300.

34. Sébastiani to Mme. Adelaide, 28 Aug. 1838; Bibliothèque Nationale, n.a.fr. 12220 ff 79-80.

The great period of Holland House began then, in 1797, with this remarkable marriage. It had united two very powerful forces in politics. First, the Fox name was, by that time, almost synonymous with the title Whig. Charles James Fox so dominated the party after the splits and divisions over the French Revolution, that his views were the party's views.[35] Accordingly, his nephew and political heir had an assured position in politics which no amount of moral disapproval could dispel. Lady Holland was attaching herself to a firm mooring in English politics. Social rehabilitation might be just one of the benefits to accrue. On the other hand, Holland had found a wife whose energy, wealth and determination made up for gaps in his own personal inheritance. The combination was formidable. Lady Holland very quickly came to grasp the essentials of the Fox family creed, and she took them over with a readiness that startled and delighted her husband.[36] The Fox family were guaranteed a third generation of political influence in the combination of Lord and Lady Holland. Either alone might have come to very little. Together they could not be ignored and the setbacks of 1797 were likely to be temporary.

Both Lord and Lady Holland saw the Holland House circle as a means of exercising power. Their European experience must have proved to them that the maintenance of a successful salon was as effective a weapon in politics as any other. The special quality of Holland House must lie in part in the fact that it most closely resembled the famous salons of Europe. It was the modus operandi for intelligent women to take a part in public affairs. Lady Holland firmly believed that 'all women of a certain age and in a situation to achieve it should take to Politicks'.[37] When Mme Recamier or Mme de Staël dined at Holland House, they must have recognised a kindred spirit. It was distinctive and uncompromising. If hearing the debate on the second reading of the Reform Bill of 1832 meant sitting with other women in the Ladies' Gallery she preferred

---

35. See below, Chapter Two.
36. Add. MSS. 51735, f 35; Holland to Caroline Fox, 26 May 1798.
37. Lady Bessborough to Lord G. Leveson Gower, 5 Feb. 1811; *The Letters of Lord G. Leveson Gower*, ii 381.

not to hear it at all.[38] As an eminent London physician observed, she preferred an arena in which she alone could hold sway:

> Supreme in her own mansion and family, she exercised a singular and seemingly capricious tyrany, even over guests of the highest rank ... Capricious it seemed, but there was in reality *intention* in all she did; and this intention was the maintenance of power, which she gained and strenuously used, though not without discretion in fixing its limits.[39]

By definition, the holding of a salon implied the wish to meddle.[40] Guests were lobbied for votes on particular issues. Ambassadors were a speciality of the House and there are cases of their reports being written immediately after dinner. The Hollands were even sufficiently close to London to allow them to host Cabinet meetings at moments of crisis. And of course, the patronage element, indispensable to any salon, was very much in evidence. An endless stream of young men were put through their paces and then found employment if their talent sufficiently impressed. These were the methods by which an energetic woman came to grips with the male-dominated world of politics. The rôle had its limitations, as someone of Talleyrand's experience knew well:

> Elle place une assertion, et sa preuve est son secret. Elle jette des propos, mais elle ne développe pas. Elle fait semblant de tout sçavoir, car cela lui donne de l'importance, et quand elle ne sçiait pas, elle invente, et la méchanceté vient de fausses nouvelles.[41]

The point is well made, but, even so, the celebrated series of Holland House dinners accumulated experience and therefore importance.

Such occasions demanded a female presidency. Lord

---

38. Lady Holland to Henry Fox, 9 April 1832; *Elizabeth, Lady Holland to her Son*, p.132.

39. Diary of Sir Henry Holland; *Sovereign Lady*, p.249.

40. Lady Bessborough to Lord G. Leveson Gower, 10 July 1805; *The Letters of Lord G. Leveson Gower*, ii 91. See also ibid., to ibid., 3 Aug. 1805; *Sovereign Lady*, p.134.

41. ed. Lady Strafford, *Leaves from the Diary of Henry Greville* (London 1905), p.23.

Holland's principal activities took place elsewhere. It was his wife who took charge of Holland House entertaining. Accounts of the dinners mention her remarks and attitudes much more frequently than those of her husband, and this was not unfair. She decided placements, when dessert would be called and when some manifestation of her hypochondria made any further social life impossible.[42] The authority she wielded was despotic rather than constitutional. Lady Caroline Lamb, believing that Lady Holland had prejudiced Byron against her, found her an easy subject for satire in her novel *Glenarvon* in which Lady Holland is made to expire with the words,

> As to confession of sins ... is there a scribbler, however contemptible, whose pen I feared might one day be turned against me that I have not silenced with the grossest flattery? Is there a man or woman of note in any kingdom that I have not crammed with dinners, and little attentions and presents, in hopes of gaining them to my side? And is there, unless the helpless, the fallen, and the idiot, appear against me, any one whom it was my interest to befriend that I have not sought for and won? What minion of fashion, what dandy in distress, what woman of intrigue, who had learned to deceive with ease, have I not assisted? Oh say, what are then my sins? ... Even if self denial be a virtue, though I have not practised it myself, have I not made ... others do so daily?'[43]

This savage description mixed an element of truth with quantities of malice to produce the maximum effect.

The imperial style was maintained in other contexts as well. She usually travelled in convoy with several maids and footmen and at least one doctor in attendance. This rule applied to travel abroad as well. On arriving in a major city,

42. Add. MSS. 52172, f 53; Lady Holland to John Allen, 29 Nov. 1822.

43. Lady Caroline Lamb, *Glenarvon* (London 1816), iii 299-300. In the novel Holland House becomes Barbary House and Lady Holland becomes the Princess of Madagascar. Both titles were designed to emphasise Lady Holland's Jamaican background. Throughout her life, she was abnormally sensitive on this point, and particularly to any suggestion that her complexion might be darker than average. The novel hurt her deeply. 'Lady H. is much hurt, and she told me that the Greys and Lansdownes, and Jerseys would cut her, and that she was two pegs lower with the Argylls and others.' Lord Broughton, *Recollections of a Long Life*, i 339.

the Hollands usually rented a large house or hotel, and immediately began to recreate the salon world they had recently left behind in England. Predictably, the Hollands were not easy guests. Elaborate arrangements had to be made to rearrange houses to Lady Holland's specifications. No flowers were allowed in drawing rooms, for example. After one visit to Woburn Abbey, Lady William Russell gave Lady Holland the title 'Lucrezia Holland'.[44] By all accounts, Lady Holland conducted visitations rather than visits.[45] The constant factor everywhere was the organisation of social life on salon principles.

Age did nothing to moderate her imperiousness. While travelling by train for the first time, she personally ordered Brunel to slow the vehicle to under twenty miles an hour 'in spite of the protestations of the passengers'.[46] Hers was not a character that worked in tandem with others, and this made partnering her at whist a nightmare. She once told Lord Auckland, 'Yes I know you wanted trumps, but my system at whist is to distrust my partner. In fact, I like to thwart him because I hate the way in which he draws the good cards out of my hand.'[47] Added to this, by the 1840s, she grew to loathe men 'covered in hair', girls 'smoking and talking slang' and even postage stamps with all the rancour of the reformed convention-breaker.[48] In view of her early life, Lady Holland's later moral attitudes excited some amusement. Guizot was taken to task for mentioning the word hell at Holland House, and was told that 'la haute poésie est la seule excuse'.[49] Lord Douro's attitude to his marriage scandalised her, in spite of the fact that her own record in that line was far from perfect,

44. Bedford to Lord William Russell, c. Aug. 1832; *Lord William Russell and his Wife*, p.258.

45. Lady Harriet Cavendish to Viscountess Morpeth, 31 Oct. 1807 and 23 Nov. 1807, *The Letters of Lady Harriet Cavendish*, p.229 and 255. See also C. Greville, *A Journal of the Reigns of George IV, William IV and Queen Victoria* (London 1888), ii 48.

46. ed. Lord Ilchester, *Chronicles of Holland House 1820-1900* (London 1937), p.187.

47. Emily Eden to Lord Clarendon, 28 Oct. 1844; Sir H. Maxwell, *Life and Letters of the Earl of Clarendon* (London 1913), i 249.

48. Lady Holland to Henry Fox, 1840; *Elizabeth, Lady Holland to her Son*, pp. 187-91.

49. Guizot to Princess Lieven, 25 May 1840; *Lettres de François Guizot et de la Princesse de Lieven*, ii 150.

The bride fainted away on her return from Church; he went riding in the Park and played a game of tennis ... On the Queen complimenting him on her beauty, he said she was all head, hands and feet (they are large), that she weighed 11 stone, and more than he did.[50]

It is not surprising that, according to Sydney Smith, London apothecaries specialised in the production of pills for people who had been frightened at Holland House.

Very few people therefore were inclined to gainsay Lady Holland on her own ground. One of the few who enjoyed this dispensation was John Allen, the librarian of the House from 1802 until his death in 1843. Through the Hollands, he became successively Warden and Master of Dulwich College. Macaulay characterised him as Lady Holland's 'Negro Slave', but this was unjust. He was vigorously independent in his views and had been known to correct Lady Holland even on the subject of her age.[51] He claimed to be both a republican and an atheist, and, in these capacities, he did much to give Holland House a reputation for unrestrained, even farouche, ways of thought.[52] His constant attendance gave rise, inevitably, to rumours that he was Lady Holland's lover, and, although such stories were almost certainly untrue, Allen was loathed by the Hollands' children. They accused him, with some justice, of supporting 'all that was bad in her ... not from selfish or interested motives, but from his own blind violence of temper and total want of judgement'.[53] He was deeply learned, something of an eccentric, and certainly not someone who would want to restrain Lady Holland's more exotic ideas.

It will be apparent therefore that the social life of Holland House was not without its problems. The essential point is that Holland himself exactly complemented his wife. Where she ruffled feathers, he smoothed them. Where she irritated,

50. Lady Holland to Henry Fox, 26 April 1839; *Elizabeth, Lady Holland to her Son*, 26 April 1839.

51. Creevey to Miss Ord, 19 March 1828; ed. Sir H. Maxwell, *The Creevey Papers* (London 1903), ii 155-6.

52. Ilchester, *Chronicles of Holland House*, p.59. See also Ilchester, *The Journal of the Hon. Henry Edward Fox, 4th Lord Holland*, pp. 124-5.

53. Henry Fox to Augusta Fox, July 1843; *Chronicles of Holland House*, p.313.

he consoled. He looked on Allen with an amused toleration. His patience and understanding were almost inexhaustible. Unlike his wife, he had no fear of solitude, and would positively look forward to evenings when 'he had no company for dinner but the parrot'.[54] His understatement moderated the effects of his wife's intemperance, and, as a man with almost no pretensions and very little ambition, he was happy to allow her great latitude in domestic arrangements. Together, they were capable of erratic kindnesses, even if these were usually directed at people outside the Fox family circle. When Romilly committed suicide, for example, his children were taken in and provided for by the Hollands.[55] Generally, however, concern was expressed, even by Lord Holland, with the head rather than the heart.

The only area where Holland seems to have been unable to exert any moderating influence concerned his own family. Easily the most uncomfortable aspect of Holland House was the complete lack of sympathy that existed between the Hollands and their children. Lady Holland lost sight of her three Webster children almost totally and this seemed to evoke no regret whatever. Their long absences abroad inevitably meant that the Hollands saw little of their one illegitimate and two legitimate children, Charles, Henry and Mary. The bringing up of children was naturally delegated to other people in aristocratic circles in the early nineteenth century, but Lady Holland's lack of maternal feelings was remarked upon frequently by contemporaries. After Holland's death, one of her sons specifically accused her of blocking access to his father,

> You know well how you have been towards all your children for years and years, you know the things you have said to them, you know the jealousy you have shown of their being with him they loved above all the world.[56]

54. Add. MSS. 51748, f 186; Holland to Henry Fox, 26 Sept. 1822.

55. Lady H. Granville to Viscountess Morpeth, 11 Nov. 1818; *The Letters of Lady Harriet Granville*, i 137.

56. Charles Richard Fox to Lady Holland, May 1841; *Chronicles of Holland House*, p.296.

Holland himself was apparently unable or unwilling to overcome this situation, and their family life was endlessly plagued by dispute and recrimination.

The quarrel between the Hollands and their eldest (legitimate) son and heir, Henry Edward Fox, turned on the question of his career. To both the Hollands, it was inconceivable that someone should have doubts about pursuing a political career, because 'there is nothing so pleasant as the satisfaction, or if you please the vanity of thinking oneself of use to one's friends or to the publick'.[57] In particular, for someone carrying the name Fox to have doubts was appalling. It represented a betrayal of the sacrifices which Charles James Fox and Holland himself had made in the cause of what they recognised as liberty. Twice Holland secured the promise of a seat in the Commons for his son and twice the offer was refused.[58] Under this pressure, even Holland lost patience:

> I must say it ill becomes one of our name who have derived so much of our consideration and our existence in the world from such connexions to speak of them as not worth having ... We Foxes owe as much to party as party can owe to us.[59]

When Henry Fox settled for a diplomatic career, this was ultimately accepted, but only as second best to Westminster.[60] There is no doubt that the strongest inducement for diplomacy, in Henry Fox's view, was the chance to live abroad and away from Holland House. Quite simply, the weight of family tradition was too much for him and he came to detest it.[61]

Such was the depth of this disappointment that the Hollands virtually adopted Lord John Russell as a substitute son. Here was someone with exactly the right tastes and abilities, who was determined to vindicate another historic

---

57. Add. MSS. 51748, ff 206-7; Holland to Henry Fox, 28 May 1823.
58. Add. MSS. 51749, ff 71-2; Holland to Henry Fox, c. Feb. 1825.
59. Add. MSS. 51749, f 169; Holland to Henry Fox, 28 Jan. 1820.
60. Add. MSS. 51749, f 138; ibid., to ibid., 21 Nov. 1825.
61. Lord John Russell to Lady Holland, 1824; *Chronicles of Holland House*, p.49.

name in the sphere of politics. He appears in Holland House
correspondence as an honorary member of the family, and his
younger brother William scarcely less so. When Russell was
sixteen, he was taken by the Hollands on their extensive tour
of Spain and Portugal. They took an almost paternal pride in
the leading part he played in the passing of the great Reform
Bill.[62] They were not inhibited from holding Russell up as a
model to their own less exciting son,

> I am glad you like Lord John. It is a victory, as you never did him
> justice. He is essentially excellent, and a model for any one to follow.
> All is sound and right about him, with great talents and ambition to
> distinguish himself in all that is laudable. Indeed I hope he will come
> into Parliament: and have very little doubt, as all must yield to him
> that matter.[63]

It was Russell who was to be entrusted with the guardianship
of Charles James Fox's letters and, by implication, of the
Foxite tradition. He was also to be a major beneficiary under
Lady Holland's will.

Inevitably, marriage was another subject for acrimony.
Almost every prospective bride for Henry Fox was objected to,
and the fact that, on one occasion, the excuse given was that
the lady was 'a Catholic foreigner'[64] demonstrates the extent
to which the Hollands' liberalism could not be applied to their
own family. Mary Fox had an even more difficult time. Even a
proposal from Lord John Russell, in 1829, had to be rejected
because of parental pressure.[65] When she finally married Lord
Lilford, an amiable if rather colourless man, Lady Holland
could not resist making verbal 'sorties' against her new son-in-
law to whoever would listen to them.[66] Not surprisingly,
neither Mary nor Henry Fox chose to be frequent visitors to
Holland House after their respective marriages.

62. Lady Holland to Henry Fox, 23 August. 1831; *Elizabeth, Lady Holland to Her Son*,
p.113.
63. Lady Holland to Henry Fox, 31 Aug. 1826; ibid., p.51.
64. Lady Holland to Henry Fox, 20 March 1827; ibid., p.61.
65. Tavistock to Lord William Russell, 1829; *Lord William Russell and his Wife*,
p.194.
66. Diary of Lady Dover, 6 Sept. 1820; Lady Leconfield and J. Gore, *Three Howard
Sisters* (London 1955), p.142.

The Holland family was therefore always a source of material for the scandalmonger in London society. After Holland's death in October 1840, their scope for action became much enlarged. To pay off outstanding debts Lady Holland immediately sold off the Ampthill estate, which her husband had inherited from his uncle, the Earl of Upper Ossory. Settling down to what she described as 'poverty on £5,000 a year',[67] Lady Holland then began to strip Holland House of its pictures and books by sending them for sale at Christie's. The legality of this spoliation of her children's inheritance was highly questionable, and Henry Fox was well aware of his mother's motives:

> She writes me most tender, sugary letters almost every post. If posterity judges of her only by these, she will pass for a second Madame de Sévigné in maternal tenderness! It is rather amusing, but it is from the extreme interest and affection so studiously repeated in her letters that I began to suspect that she was employed in some business of the sort, for these effusions are always sure precursors of some mischief.[68]

When Lady Holland herself died, in 1845, Henry Fox was left £7,000 a year and the Jamaican estates, which were by that time virtually worthless.[69] Mary Fox received nothing but her mother's jewellery, and Charles Richard Fox only £1,000. The estate at Kennington, on which the Oval now stands and which was easily the most valuable thing she possessed, was left to Lord John Russell. When he heard the terms of the will in advance, Russell was moved to protest, but he was met by the firm statement, 'I hate my son; I don't like my daughter.'[70] As this remark suggests, Holland House was not the place for a family. Commonplace people like Henry and Mary Fox were seen as something of an encumbrance in the sharp world of the salon. Their lack of interest in political and literary life was, for their parents, almost crushing. They accordingly first tried to force them to conform to a pattern of which they

67. *Chronicles of Holland House*, pp. 287-90.
68. Holland to Clarendon, 20 April 1842; *Life and Letters of Lord Clarendon*, i 230.
69. See below, Chapter Four.
70. ed. E. Peel, *The Recollections of Lady Georgiana Peel* (London 1920), p.71.

approved, and ultimately ignored them. Whole nations would
evoke genuine sympathy in the Hollands but the refusal of
their children to acknowledge a family lead was met with
something approaching brutality.

It is, however, the relationship between Lord and Lady
Holland themselves which must be of most interest in a
description of Holland House society. Superficially, the same,
brisk matriarchy seemed to obtain. Holland was, on
occasions, forbidden to go out to dinner with particular
individuals or to invite them as guests. Thomas Coke of
Holkham came into this category for once having made a
remark about the purity of Lady Holland's past life.[71]
Holland's gout could not be alleviated by crutches because his
wife disapproved of them.[72] He was sometimes left completely
alone for the evening with 'une bougie, ses lunettes, et du
papier pour écrire, pas autre chose'.[73] When, by the
intercession of Grey, he was once allowed a second slice of
melon, Lord Holland murmured, 'Ah, Lord Grey, I wish you
were always here. It is a fine thing to be Prime Minister.'[74]
The balance of power was unchanging outside Holland
House. The following is a description of a visit to the Duke of
Argyll:

> The Hollands ... were delighted with Inverary, and she all smiles and
> graciousness, pleas'd with every thing, without wants, displeasures,
> or difficulties. Lord Holland was allow'd to fish a whole morning
> without being sent home for thick shoes or a silk handkerchief, to play
> chess all evening without the men being thrown down in the most
> interesting moment of the game, and to sit up till near three o'clock in
> the morning without Amélie once appearing at the door to say, My
> Lord, Miladi dit que c'est bien tard.[75]

There was much in these public displays of play-acting, and
there is little doubt that Holland himself was willing to

71. Creevey to Miss Ord, 1 March 1824; *Creevey Diaries*, ii 74-5.
72. Lady Granville to Lady Carlisle, 16 Sept. 1828; ed. F. Leveson Gower, *The
Letters of Harriet, Countess Granville* (London 1894), ii 128.
73. Princess Lieven to Guizot, 15 July 1837; *Guizot-Lieven Letters*, i 30.
74. T.B. Macaulay to Hannah Macaulay, 14 Aug. 1832; G.O. Trevelyan, *The Life
and Letters of Lord Macaulay* (London 1959), p.194.
75. Lady Bessborough to Lord Granville Leveson Gower, 2 Oct. 1807; *The Letters of
Lord Granville Leveson Gower*, ii 290.

indulge his wife's tantrums, finding them more amusing than irritating. They had, however, one serious consequence. Many contemporaries believed that these minor acts of despotism implied that Holland was unduly influenced by his wife in more important matters. At critical moments in Holland's political career, the question of Lady Holland's behaviour was raised, and raised to their disadvantage. In 1811 for example, James Perry believed that Holland could not become leader of the Whig party, 'while he is completely under the dominion of his wife'.[76] More important, the tangled ministerial negotiations of 1827-8 were complicated further by this consideration. When Lady Holland complained that her husband had been passed over for the Foreign Office, she was told rather bluntly by Lord John Russell that, 'If you must know, it is because no man will act in a Cabinet with a person whose wife opens all his letters.'[77] In the opinion of many people, it was impossible in any context to consider both Lord and Lady Holland as anything but a single unit.

These were genuine reservations and had impact, but they were probably based on a misreading of the situation. Holland was by nature a pliant man who had no wish to meddle in domestic detail. He was also devoted to his wife and it pleased him to tolerate her wilfulness. But, whenever their views on a particular subject diverged, there is no evidence whatever that Lady Holland's view was likely to prevail. As will be seen, Holland was occasionally badgered by his wife to take a different attitude towards a particular issue or person, but there is no example of him falling in with her wishes. He had after all the trump card. The family's influence in the Whig party and in politics at large was built on the name Fox and the tradition which it enshrined. Holland had a place in national life because he now represented that tradition. Lady Holland's standing was in turn dependent on her husband. Her origins and early life had not equipped her for the possibility of acquiring influence in later life. That influence came to her only because she had attached herself to an

76. Lord Glenbervie's Diary, 21 Jan. 1811; ed. F. Bickley, *The Diaries of Sylvester Douglas* (London 1928), ii 118.

77. *Sovereign Lady*, pp. 256-7. A slightly different account of this conversation is to be found in *The Croker Diaries*, i 400.

assured political dynasty. It is to be noted that, although she found some members of the Fox family tiresome, they were never subjected to Lady Holland's wrath or sarcasm. Holland, as head of this clan, knew his ultimate authority to be secure.

The outcome of all this was that Holland House society was never comfortable. It was certainly no place for the slow-witted or oversensitive. For beginners, the experience of dining at Holland House could be terrifying.[78] Even actresses like Fanny Kemble found the tension unbearable.[79] In addition to the family turbulence between the Hollands, their children and John Allen, there was always the proximity to national affairs, which, at moments of crisis, produced pandemonium. The sort of scene described by Sydney Smith, in 1811, was not uncommon:

> Never was such a ferment as Pall Mall and Holland House is in! John Allen, wild and staring – Antonio[80] and Thomas the porter, worked off their legs – Lord Lauderdale sleeps with his clothes on, and a pan full of ink close to his bedside, with a string tied to the wrist of his secretary in the next room. Expresses arriving at Pall Mall every ten minutes from the House of Commons, and the Whig nobility and commonalty dropping in at all hours to dinner and supper.[81]

On many occasions, the number of people dining and the number staying overnight were open questions.

In this maelstrom, guests were treated with an extraordinary lack of attention. There were frequently so many people sitting down to meals, that it was actually difficult to manipulate cutlery in the press.[82] If, then, an important person arrived, some lesser mortal was simply told to go away. On one occasion, even Samuel Rogers, one of the Hollands' most devoted attendants, was dismissed with the words, 'Go away. There is something on your handkerchief I do not quite

78. Diary of Lady Frances Elliot, 6 Sept. 1836; D. MacCarthy, *Lady John Russell, A Memoir* (London 1910), pp. 25-6.

79. P. Clayden, *Samuel Rogers and his Contemporaries* (London 1889), ii 151-2.

80. Lady Holland's manservant.

81. S. Smith to Lady Grey, 24 Jan. 1811; P. Nowell Smith, *The Letters of Sydney Smith* (Oxford 1953), i 202.

82. *The Greville Diaries*, ii 323.

like.'[83] The snubbing of guests seemed to have been worked upon almost as an art form.[84] In addition, Byron always complained bitterly about the cold, because Lady Holland would never allow a fire to be unscreened,[85] and Thomas Grenville always came away with indigestion.[86] Physical injury was added to wounded pride when, in 1822, Lady Holland took on a cat:

> Rogers it seems, has already sustained considerable injury in a personal affair with this animal. Brougham only keeps him or her at arm's length with snuff, and Luttrell has sent in a formal resignation of all further visits till this odious new favourite is dismissed from the Cabinet.[87]

Such events were not uncommon, and early nineteenth-century letters and diaries are full of entries recording scenes of acute discomfort.

Not surprisingly, many people chose to describe a visit to Holland House as a calling on majesty. Lord Campbell for example, found 'the Circle very brilliant. *Her Majesty* was seated on her throne, a pony chaise on the lawn, and there she received her subjects who came to be presented or to pay their respects. It was a much more formal ceremony than going to kiss the King's hands.'[88] Another guest called Lady Holland 'the only really undisputed monarchy in Europe ... [with] courtiers and dames d'honneur, all dans les règles.'[89] As an act of prerogative, Lady Holland decreed, after 1830, that Holland House would dine at five o'clock, while the rest of London had by that date moved on to six or seven. The motive for this decision was, in Talleyrand's words, 'pour gêner tout le monde'.[90] Not everyone could sustain unquestioning

83. *Samuel Rogers and his Contemporaries*, i 35-6.

84. Lord Broughton, *Recollections of a Long Life*, i 84-5, and Lady H. Granville to Viscountess Morpeth, Sept. 1815; *Letters of Lady H. Granville*, i 80.

85. R. Prothero, *The Works of Lord Byron* (London 1901), ii 353.

86. T. Grenville to Lord Grenville, 20 Jan. 1819; Hist. Mss. Comm. 30 *Fortescue* x p.443.

87. Creevey to Miss Ord, 23 Dec. 1822; *Creevey Diaries*, ii 58.

88. Mrs Hardcastle, *The Life of John, Lord Campbell* (London 1881), i 469-70.

89. Lady H. Granville to Viscountess Morpeth, *Letters of Lady Granville*, i 169.

90. L. Sanders, *The Holland House Circle*, p.65.

subservience however. The history of Holland House is punctuated with rebellion and nonjuring. The major clashes with Brougham and Byron are well-known, but few people escaped some dispute or period of estrangement.[91]

As has been suggested above, there was no moderation in the display when abroad. The Hollands travelled with great ceremony. At Paris, the entertaining followed familiar patterns,[92] and some people 'supposed themselves in the presence of Marie Theresa at least'.[93] The pretension involved was such that it could not fail to catch the satirist's eye. Lady Caroline Lamb, in '*Glenarvon*', found the task almost too easy:

> A small fleet had been seen approaching the coast; it was rumoured that the French in open boats were preparing to invade Ireland; but it proved, though it may sound rather ludicrous to say so, only the Princess of Madagascar. Their immense retinue and baggage, which the common people took for the heavy artillery, arrived without incident, or accident, at Belmont.[94]

In the same novel, Barbary House is spoken of as a Court, in which Rogers, Luttrell, 'Conversation' Sharp and all the other regular members of the Holland House circle were depicted as courtiers and jesters.

This raises the most important question of all. In view of the embarrassments and inconveniences of Holland House, the fact that most people positively looked forward to an invitation stands in need of some explanation. In spite of the brow-beatings, Holland House became one of the great social centres of early nineteenth-century London. The simplest answer to this problem is to emphasise the disparate nature of its gatherings. The Hollands collected distinction of any kind. Science, literature, art and politics, both English and European, were represented by their most celebrated exponents. The Dinner Books of Holland House are

91. *The Greville Diaries*, iii pp. 130 seq.

92. Lady H. Granville to Viscountess Morpeth, June 1817; *Letters of Lady H. Granville*, i 121. See also, *The Journal of Henry Edward Fox*, March 1825, p. 223 seq.

93. Lady H. Granville to Lady Carlisle, 14 Dec. 1825; *Letters of Lady H. Granville*, i 370.

94. Lady C. Lamb, *Glenarvon*, ii 57-8.

catalogues of talent. A successful evening for the Hollands was one in which the commonplace had no part. Lady Holland reported an evening that was particularly successful to her son, because there had been 'not one person who was not remarkable for sense, wit, acquirement or some distinguishing quality'.[95] Poets and ambassadors, the Royal Academy and the Royal Society, politicians and failed revolutionaries were mixed in together at Holland House dinner parties, which could be nerve-racking but never dull.

The company found there made Holland House one of the great Houses in England. Some measure of its reputation may be gauged from the lamentations voiced when, with Holland's death, the entertaining died away. Jeffrey, the editor of the *Edinburgh Review*, was appalled at 'the extinction of all that light' and at 'the conversion of that place, which, for fifty years has been the resort of all that was distinguished, and 'the school of all that was amiable and honourable into a house of mourning and desolation'.[96] Jeffrey had been a long-standing friend and protégé of the Hollands, but even the diarist Greville, who was at times among their most severe critics, had to record that

> Never was popularity so great and so general, and his death will produce a social revolution, utterly extinguishing not only the most brilliant, but the only great house of reception and constant society in England ... This event may be said with prefect truth 'to eclipse the gaiety of nations' ... It is impossible to overrate the privation, the blank, which it will make to the old friends and associates, political and personal, to whom Holland House has always been open like a home.[97]

All kinds of people had no hesitation in running the risks of visiting Holland House, because it was easily one of the most exciting places in London.

With pre-eminence in social life went power and influence. These two aspects of society were inextricably mixed together

95. Lady Holland to Henry Fox, 2 April 1839; *Elizabeth, Lady Holland to her Son*, p.175.
96. Add. MSS. 52181, f 181; J. Jeffrey to J. Allen, 25 Oct. 1840.
97. Greville *Memoirs*, iv 351-2.

in the early nineteenth century, and this was particularly true of parties in opposition. The Whigs, in opposition from 1784 to 1806 and from 1807 to 1830, had none of the cohesion which comes from an experience of government. Historians agree that its organisation at Westminster and in the constituencies was rudimentary and friable.[98] Grey's and Holland's careers in politics are abnormal in the sense that they were largely spent in opposition and with no prospect of ever returning to government. The events of 1830, which propelled them back into office late in life, came as something of a shock. In this context, the organisational vacuum was filled, however imperfectly, by social functions. The dinner parties at Holland House stood in marked contrast to the drums, routs and balls popular in the rest of London. Lady Holland's preferences were clear:

> What a sad waste of health and animal powers are these numerous assemblages of persons, how little pleasure and gratification. A sociable chat for a few hours with a few well-informed persons is worth all that a thronged room can furnish.[99]

By contract, a dinner was often organised to discuss a particular topic, and guests were invited who might be thought to have something to contribute. Even Lady Palmerston, no friend of the Hollands, had to admit that the 'House kept the Party together'.[100] In short, Holland House had a political function of the greatest importance.

Finally, as a centre of Whig life, Holland House influenced the development of party thinking in dramatic ways. The Whig party in the early nineteenth century was a strange mixture of the static and the evolutionary. Much of its thinking was static because experience of the French

---

98. A. Mitchell, *The Whigs in Opposition 1815-1830* (Oxford 1967).

99. Ilchester, *Chronicles of Holland House*, p.35. Her husband was equally alive to the close relationship between politics and social life. 'Private dinners, tavern suppers, convivial meetings, perhaps intemperance itself, constituted a large portion of the ways and means of public men some thirty or forty years ago.' Holland, *Further Memoirs of the Whig Party*, p.354.

100. Lady Palmerston to Lord Beauvale, 23 Oct. 1840; T. Lever, *The Letters of Lady Palmerston* (London 1957), pp. 237-8.

Revolution and Bonaparte froze English politics for a generation. The issues on which Fox and Pitt had pronounced in the 1780s and 1790s were still current in the 1820s and early 1830s. 'Foxite' and 'Pittite' are more often used to describe loyalties than 'Whig' or 'Tory'. The intellectual positions adopted by Pitt and Fox on the great issues of Catholic Emancipation, Parliamentary Reform and the Abolition of Slavery for example were so comprehensive that there was really nothing new to say. Holland, Fox's nephew and heir, became the high priest of this tradition, and Holland House became a temple of Fox worship, where the ideas and sufferings of Uncle Charles were retailed to new generations of Whigs. In this sense, Whig thinking was static and embalmed in Holland House.

Reinforcing and enlarging this Foxite faith were new strains of thinking and new experiences. From Scotland came the products of Edinburgh and Glasgow universities, who, with their mouthpiece, the *Edinburgh Review*, brought to the Whig cause a kind of writing that had not been seen before. With them came the full force of the Scottish Enlightenment which, they believed, could substantiate Whig ideas on an almost scientific base.[101] From Europe, as ambassadors or refugees, came nationalists and liberals who offered new contexts for the application of Foxite prejudices. Foxite views on constitutionalism for example could now be worked out in exciting situations in Spain, Portugal, France and even Italy and Poland. Arguably, England has never, until recently, been so˜close to Europe as it was between 1789 and 1830, and the Hollands with their much travelled past were magnificently equipped to take advantage of this fact.[102] Scots and Europeans were an indispensable part of any Holland House gathering.

In spite of Lady Holland's tantrums and real doubts about Lord Holland's easygoing judgment, their House acquired a quite extraordinary preeminence and popularity. Their dinner parties united the Foxite core of the Whig party with

101. See below, Chapter Seven.
102. See below, Chapters Eight to Eleven.

the new ideas and situations in Scotland and Europe. The Fox name was a guarantee of stability and the Holland experience gave it freshness and a wider intellectual base. All these streams of thinking flowed into Holland House and were represented by their best exponents. Such a mixture was inevitably informative and exciting. The ability to orchestrate such performances gave power to the Hollands. Each of the separate types of thought represented at Holland House must be investigated in turn, but it is always necessary to remember that it is their admixture at a dinner table which gave the House its piquancy and real character.

2

The Foxite Legacy

Everything that happened at Holland House happened under the shadow of Charles James Fox. He never liked his nephew's wife, and she, in turn, expressed herself 'extremely afraid of my Uncle Charles'.[1] He blamed her exclusively for the scandals and trials of 1796 and 1797, and she resented the rival influence which he exerted over her husband, realising at the same time that she had to accommodate herself to it, because it was Fox's name that guaranteed her own position in society and politics. Lord Lauderdale was accorded a special position at Holland House, because 'he was indefatigable in carrying through law proceedings in the H. of Lords, which enabled me to be what I am in this family. He reconciled Mr Fox and all his connections to the measure by receiving me; and in short I owe to him every advantage and comfort I enjoy.'[2] Reconciliation only went so far. Fox, on his deathbed, refused to see Lady Holland at all. Her only recourse on this occasion was 'to plant herself in one of the rooms below stairs under pretence of waiting for Lord Holland', preventing 'his admitting any other woman'.[3]

For nearly forty years after Fox's death, the defence of his uncle's every political statement became one of Holland's

1. Add. MSS. 51734, f 25; Lady Holland to Caroline Fox, 20 July 1796. See also Add. MSS. 51734, f 14; Holland to Caroline Fox, 8 July 1796.
2. Lady Holland to Henry Fox, Sept. 1839; *Chronicles of Holland House*, p.261.
3. Creevey to Miss Ord, 30 July 1806; *Creevey Diaries*, i 82.

principal duties in politics. His speeches and letters make
endless references to Fox's beliefs and draw comparisons with
situations that Fox himself faced. There was a vehemence in
Holland's defence of his uncle's career that some
contemporaries found a little unbalanced.[4] Certainly, Holland
felt an intellectual dependence on Fox that marked his whole
career. This is not surprising if it is remembered how close a
supervision of Holland's intellectual formation was
undertaken by Fox. His letters to his nephew in the 1790s are
tutorials of the most painstaking kind. Not only is the true
nature of Whig politics set out and explained, but there are
also lists of books and pictures that a Whig should admire and
lists of books and pictures that he should not. During
Holland's travels in Europe in the early 1790s, Fox arranged
meetings with men like Lafayette and la Rochefoucauld, and
his letters to his nephew almost rival those of Lord
Chesterfield in their comprehensiveness.

In a very real sense, Holland, after 1791, became his uncle's
major political confidant, which was both flattering and
compromising to the younger man.[5] However, in defending
the Foxite tradition of the 1790s, he was defending something
to which he had in some small measure contributed. In the
process he assumed the same friends and foes as his uncle.
William Pitt was consigned to the lowest circle of Hell. George
Canning and the Lansdowne family, who had presented
problems to Fox in the 1790s were to present very similar
types of problem to Holland in the 1820s.[6] Those Whigs who
took up an anti-Foxite position in the Whig schism of 1794
were pursued by Holland ever after with charges of treason.[7]
Uncle and nephew occasionally disagreed on small points of
tactics, but they walked absolutely in step along the main lines
of policy. Holland joyfully admitted the fact:

4. Aberdeen to Croker, 2 Feb. 1851; *Croker Diaries*, iii 225.
5. Add. MSS. 51731, f 46; Holland to Caroline Fox, 18 July 1791. Emily Leinster to
W. Ogilvie, 29 June 1792; *Emily Duchess of Leinster*, p.199. Add. MSS. 47571, f 22; Fox
to Holland, 23 Nov. 1792.
6. See below, Chapter Five.
7. Add. MSS. 47571, f 143; Fox to Holland, 10 Aug. 1794.

I was, no doubt, swayed by my affection for him, as well as convinced by his arguments, to espouse the principles which have generally guided the popular party in this country called Whigs. He seemed to take pleasure in awakening my ambition, and directing it, both by conversation and correspondence.[8]

When Holland came to write memoirs, therefore, it is not surprising to discover that much space is taken up with the most pious vindication of his uncle's career. Most of the first volume of the *Memoirs of the Whig Party during my Time* takes the form of a character-by-character account of the Whig party of the 1790s, and all of them are described in terms of their relations with Fox. The last thirty pages of the same volume are devoted to a description of Fox's last illness and death. The piety of the work is overwhelming. Holland again and again acknowledges an unquestioning obedience to the lessons imparted by his uncle. He wrote the work 'in veneration of one whose memory furnished me with the strongest motive for continuing in publick life, as well as the best regulation for my conduct therein.'[9] The prejudices of the book are broad and were much criticised at the time of its publication. In almost every respect, they faithfully reflected a received family view.

Naturally, Holland's early political career was stage-managed by his uncle. His future rôle in politics was accepted without question by both sides, and Fox encouraged, flattered and lectured in equal proportion. When Holland was still only seventeen, Fox professed 'the greatest pleasure' to hear the young man's 'opinion upon general Politics'.[10] In turn, Holland's only regret at being abroad so much was that he was prevented from helping 'my U. Charles ... to be of service in any way to whom would be of the greatest gratification to my vanity and the most immediate object of my ambition'.[11] The timing and nature of Holland's maiden speech on 9 January 1798 were again decided by Fox. He took the view

8. Holland, *Memoirs of the Whig Party during my Time*, pp. 3-4.
9. Holland, *Memoirs of the Whig Party during my Time*, i 272.
10. Add. MSS. 47571, f 1; Fox to Holland, May 1791.
11. Add. MSS. 51732, f 132; Holland to Caroline Fox, Dec. 1794.

that Pitt's Assessed Taxes Bill would provide an admirable opportunity to attack both the bill and the war policy which had made it necessary.[12] Holland made the most of his opportunity. At the suggestion of his uncle, the war with France became 'a calamitous contest', Pitt's system of government the organisation of 'terror and coercion' and the Bill itself, in requiring disclosures of personal income, was 'contrary to the customs and prejudices of Englishmen, and repugnant to the principles of the constitution'.[13] The entering of an official Protest in the Lords' Journal was also done at Fox's suggestion.[14]

Similarly, in the brief Whig-Grenville Ministry of 1806-7, Fox was very anxious that his protégé should have the experience of holding office:

> Mr Fox asked me what I wished for myself? I answered, an office of business, in which I could be useful. I added, that Lady Holland's predilection for foreign modes of living would make me prefer a diplomatick station to any other, and that the embassy in Paris, when peace came, would of course be my ultimate object in that line.[15]

In fact, Holland became Lord Privy Seal for the brief life of the Talents Ministry, where his principal occupation was conducting negotiations with the American Government over the rights of neutral shipping. Fox's death in 1806 removed this kind of supervision, but the debts owed to the dead were almost more poignant than those which had been paid to the living. To understand fully the Foxite legacy to Holland House, it is necessary to explain the politics of the 1780s and 1790s, and to describe in some detail the remodelling of Whig ideas that went on under Fox's nominal leadership.

The most important of these was a rediscovery in dramatic terms of the fear of the executive power of the Crown. If the radical, between 1760 and 1832, took as his starting point in politics some notion about popular rights, whatever was

---

12. Fox to Holland, 14 Dec. 1797; Lord J. Russell, *Memorials and Correspondence of C.J. Fox* (London 1853-1857), iii 139.
13. *Parl. Deb.*, vol. XXX.
14. Holland, *Memoirs of the Whig Party during my Time*, p.99.
15. Holland, *Memoirs of the Whig Party during my Time*, i 232.

meant by that expression, the Whig started from the other end of the political spectrum. Fox insisted that it was the executive powers of the Crown that underlay all difficulties. Holland inherited a family interpretation of the reign of George III that was almost demonic. Even when George died, in 1820, Holland had no charity:

> The lavish and unmerited praises bestowed on the late King make me sick and almost angry, and as many are meant as sneers at His present Majesty they soften me to him ... There was nothing good done in his reign that was not done against his will and some of the worst things, the Royal Marriage Act, the American War, were peculiarly his own measures.[16]

The record of 1761-3 and 1765-7,[17] when Whig leaders were used 'like tennis balls', to use Edmund Burke's expression, proved that George III was only too willing to use the powers of the executive to break governments and destroy public men. George, an absolutist as Elector of Hanover, was all too anxious to import that Continental fashion into England. He had expressly forbidden his son, the future George IV, to attend Fox's funeral.[18] This reading of events was adopted as part of the Holland House faith, and the first Lord Holland's assistance to George III in many of his early manoeuvrings was conveniently forgotten.

For Charles James Fox and later his nephew, concern about executive power was usually expressed in discussions about the events of 1782-4, which were for the whole family the turning point of eighteenth-century politics.[19] Even the French Revolution and subsequent events in Europe were merely codas on the theme of the tale of the Fox-North Coalition rather than anything new or more important. In 1805, Lord Cowper was persona grata in the Fox family because 'his

16. Add. MSS. 51748, ff 78-9; Holland to Henry Fox, 20 Feb. 1820.
17. It was believed that, during these years, Whig ministries were deliberately destroyed by a well-concerted plan devised by George III and his principal adviser, the Earl of Bute. See J. Brewer, *Party Ideology and Popular Politics at the Accession of George III* and P. Langford, *The Rockingham Administration*.
18. Add. MSS. 51520, f 12; The Prince of Wales to Holland, 12 Sept. 1806.
19. See J. Cannon, *The Fox-North Coalition*, and L. Mitchell, *Charles James Fox and the Disintegration of the Whig Party*.

justice candour and liberality about the Coalition is one of the strongest proofs of good sense and rooted Whiggism'.[20] Twice within two years, Charles Fox saw ministries of which he was a leading member destroyed by the open use of prerogative powers. George had undermined Cabinet cohesion, he had intervened in the deliberations of the House of Lords and he had terminated the life of a Parliament three years early to rid himself of an adverse majority. Fox, whose career was shattered by these events, likened George to James II, and argued that if the executive could assault the legislative branch of government in this way, the much vaunted 'balance' in the eighteenth-century constitution was gone forever. To defend the legislature, even Parliamentary Reform might have to be taken more seriously.

Holland grew up to accept this interpretation completely. There was enough history in it to make it plausible and enough myth to obscure the mistakes of his uncle and grandfather. The fact that the Whigs were out of office from 1784 to 1830, with only the break of the Talents Ministry from 1806 to 1807, illustrated the measure of George III's success. It is important to remember that Holland grew to political maturity, in the 1790s, in an atmosphere of hopelessness. Charles Fox believed, at the time of his secession from Parliament in 1797, that the battle had been lost, and that his probable fate would be the Tower. The apocalypse, springing from the gross misuse of executive power, was never far from Fox family thinking. Holland himself believed that the executive was continuing to grow stronger all through the first three decades of the nineteenth century. Much of the idiosyncrasy of Holland House lies in the fact that, while most people were alarmed by radicals and the first stirrings of democratic ideas, the Hollands clung to the view that executive power, which had ruined Charles Fox, was still the principal danger. References back to 1784 are everywhere in Holland's letters and speeches.

If the balance of the constitution had been upset, it was not surprising to Whig minds that the other extreme of radicalism

20. Add. MSS. 51737, f 168; Holland to Caroline Fox, 9 March 1805.

should gain in weight and importance in the early nineteenth century. Unrestrained monarchy and unrestrained democracy were two aspects of the same lunacy. True liberty could survive in neither. Direct parallels could be drawn between 'the Jacobins of France and the Crown party here'.[21] The balanced idea of the constitution lay in the mixing in due proportion of monarchy, aristocracy and popular views. Fox, in the 1790s, saw himself as situated in the middle of politics, as the last hope of maintaining the balance. As his nephew observed in 1796:

> How nobly my Uncle has acted. How little we aristocrats deserve such an advocate, for, if our destruction from above or below is not effected, to him we owe our deliverance.[22]

The conservative element in Holland House thinking stems from this fact. As the English constitution was assailed first by George III and later by democrats, Fox and the Whigs saw themselves as the group in the middle anxiously trying to maintain and preserve the traditional idea of balance.

In the trio of concepts, monarchy, aristocracy and democracy, it is the aristocratic principle which balances the other two. The Hollands believed absolutely that the obligations of the aristocracy stemmed from this fact. If the executive was too powerful, the popular cause should be supported. Notionally at least, it was also possible to lean the other way. As Brougham noted, 'both uncle and nephew had the genuine Whig predilection for the kind of support given by the union of great families, considering this as absolutely necessary to maintain the popular cause against the Court'.[23] Their son's refusal to accept this rôle was therefore deeply distressing. The ownership of title and property imposed irresistible obligations, in a constitutional context where all values still stemmed largely from the ownership of property. If Whigs refused to fulfil this duty, unrestrained monarchy or

21. Fox to Holland, 23 June 1794; *Memorials and Correspondence of C.J. Fox*, iii 74.
22. Add. MSS. 51733, f 161; Holland to Caroline Fox, 5 Jan. 1796.
23. *Life and Letters of Lord Brougham*, iii 465.

democracy must be the result, and either would mean the end of civil liberties and constitutional practice.

George III's major weapon in what the Whigs took to be his assault on constitutionalism was war. The struggle against Revolutionary and Napoleonic France, begun in 1793 and carried on with only short breaks until 1815, was primarily undertaken as an excuse or cover for the abolition of civil liberties. Fox's letters of the 1790s, which discuss the suspension of Habeas Corpus, the Traitrous Correspondence Bill or the transportations, always link these events to the war and the King's long term intentions.[24] Inevitably, war and the tensions it produced made the Whig emphasis on balancing the constitution virtually unrealistic. As Holland complained, as early as 1794:

> As to Politicks they are very melancoly indeed. It is not merely the success of Jacobinism or the triumph of Toryism that I fear but it is a spirit of mistrust suspicion ill nature and intolerance which is gaining ground all over Europe. We are all grown so savage and bloodthirsty and so suspicious that Politicks do not as formerly confine themselves to the splendor or poverty of a nation but in some measure affect the happiness of every individual.[25]

This fact and the Whig schism of 1794, which left him with only fifty or sixty supporters in the House of Commons, gave Fox a feeling of complete hopelessness. His secession from Parliament in 1797, as a desperate attempt to highlight the total impotence into which the House of Commons had fallen, had been suggested as early as 1794.[26] Holland, a younger man, always believed that the struggle should be continued, but his formative years were spent in the company of people who believed that executive power, aided by a seemingly endless war, must prevail.

England's entry into the war against France, in 1793, brought the question of executive power into a European-wide

24. Fox to Holland, 12 April 1795; *Memorials and Correspondence of C.J. Fox*, iii 105, and ibid., 17 Nov. 1795; ibid, iii 126.

25. Add. MSS. 48226, ff 122-3; Holland to Boringdon, 6 July 1794.

26. Add. MSS. 51732, f 10; Caroline Fox to Holland, 19 May 1794, and Add. MSS. 51732, f 24; Caroline Fox to Holland, 19 June 1794.

context. Up to the outbreak of the French Revolution, England had largely stood apart from the rest of Europe. Its constitutional development stood in marked and noted contrast to the despotisms, benevolent or otherwise, on the Continent. Fox feared that Pitt and George III, in joining the First Coalition of Austria, Prussia and Russia against France, wished to change this pattern fundamentally. It produced, in his mind, a black and white view of Europe, in which the same battle between constitutionalism and autocracy would be fought from London to Moscow. Fox never doubted that Pitt had joined in the war for the ideological purposes of restoring the French monarchy and reversing the constitutional gains of the seventeenth and eighteenth centuries in England. Concern for the future of the Low Countries, which was the ostensible casus belli, was never seen by Fox as anything but a limp excuse.[27] The stakes were very much higher. As he told his nephew, in 1794,

> I can not help thinking now and then of the dreadful state of things in Europe and the real danger which exists in my opinion of the fatal extinction of Liberty and possibly of civilization too, if this war is to go on upon the principles which are held out.[28]

Fox, developing the theme of the predominance of executive power, therefore laid the basis for that manichaean view of Europe which became a hallmark of Holland House. From London to Moscow, there was battle joined between good and bad, light and darkness. The Coalitions against the French and, later, the victorious powers at Vienna in 1815 represented the evil of autocracy. Only the ultimate barbarism of Turkey could outdo, in Fox family thinking, the awfulness of Russia, Austria and Prussia. Inevitably, in order to oppose these Empires, the Fox family had in some way to support the French. The francophilism of Holland House became notorious. Quite simply, France after 1789 represented, in however perverted a form, the cause of 'liberty' against

27. Fox to Holland, 21 Aug. 1794, *Memorials and Correspondence of C.J. Fox,* iii pp. 83-6.
28. Add. MSS. 47571, f 120; Fox to Holland, 25 April 1794.

'autocracy'. There was no French crime that was not outweighed by the actions of the Coalition powers. If the French became expansionist at the expense of surrounding countries, Poland had been entirely obliterated by the despots. If the Terror was deeply alarming, English judicial practice was worse. The enormity of the state trials after 1793 surpassed even 'French soidisant judicial proceedings'.[29] The Coalition Wars against France left the Whigs with no ideal solutions. In choosing to support France, the Fox family was choosing very clearly between evils, in the hope of a future good. They were often fiercely critical of French behaviour, but the alternative was always worse.

The longevity of Fox's views and their impact on the next generation depended on seeing the battle begun in 1789 as continuing into the 1820s and 1830s. Holland certainly believed this. In his view, the challenge of 1789 to the principles of autocracy went on, after hostilities ended in 1815, in the nationalist movements of the early nineteenth century. It was entirely appropriate to form a view on a crisis in the Middle East in 1836 by reference to Fox's remarks on the Oczakov Affair forty-five years earlier.[30] Further, the growth and extension of executive power under George III brought England very firmly into the front line of battle. Holland's close links with many European liberals was the camaraderie of arms. This ideological interpretation often came close to the naive. Holland created in his mind a spectrum of powers on a line between good and evil, and, in each crisis, simply supported the least bad or most good. The frequent refusal to allow British national interests to modify these ideological criteria was always bewildering, and often irritating, to professional diplomats. The line of moral distinction was sometimes so thin as to be unusable. During the Hundred Days for example, the choice between renewed war if Bonaparte was successful and victory for the depots if he was not left Holland an embarrassed neuter. It demonstrates,

29. Fox to Holland, c 28 Dec. 1793; *Memorials and Correspondence of C.J. Fox*, iii 57. See also Add. MSS. 47571, f 58; Fox to Holland, 17 Sept. 1793.

30. Add. MSS. 51755, ff 73-4; Holland to Henry Fox, 8 April 1836.

however, the extent to which Holland had accepted his uncle's principal article of faith that the most dangerous factor in English or European politics was an overweening executive.

Taking executive power as the main enemy, Fox was able to set the experiences of the 1780s and 1790s into a much wider tradition. Many Whig families had an ancestor who had been maltreated by a despotic Stuart king. The Hollands lacked this particular credential, but the iconography of Whig houses put Fox very much into an Apostolic succession. At Holkham Hall in Norfolk for example, the celebrated Nollekens bust of Fox stands amid those of Demosthenes, Alexander the Great, T.W. Coke and Francis, Duke of Bedford. There was a similar Pantheon at Woburn Abbey. As such a list indicates, the historical sensitivity of the Whigs is sometimes at fault, but the determination to give their ideas the benefit of a long pedigree is clear. In the hall at Holkham, there are four bas-reliefs depicting the death of Socrates, the death of Germanicus, the delivery of the keys of Florence to Cosmo the Great and William IV signing the Reform Bill. In the latter, William is rather unkindly dressed as King John and the Whig aristocracy as the barons at Runneymede. On this evidence, Fox's trumpeting of the dangers of executive power in the hands of George III was the latest episode in a long struggle.

The second article of faith in the Foxite creed was by contrast rather new. The fact that, by 1806, most Whigs saw themselves as guardians of many reform movements would have surprised their fathers and grandfathers. As Fox lectured his nephew, in 1801:

> The line of conduct to be taken seems quite clear, as Lansdowne would say, simplicity and consistency. Removal and censure of Pitt and his associates, Religious Liberty to its utmost extent, Reform in Parliament, Liberty of the Press ... not only peace, but a good understanding if it can be had, with Bonaparte.[31]

The cause of slavery abolition should properly be added to this list, but, to call these issues distinctly or largely Foxite was a very recent development. In the 1780s practically all of

---

31. Fox to Holland, 8 Feb. 1801; *Memorials and Correspondence of C.J. Fox*, iii 186-7.

them had been disputed between Pitt and Fox, but the French Revolution had the effect of defining attitudes in the most clinical way. To be against the French was to be against all reform. To say anything in their favour was to be associated in the popular mind with all reform. By this process, the Foxite became a reformer and the Pittite an anti-reformer.

Such a simplistic reading of course does great violence to a much more subtle sequence of events. The slave issue remained bipartisan. Pitt had as lively an interest in the problems of Irish Catholics as Fox, if for different motives. Equally, Fox's views on Parliamentary Reform, when expressed in private, were usually tepid and uncertain. None of these distinctions, however, influence the cruder assumptions of popular opinion, and all traces of equivocation were obliterated by the passage of time. The Foxite creed which Holland House inherited was cast in much bolder colours. When Fox's views were invoked in Parliamentary debates in the 1820s on issues like religious toleration or parliamentary reform, he was quoted as an uncompromising champion of these movements, and indeed as the only major English politician not to abandon them in the reactionary decade of the 1790s. The historical truth of this statement could be questioned on practically every point, but Whigs came to believe it implicitly. When Holland referred to 'members of the old opposition who had uniformly maintained the principles of peace and reform',[32] there were few qualifications to be made. The Foxite creed postulated a Fox who was a committed reformer and the greatest defender of English liberties against the assaults of the Crown.

In speaking of a Fox creed or a Fox cult, theological metaphors are used and this is not accident. The adoration of Fox in the early nineteenth century had much of a religious flavour about it. In no small measure for example, Holland's binding debt to a family past developed from the fact that the mantle of martyrs devolved upon him. To stay with Fox through the 1790s was to suffer loss. Whig doctors were denied patients and Whig lawyers were denied briefs. More

32. Add. MSS. 51869, f 520; Holland's Political Journal, 7 June 1832.

particularly, able young men like Grey, by adhering to Fox, consigned themselves to a career in the wastes of opposition. He eventually became prime minister in old age. Many others died without ever achieving office at all. Fox himself called these men

> ... the few who are neither subdued enough to be silent through fear, nor desperate enough to give up regular opposition, in expectation of more violent measures. [They were] weak in number and weight; but though weak, are right, and that must be our comfort.[33]

Holland, in 1831, called them 'the old ones of Claret and Foxite memory', and felt strongly that the Grey government 'should reward ... the old set who went through the persecutions of 1793 to 1800'.[34] The invocation of Fox's name, and the defence of the issues which it was believed he had defended, was also therefore the vindication of the sufferings of the faithful. Most Whig families would have had a representative among the martyrs. If the Hollands' eldest son refused a political career, he could be accused among other things of turning his back on martyrs.[35]

To understand the significance of Holland House, it is necessary to describe, in some detail, the elaboration of this cult in the early nineteenth century into its many diversified forms. The possession of a bust or portrait of Fox was a declaration of loyalty, whether in the Pantheon of Whig Worthies at Woburn Abbey or in the dressing room of Sarah Siddons. The first thing Whitbread did, on the death of his father, was to sell the family's portrait of Pitt. Large numbers of boys were christened Charles James or Charles James Fox after 1806. Copies of Fox's speeches were often presented to children in Whig families as a twenty-first birthday present.

33. Fox to Holland, 18 March 1794; *Memorials and Correspondence of C.J. Fox*, iii 69.

34. Holland to Grey, 19 Dec. 1831; Grey MSS. Box 34.

35. See L. Mitchell, *Charles James Fox and the Disintegration of the Whig Party*, vii. Holland felt these obligations keenly: 'I own I feel very strongly about .these old Edinburgh Foxites ... they resisted discountenance amounting to persecution from the period of the French Revolution to 1800 ... these reasons make me feel that I am bound as My Uncle's nephew and in some sort representative to secure their pretensions a favourable hearing.' Holland to Brougham, 27 Dec. 1831; Brougham MSS. 14966.

In *Vanity Fair*, Thackeray, in building up the character of Miss Crawley as 'a bel esprit and a dreadful Radical for those days', makes the point that she had a picture of Charles Fox in every room of her house.

Most important, the invocation of Fox's name and beliefs could take institutional form. The first record of a Fox Club is to be found in 1790.[36] Although there is no evidence that this club had a continuous life, on 24 January 1798, Fox's birthday, some two thousand people sat down to dinner to do their hero honour.[37] In 1808, a few of Fox's closest friends held a dinner to celebrate Fox's memory, and, from 1812 onwards, these functions were held under the auspices of a new Fox Club. The practice of dining on Fox's birthday rapidly spread outside London, and between 1815 and 1830, there are reports of such gatherings in almost every part of the country. The last dinner seems to have been held in Brooks's Club in 1907.[38] The numbers of people attending varied greatly and the dinners die out rapidly after the Whigs returned to power, but, in their years of opposition, they had a certain importance and usefulness.

Most obviously, Fox's name and Fox's history, when invoked at a Fox dinner, gave some minimum cohesion to a party in eternal opposition and much fissured by personal and political antagonisms. Grey, speaking at the Newcastle Fox Dinner in 1819, asked:

> What subject is there, whether of foreign or domestic interest, or that in the smallest degree affects our Constitution, which does not immediately associate itself with the memory of Mr Fox; and what moment so fit to address to you the observations which may be thought proper on such an occasion as that in which your feelings are most excited by his name.[39]

The toasts at these meetings were almost standardised, in that they intoned the catechism of 'Mr Fox and Parliamentary Reform', 'Mr Fox and religious toleration', 'Mr Fox and an

36. Add. MSS. 51516. A list of Fox Club members.
37. *Morning Chronicle*, 25 Jan. 1798.
38. V. Williamson, *Memorials of Brooks's*, pp. xix-xx.
39. *The Times*, 7 Jan. 1819.

end to Slavery'. In addition, Fox's name was employed to give respectability to ideas on which he had never pronounced at all. The Earl of Albemarle, at the Norwich Fox Dinner in 1821, after declaring that he had gone into politics 'as a man educated in the principles of Mr Fox must always go, with a mind abhorring persecution', went on to give a toast associating Fox with the cause of liberalism in Spain and Naples.[40]

For obvious reasons, it is not possible to push this argument very far. Annual meetings on Fox's birthday were more likely to be exercises in nostalgia than real contributions to Whig party organisation. Even so for a party out of office these opportunities were better than nothing. Further, as a political tactic, they avoided recourse to public meetings which were hard to manage and too often resulted in radical resolutions. Men who could afford to discuss politics over a dinner table were by definition within the political pale. In the crisis following Peterloo, Grey believed that 'the expression of views should be confined to such opportunities as Fox Club dinners might provide'.[41] Francis Place himself acknowledged that the Fox Dinners were an effective anti-radical device, if nothing else.[42] Lord Cockburn made larger claims for them:

> These Fox Dinners did incalculable good. They animated, and instructed, and consolidated the Whig party with less trouble and more effect than anything else that could have been devised.[43]

Whoever was right, however, the retention of the Fox cult was central to either purpose.

Holland himself set great store by these dinners, and he faithfully attended them every year when he was in England. Although granting their nostalgic character,[44] he seems to have agreed with Cockburn that they also served some

40. ibid., 21 Jan. 1821.
41. Grey to Holland, 10 Sept. 1819; A. Mitchell, *The Whigs in Opposition 1815-1830*, pp. 127-8.
42. Add. MSS. 36627, f 5; Diary of Francis Place.
43. Lord Cockburn, *Memorials of his Time*, pp. 397-8.
44. Add. MSS. 51869, f 78; Holland's Political Journal, 13 Aug. 1831.

organisational function. The question of finding a new
Secretary and Treasurer for the London Fox Club, in 1821,
led him to set out very broad requirements for prospective
candidates,

> I think that as far as the Fox Club is of any use it is essential to have
> some one ... who is in habits and intimacy with persons in both
> houses of Parliament, and not averse, nor unused, to communicate
> with those connected with Newspapers and agents in Elections.[45]

Holland also agreed that when the Radical challenge became
formidable, the Fox dinners were 'a proof of the comparative
strength in the Whiggish or aristocratical wing of the Reform
party'.[46] For all these reasons, Holland was much in demand
as guest of honour at Fox Dinners, and it was yet another
point of difference between him and his son that the latter
found these occasions tedious and uninspiring.

Whatever the purpose of the Foxite cult and the political
myths it propagated, its existence gave prominence to Holland
House which became something of a shrine. As soon as a
visitor entered the lobby, he was confronted by Westmacott's
statue of Fox,[47] on the plinth of which was inscribed the
following verse:

> Read history's page – there stranger you will find,
> The lasting record of a Fox's mind –
> Behold this form – the sculptor's magic art
> Has here preserved his frail or mortal part –
> Yet ask you still the charm which all subdued?
> Then enter here and see that charm renewed.[48]

---

45. Add. MSS. 51546, f 159; Holland to Grey, 15 Dec. 1821.
46. Add. MSS. 51756, f 5; Holland to Henry Fox, 17 Jan. 1837.
47. E. Vincent, *Ugo Foscolo*, p.25.
48. Add. MSS. 51677, f 40. This should be compared with the epitaph which
Holland wrote for himself shortly before his death:

> Nephew of Fox and friend of Grey
> Enough my Need of fame
> If those who deigned t'observe me Say
> I've tarnished neither name.

Bod. Lib., MSS. Eng. Lett. c 234, f 113.

The Hollands openly saw their House as the forum in which memories of Fox could be kept alive and where his views could be retailed to new generations. The influence of Holland House was open to anyone of whom Fox had spoken well,[49] and new protégés were brought within his shadow. The dependence of Holland on the intellectual lead given by his uncle was seen by him as repaying Foxite kindness. As he remarked to his sister,

> ... both you and I have found that most of our Uncle's political adherents male or female have shown us through life a sort of parental interest and regard difficult to be maintained and unusual to be sought for, between persons so much and necessarily separated by differences of age and habit.[50]

Here was the guarantee of the Hollands' position in politics. If the Foxite cult was a central aspect of the Whig party in the early nineteenth century, Holland, as the interpreter of Fox, was indispensable in Whig discussions. Holland was in fact sole heir to the whole political legacy. Within a month of Fox's death, the Duke of Bedford had written to Holland as follows:

> I will only add that I shall look to you as the natural heir to your Uncle's principles and station, as the Repository of his great Mind, from which all our Stores of political action and political wisdom must now be drawn, and if I do not say to you that I shall feel towards you all I felt for him (for I never can feel for any other man what I felt for him) you will at least allow me to consult your opinions and seek such assistance and advice, in all things when I may be in need of them.[51]

The Hollands were to elaborate and develop this inheritance in many interesting directions, but it was in every way fundamental to their standing. Lord Holland, almost by definition, was 'the only statesman ... who has the great manly views of Mr Fox'.[52] He had been so conscientious and

49. Holland to Whitbread, 12 Oct. 1812; Whitbread MSS 1925.

50. Add. MSS. 51741, f 223; Holland to Caroline Fox, 4 Dec. 1825.

51. Add. MSS. 51661, ff 33-4; Bedford to Holland, 28 Sept. 1806. See also Add. MSS. 51520, f 12; Prince of Wales to Holland, 12 Sept. 1806.

52. Lord William Russell to Lady Holland, 26 Sept. 1828; *Lord W. Russell and his Wife*, p.171.

unquestioning a pupil of his uncle, that other Whigs could regard him almost as a political reincarnation of Fox himself.

So universal was this feeling that when, in 1806 or 1830, the Whigs were called upon to form a Cabinet, Holland's claims to office were irrefutable. In spite of the doubts about Holland's own judgment and fears about Lady Holland's influence, the representative of the Fox name simply could not be excluded. Holland himself was aware of this position. Reflecting on the Ministry of the Talents, he told Lauderdale that

> ... my uncle's friends felt very jealous of the Grenvilles, and thought that my name in the Cabinet was absolutely *necessary*, and in the Foreign Office *desirable*, to prove that there was a disposition to cultivate my uncle's friends, to preserve his system and principles, and to give to his memory a portion of that influence which his superiority had hitherto secured to his party.[53]

The same point held in 1830. In both cases, the answer to the problem of employing an unavoidable man, about whose capacity for office there was real doubt, was to appoint him to minor office only. Holland was only Lord Privy Seal in 1806-7 and Chancellor of the Duchy of Lancaster in 1830-40. It was the only sensible way of reconciling the claims of a great name with the realities of politics.

Holland readily accepted the obligations of his inheritance. The quality of Charles Fox's tuition was such that it had produced devotion rather than rebellion. In 1809 for example, he accepted the Recordership of Nottingham, 'which however I may laught at it, I like very much because there never was a body of Men more firmly attached to the cause of freedom and in the very worst times more devoted to my Uncle than the corporation of that town'.[54] More seriously, he had to defend his uncle's memory against his first biographer. In 1811, John Trotter, who had become Fox's secretary in 1802, solved

---

53. Holland to Lauderdale, 22 Sept. 1806; *Memoirs of the Whig Party during my Time*, ii 53. See also, Henry Fox to Lady S. Napier, 2 April 1807; Bod. Lib. MSS. Eng. Lett. c 238, f 150, and J. Wishaw to Brougham, 19 Sept. 1806; *Life and Times of Lord Brougham*, i 373.

54. Add. MSS. 51739, f 24; Holland to Caroline Fox, 26 Nov. 1809.

pressing financial problems by publishing a life of his late employer. The picture of Fox presented was not, as Holland himself admitted,[55] wholly unfavourable, but it still caused Holland House much pain. In their view, Trotter had totally missed the point of Fox's career, namely his great sacrifices in the face of the overwhelming forces in the service of the Crown. In a series of agitated letters[56] to Jeffrey, the editor of the *Edinburgh Review*, Holland pointed out the weaknesses of the book and made long suggestions about who should review the book and how. It was, in sum, an early example of that jealous guardianship of Fox's memory that was to mark Holland's career for the next thirty years.

For the same reason, Holland was always against the tactic of seceding from the House of Commons by way of demonstrating the ineffectiveness of that institution. For him, it was always necessary to vindicate the Foxite past whenever possible. Although the cause of opposition might be hopeless in the conventional sense of seeking to obtain power, there was still a perfectly plausible rôle for it to play in the demonstration of Foxite consistency. Holland was alarmed by Charles Fox's absence from Parliament after 1797, until his uncle specifically asked him to remain at his post in the House of Lords to represent the family line.[57] This sense of obligation was always present thereafter. When, later in his career, Holland had to contend repeatedly with Grey's reluctance to come to London and give time to Westminster, he always fell back on the argument that their joint debt to Fox demanded continued exertion. In 1820 for example, although severe attacks of gout made him 'more of a passenger ... every day',

---

55. Add. MSS. 51739, ff 69-70; Holland to Caroline Fox, 3 Nov. 1811.

56. Add. MSS. 51644, ff 131-52; Holland to Jeffrey, Oct./Nov. 1811. This letter ends with a menacing Greek epigram

Εἰ πὲρ γάρ τε χόλον γε καὶ αὐτῆμαρ καταπέψῃ
ἀλλά τε καὶ μετόπισθεν ἔχει κότον, ὄφρα τελέσσῃ

(If a man digests his wrath even for a day
Yet he will keep it alive for future revenge)
Iliad i 81-2.

57. Fox to Holland, 1797; *Memorials and Correspondence of C.J. Fox*, iii 138. See also Fox to Holland, 19 Nov. 1797; ibid., iii 138.

Holland did 'not like the prospect of seeing a party of which my Uncle was and you are the head, crumble to pieces for want of exertion to keep it together'.[58] In the long Holland-Grey correspondence, the point is again and again made that mounting an opposition to Pitt's political descendants had a purpose outside the mere acquisition of power.

Holland's piety towards his uncle's memory was basically acceptable because the context and the issues of political life were much the same for both uncle and nephew. Inevitably, however, over a fifty-year period, the reference points in politics changed to some degree. Different factors, for example, affected the Turkish problem in the 1830s from the ones that had been discussed in the 1790s, even though the conclusions drawn might be the same. Holland's Hamlet-like devotion to Fox's ghost carried the real danger that these distinctions would not be drawn. His judgment would often be questioned in the future, and quite frequently such doubts arose simply because Holland was applying Foxite views to situations which they no longer neatly fitted. On one or two occasions, an overwhelming debt to the past made accommodation to the present difficult. In addition, after Fox's death, it was not always easy to remember detail, and Holland admitted that he 'could only discern the path by such light as recollection, possibly indistinct and erroneous, could supply'.[59]

In spite of these drawbacks, however, Holland, as Fox's sole heir, was in an enviable position. The Foxite faith in 1806 involved the championship of some kind of Parliamentary Reform, the extension of religious toleration to Catholics and the defence of slaves. It clearly maintained that executive power was the greatest enemy of civil liberty, and it demanded that English politics should be debated within the context of European events. Each of these points had a historical perspective, and each could be explained in terms of the practical responses Fox made to the problems of the 1780s and 1790s. With every year that passed after 1806, the

58. Add. MSS. 51546, ff 95-6; Lord and Lady Holland to Grey, 5 April 1820.
59. Holland, *Memoirs of the Whig Party during my Time*, pp. 2-3.

identification of these issues with Fox becames closer. His doubts and equivocations were forgotten or smoothed over. All of this was handed over to Holland House for safekeeping.

To argue that the Whigs had a set of beliefs, however badly defined, is to qualify the picture of a badly organised and factionalised party which has properly been presented by a number of modern historians.[60] In fact, the two statements complement each other rather than conflict. The Whig performance at Westminster and in the constituencies was often incoherent and feeble. They argued about tactics and found it almost impossible to find satisfactory leadership. Yet Westminster was only one area of political life, and one in which the Whigs recognised their cause to be hopeless. Even Holland agreed that their role was 'to be spectators rather than actors in many of these exhibitions and to assist rather by applauding those we approve and hissing those we condemn than by suggesting much of our own'.[61] It was worth attending at Westminster because there were always Foxite points to be made and because there was 'some sport' in irritating Radicals and Tories, but undue effort was redundant because power could never be theirs. The organisational aspects of the party are therefore correctly described as ramshackle and amateurish.

Westminster, however, was never the sole arena for political action. It was no accident for example that the Parliamentary Session was roughly coterminous with the London Season, thereby illustrating the inter-reaction of social and political activities. The salon was the obvious forum for mixing these two elements, and Holland House became the supreme example of this principle operating. Here, the Hollands could peddle the Foxite faith, as outlined above, and could display, as it were, the full magnificence of their political legacy. Most despaired of power and some even disliked the idea of office, preferring to see politics as something which might interest the amateur among all the other diversions of the Season. Pittites were often accused by Whigs of actually needing

60. A Mitchell, *The Whigs in Opposition 1815-1830.*
61. Add. MSS. 51653, f 112; Holland to Mackintosh, 29 Dec. 1821.

government salaries to support themselves. None of this means, however, that they were intellectually bankrupt. The Foxite articles of faith were always there. Their interpretation could be disputed, and their claims would be substantiated by new ideas from Scotland and Europe, but they provided the basis for action when the vagaries of politics wafted the Whigs back into office in 1830. The continuing impact of Fox's career guaranteed the Hollands' place in politics and was the rock on which Holland House itself was built.

3

Whig Beliefs and Whig Myths

There is an obvious difficulty about trying to generalise about a man's political outlook over half a century. Inevitably, such views change with the passage of time, some being held more fervently and some being abandoned altogether. In Holland's case, however, the exercise is worth undertaking, because his politics were determined by two abnormal factors, namely the unusually static preoccupations of politics between 1789 and 1830 and the dominating influence of his uncle. For most of his career, the great issues in English politics remained the same. Any stimulus for the development of attitudes came from abroad. The pupil of Charles Fox could therefore coast along happily, applying the lessons of the master in debates about old issues on which he had so finally pronounced. In describing the political attitudes of Holland House, one is really describing the working out of the Foxite legacy in the next generation.

Like Fox, Holland took as his starting point the crisis of 1784. The events of that year convinced the Fox family that the old shibboleth of the English constitution being 'in balance' could no longer be held. It was too obvious that the House of Commons could not 'balance' the power of the Crown. George III dismissed the Coalition ministry when its majority in the Commons was over a hundred. William IV would attempt the same thing in 1834. The logic of all this was inescapable. If the idea of 'balance' ever had worked in the English constitution, George III had successfully overturned it. The only answer was to build up the power of the House of Commons to a position of pre-eminence within the constitution. As Holland told his sister, in 1793, 'Now the object of my Uncle's Political sentiments is to give influence, authority, weight and responsibility to the House of Commons'.[1] This conclusion was not arrived at speculatively, but in response to hard experience. To Holland, the dismissal of the Talents Ministry, in 1807, echoed that of his uncle in 1784. He told the Lords that 'Caesar made way for Catiline and the Duke of Portland imitated Mr Pitt in establishing himself in power against the constitution'.[2]

Both these occasions involved the question of who should be in government and by what authority. It was obvious to the Whigs that Pitt and Portland depended basically on the support of kings. Pitt's cavalier dismissal in 1801, after seventeen years service to George III, seemed to emphasise the point that any real element of balance within the constitution had gone. In this new situation, the House of Commons must be elevated to the leading place in the triumvirate of King, Lords and Commons. In all the wrangles over the Whig party leadership, Holland endlessly made the point that most of the party's leaders should be in the House of Commons.[3] The House of Lords was still an essential feature of the legislative process, but, since its membership had doubled between 1784 and 1801, that body could not be counted on to stand up to George III. The House of Commons, possibly purged by Parliamentary Reform, was the only possibility. If no change were made, executive power would sweep away civil liberty and the awfulness of the 1790s would be perpetuated.

Over a period, the theme develops. In 1828, it is 'parliament', which should predominate, presumably reserving some authority for the Lords:

> The supreme power of parliament must, in my judgement, be always left at full liberty to legislate for the good of the country ... No shackles, no promises, no pledge, ought to bind a legislature, which, unless it is free and unfettered, cannot, in the vicissitude of human affairs, be sufficient to provide for the security and welfare of the community.[4]

1. Add. MSS. 51731, f 105; Holland to Caroline Fox, 5 Jan. 1793.
2. *Parl. Deb.* vol. XLV, 412-7; 13 April 1807.
3. Add. MSS. 51544, ff 91-102; Holland to Grey, 30 Nov. 1807.
4. *Speech of Lord Holland in the House of Lords on the Second Reading of the Bill for the Repeal of the Corporation and Test Acts* (London 1828), p.42.

After the passing of the Reform Bill, however, the tone changes, and it is the supremacy of the House of Commons which is specifically referred to. Sovereignty has come to reside in an adequate representation of 'the people', although that expression has still not taken on a full democratic meaning.[5] Holland comes to the idea of the sovereignty of 'the people' as the answer to the problem of executive power, rather than starting from any democratic premise:

> ... the objection felt as well as stated to Ld Melbourne's government is that the House of Commons do really represent the people and so representing them have necessarily the virtual supreme government in their hands. They forget that such is the intention of a popular representative Monarchy and they shut their eyes to the obvious truth that such must be the effect of a reform which gave to the Community a real and positive and not a mere nominal representation. It is to be hoped that the Hse of Lords will ere long discover and act upon this undeniable truth.[6]

By 'the people', Holland is still referring to a political nation composed of property owners. He never subscribed to the idea of the right of every man to take part in politics. The crucial point is, however, that the House of Commons, in representing 'the people' should now be the preponderant influence in the constitution.

In thus elevating the claims of the Commons, the Fox family was clinging to the idea of balance, but in a new form. Traditionally, the old notion of the legislature balancing the executive had been designed to avert the danger of executive power which had been repeatedly demonstrated under the Stuarts. After 1789, there was another danger, namely the claims for democracy. In the Whig view, the unbridled licence of the Crown or the violence of a mob meant the end of all civil liberty. Further, the one tended to act as an excuse for the activities of the other. Fox and his nephew loathed both. In the 1790s Fox had been accused of thinking 'in such a half way ...

5. Throughout his writings and speeches, Holland uses the word 'people' to describe those who owned forms of property. He would fully have agreed with his friend Lord Cockburn, when he insisted that 'by the word people, we mean the great central mass of property and knowledge'. K. Miller, *Cockburn's Millennium*, p.106.

6. Add. MSS. 51871, ff 971-2; Holland's Political Journal, 1836.

he is neither for the broad idea of public government, nor for the Court, [and] if he really thinks it the People's interest to have the Court opposed by a union of moderate men, he can never expect to find that union as he [is] now almost single in his opinions'.[7] The forum for this 'union of moderate men' was to be the House of Commons. If that body could be brought to represent properly the political nation, its credibility would be irresistible to all except those who believed in the political pretensions of autocracy or democracy. The Fox family assumed that they stood on the middle ground of politics, balancing the dangers of executive power and mob rule.

It is therefore very important, at the outset, to understand what Holland meant by 'the people' and 'democracy'. The terms are freely used in his speeches and letters. In the *Memoirs* for example, Holland refers to 'the People' as 'that Sovereign whom Mr Fox acknowledged, and from whom George the Third himself derived the power of dismissing or replacing him'.[8] Equally, 'he thought, that for defence no government could be too free; by that he meant too democratic; the words might not be synonymous, but it was in such governments that men felt of what they were capable'.[9] With regard to both terms, however, there are two meanings depending on context. When Holland talks of 'the people' with approbation, he is talking of those, who qualify for political consciousness by meeting the criteria set by the times, in other words a *pays légal*. When he uses the term disparagingly, he is simply referring to the total number of people in the state, most of whom could never qualify for political life. On the same level, his use of the word democracy describes government *for* or on behalf of the broad mass of the citizenry and never government *by* such people. He once rebuked an opponent for using 'the word democracy in a very fallacious sense when he applied it to the mass of the people. Though the opinion of the mass of the people was not to be

---

7. Add. MSS. 51731, f 100; Holland to Caroline Fox, 25 Dec. 1792. See also, Add. MSS. 51732, f 161; Holland to Caroline Fox, 28 Jan. 1795.
8. Holland, *Memoirs of the Whig Party during my Time*, p.133.
9. *Parl. Deb.*, LI 535-6, 22 Feb. 1810.

followed in every case, yet every government was made for the benefit of the mass of the people.'[10]

There was an insuperable objection to using democracy, in the widest definition of the term, to forestall difficult kings. The people in the mass were too uneducated and unleisured to have either the training or the time to form mature political opinions. Their views were incoherent, irrational and all too often the echos of demagogic minds. Once again, as Holland noted, his uncle had given a lead in refusing 'to derive popularity from espousing opinions which [he] thought unsound, though generally held by the people'.[11] The King and Church crowds of the 1790s had demonstrated how the political extreme of despotism could manipulate the other extreme of mob rule. Holland's advocacy of an extension of the franchise was never conceived in a democratic context therefore. Rather it was an attempt to bring all 'the people', meaning the 'political nation', within the constitution. Property holding[12] was still the qualification for admission to the political nation, because only that created the conditions in which rational judgments could be formed. The consolidation of the political nation in the House of Commons was the guarantee against extremes and the ultimate defence of civil liberty.

Constitutional government therefore, properly conducted, was a trust on behalf of the broad mass of the population. The possession of property demanded that a man accept this responsibility. The moral promptings for such a course were strong:

> I am particularly glad you said what you did about property, because I see on all sides a tendency to disregard the happiness and security of the Poor, otherwise as in good policy, it may be supposed to contribute to that of the rich.[13]

10. ibid., **XXXV** 1239, 23 March 1801.

11. Holland, *Memoirs of the Whig Party during my Time*, p.168.

12. More particularly, in Holland's writings, property is still often equated with landed property. He was happy to recommend a man for the J.P's bench once he was assured 'that he is not engaged in trade'. Holland to William Shepherd, 15 Nov. 1831; Shepherd MSS. vol. 7, f 55.

13. Add. MSS. 51734, f 52; Caroline Fox to Holland, 9 July 1798.

Holland himself was keenly aware, however, that, unless these obligations were fulfilled, the penalty to be paid by the propertied classes would be grievous:

> Great Lords should learn that to retain their importance in the country some attention to popular rights, aye and popular wishes too, is as necessary as condescension to the views of Ministers and Courts – Every one can understand that a Personality to a King can be resented but they seem to think that the people should not be angry at being called and treated like a rabble when distress or mistake hurry them into imprudent excesses.[14]

If this concept of government as trust was spurned and if the House of Commons did not 'balance' politics by defending popular rights against the depredations of the executive, the result would be democratic revolution. The example of France was too close.

Now Holland naturally believed that the Whigs were uniquely qualified to fulfil this trust. The historians of the party, among whom had figured Fox himself,[15] told him that Whigs had already performed this task for generations. If property remained the qualification for admission to the political nation, the Whigs, as men of great property, had a special rôle to play. They found it very difficult to move away from the idea that part of the quality of an argument lay in the name of the man who put it forward. As late as 1829, Lord John Russell concluded a letter to Holland with the words, '*Measures not men* is the maxim of a *tailor* and not a *man*.'[16] By this he meant that, in assessing candidates for office, who a man was had at least as much importance as the programme he hoped to implement. The divine right of the Whigs to govern, a notion which so many of their critics found smug and self-satisfied, was based on these assumptions. By prescription, the Whigs alone knew how to fulfil the trust implied in government and to avoid the dangers of popular and executive excess.

Holland House in no way accepted however, the charge that

14. Add. MSS. 51848, ff 86-7; Holland to Henry Fox, March 1820. See also Holland, *Memoirs of the Whig Party during my Time*, ii 66-7.

15. Fox, at his death, left an uncompleted *History of the Reign of James II*.

16. Add. MSS. 51677, f 67; Lord J. Russell to Holland, January 1829.

the Whigs championed exclusiveness based on the accidents of birth. When Thomas Moore suggested, in his biography of Sheridan, that Fox had only been preferred to Sheridan because of his family connections, Holland reacted angrily by saying that if distinctions based on birth 'were greater than right reason can justify the Times, the country, the Parliament and the publick are responsible. They were in fact less in the real and practical estimation of the Party called Whigs than in that of the Society in which they lived.'[17] The promotion of talent, from Burke and Sheridan to Macaulay and the Edinburgh Reviewers had been a consistent feature of the Whig tradition and one in which the Hollands took pride. The objection to someone like Goderich was that he was incompetent, not that he had once been called Robinson.[18] Holland liked to believe quite simply that 'it is the Whiggism of particular men that makes me respect them'.[19] If Sheridan had not reached the highest levels of party leadership, it was personal 'peculiarities',[20] notably his notorious insobriety, which was to blame.

Holland House was therefore able to hold in tandem both that the holding of office as a trust was something prescriptively Whiggish and that they had a splendid record of encouraging ability from whatever social level. Their opponents found this frankly hypocritical, and there is much force in their criticism. The Whigs, and Holland House in particular, certainly patronised ability, but not beyond certain limits. Burke and Macaulay were admirable in the sense that they were happy with minor government office. Sheridan and Brougham aimed higher and were therefore thought difficult. Canning was most difficult of all because he believed that ability was a sufficient qualification actually to lead a party. Much of the tension about the Canning ministry in 1827 stems from this fact. As will be seen, for the Hollands this problem was particularly acute.[21] Men of talent certainly had a part to play in Holland House, but in general the Hollands shared

17. Add. MSS. 51653, ff 128-33; Holland to Sir James Mackintosh, 1825.
18. Add. MSS. 52173, f 121; Lady Holland to Allen, 25 April 1828.
19. Add. MSS. 51731, ff 96-7; Holland to Caroline Fox, 9 Nov. 1792.
20. Add. MSS. 51653, ff 128-33; Holland to Mackintosh, 1825.
21. See below, Chapter Five.

that Whig pride of caste which suggested that government, on the terms described above, was best left in the experienced hands of great families. They were not, as John Allen observed, 'a mere Aristocracy',[22] and the Hollands watched with real distress the appearance of 'divisions of Classes and great interests',[23] but there was no escaping the fact that their prescriptive right to government was uppermost in their minds.

If there was some ambiguity about Whig rankings, however, the Whigs of the early nineteenth century were clear that their self-appointed task of defending constitutional practice against political extremes could only be done through the agency of a party. There is not a trace in the Hollands' writings of the eighteenth-century tendency to see party as faction and an organised opposition to the King's chosen ministers as treason. The necessity of party, which Burke had darkly hinted at in the 1770s is now trumpeted everywhere. It was a logical extension of the new-found importance of the House of Commons that Whig strength should be mobilised within it. As Holland put it, in passing on another of his uncle's lessons to his own son,

I therefore think that if you have any publick object for yourself or others you will, you ought, nay you infallibly must, under whatever name you disguise it, persue it by party means.[24]

It was a maxim which he himself learned back in the 1790s.[25]

In Holland's thinking about party, there is an intellectual progression from Fox, however. After 1815, his belief in the value and necessity of party is reinforced by the presentation of it as the alternative to the politics of class and faction. In his view, the real danger of revolution stemmed in part from the breakdown of party and the ensuing fragmentation of interests:

22. J. Allen to Sir Charles Vaughan, 1809; Vaughan MSS c 9/3.
23. Add. MSS. 51547, ff 93-4; Holland to Grey, 22 Dec. 1826.
24. Add. MSS. 51749, ff 42-3; Holland to Henry Fox, 22 Oct. 1824.
25. Add. MSS. 51732, ff 45-6; Holland to Caroline Fox, 22 July 1794.

We have indeed got rid of party government and we shall now see if an Empire divided between Interests and Countries and religions, grower and consumer, Irishmen and Englishmen, Protestants and Catholicks, constitutes a happier wiser or stronger community than one where the only distinctions were attachment to different systems of policy or adherence to opposite leaders in the state.[26]

When, from time to time, negotiations were started to consider the question of a Whig re-entry into government, Holland usually viewed them with great suspicion. For him, there was no question of a partial re-entry into office. Rather the Whigs should come in as a party.[27] The Whigs of course never achieved this level of cohesion, least of all in 1827 when Holland himself was somewhat at sea, but this was distressing. A wicked executive naturally preferred to deal with factions, among whom it could manoeuvre, than with firm parties based on a set of political principles. But it was precisely this fact that Holland feared. The division of a community into endless competing factions was a step, in his view, towards final political collapse.

The main enemy of the Whig party, even after 1789, was the Crown. Holland endlessly repeated his uncle's homilies on the dangers of executive power:

I remember Stanhope said of the French Republick once to me, when they're right I praise them and when they're wrong then I say nothing about them, and that you see is candid – I own my disposition is to shew this sort of candour to the Jacobins or to any people who oppose the influence of the Crown, and now you have my creed.[28]

The principal aim of any reform of the constitution must be the further diminution of royal influence.[29] Indeed, Holland believed, against the wisdom of current research, that the power of the Crown was actually increasing in the early

26. Add. MSS. 51749, f 203 and f 217; Holland to Henry Fox, 3 Oct. and 30 Nov. 1826.
27. Princess Charlotte to Miss Elphinstone, 2 Jan. 1812; *The Letters of Princess Charlotte*, p.21 and Add. MSS. 51661, f 104; Bedford to Holland, 4 Feb. 1808.
28. Add. MSS. 51738, ff 65-6; Holland to Caroline Fox, 1 Jan. 1808.
29. Holland to F. Horner, 10 Jan. 1817; *The Letters of F. Horner*, ii 395-6.

nineteenth century. Against a background of the French Revolution, such views were thought idiosyncratic or downright perverse by many contemporaries. Seen in an exclusively English context, the Hollands' attitude might well appear eccentric. Their defence lies in the fact that they insisted on putting England in a European context, where theories based on the misuse of autocratic power carried more credibility.

The danger was all the more acute because the Hanoverians were, in the Hollands' eyes, fundamentally undesirable. George III's only quality had been stubbornness and that had been most employed in thwarting Uncle Charles's defence of English liberty. George IV was idle, emotionally unstable and given over to a Byzantine dependence on overweight mistresses:

> Who gave private advice to the Prince of Wales? The M. of Hertford. Who seduced him from his early friends? – the M. of Hertford. Who defeated the prospect of a strong administration? The M. of Hertford – Who debauched away my Cook? The M. of Hertford.[30]

The Hollands had a closer relationship with William IV, if only because their illegitimate son, Charles Richard, married the eldest of William's illegitimate daughters. Described as a political booby, he was taken to be less menacing than his father and brother. The events of 1834-5, however, convinced the Hollands that even boobies could turn vicious.

The only Hanoverians in whom the Hollands had any confidence were Princess Charlotte and the young Victoria. Holland House was delighted to discover that the latter

> ... identified her family interests with those of representative government and constitutional or parliamentary monarchy – This is lucky for the interests of freedom though perhaps it is rather mortifying to philosophy to perceive how much the destinies of Europe, and the institutions and happiness of mankind still depend in spite of the pretended march of intellect, the schoolmaster, the representative system, the press or what not on the accidental and personal character and will of a girl of 18.[31]

30. Add. MSS. 51739, f 96; Holland to Caroline Fox, 29 Aug. 1812. See also T. Moore to Lady Donegal, *The Letters of Thomas Moore*, i 175.
31. Add. MSS. 51871, f 1047; Holland's Political Journal, 3 Aug. 1837.

Her reign opened marvellously, and Victoria's backing was invaluable to Melbourne's shaky administration. In particular, her behaviour during the Bedchamber Crisis of 1839 was impeccable.[32] Very soon, however, in Lady Holland's opinion, the family tradition reasserted itself. By 1842, she was suggesting that 'best beware of Princes is a maxim as old as Monarchies, they are not to be trusted and never faithful to friends'.[33] It's fair to predict that the Hollands would not have been surprised by Victoria's later association with Disraeli.

If challenged on these prejudices, the Hollands would have replied with a long list of examples demonstrating, in their view, the ways in which the Hanoverians had cheated politicians and twisted constitutional practice to their own ends. The prorogation of Parliament for ninety days in 1816 during the discussion of peace terms was 'a measure that has no precedent since James 2nds time'.[34] George III and his sons were masters of the game of breaking parties by 'playing one against the other', and this 'picking out individuals from each and sharing anything like power with none'[35] gave monarchy power at the expense of constitutional practice. Above all, if questioned on their conviction that executive power was still the greatest danger to English liberty and that it was annually growing stronger, the Fox family always pointed to the elevation of Addington. The fact that a virtual nonentity could become first minister against the combined wishes of Fox, Pitt and Grenville, demonstrated the truth of the situation for Holland House. As Fox exclaimed, 'Was there ever anything like this? ... what is, or rather what is not the power of the crown?'[36]

In listing royal misdemeanour, family history and experience came necessarily to the fore. The tribulations of Charles Fox and the Coalition ministry have already been referred to. The Talents Ministry of 1806-7, of which he was a

32. Add. MSS. 51757, ff 48 seq; Holland to Henry Fox, 3 May 1839, and ff 56 seq; ibid., 25 June 1839.

33. Add. MSS. 51747, f 260; Lady Holland to Caroline Fox, 23 Sept. 1842.

34. Add. MSS. 51653, ff 55-8; Holland to Mackintosh, 23 Jan. 1816.

35. Add. MSS. 51751, f 25; Holland to Henry Fox, 8 July 1830.

36. Fox to Holland, 24 Jan. 1803; *Memorials and Correspondence of C.J. Fox*, iii 211-12.

part, presented, in Holland's view, an exact parallel. It was conceived without love: 'H Mty [is] resigned to his fate saying if God's will is to deprive him of his dominions God's will be done, which is very pious but somewhat hard on his subjects.'[37] It was endlessly menaced by the threat of dissolution,[38] and was finally destroyed by royal intrigue.[39] Uncle and nephew had had the same experience. The same sad tale was to be repeated in 1834-5, though this time it was to have a happier ending.[40] On this occasion, Holland read of the dismissal of the Whig ministry in *The Times*, and this was his first indication that he was no longer a Minister.[41] William IV had not only chosen to turn out a government enjoying the confidence of the House of Commons, but he had done it in a manner 'so abrupt, so unlike anything gentlemanlike'.[42] The Fox family believed that executive power was their enemy because, in their own bitter experience, this had so often been the case.

The Holland House view of Pittites and Tories was a logical extension of this idea. The heirs of Pitt were the aiders and abetters of designing kings. They believed neither in government for the people nor by the people. Frequently, their social origins and a lack of a financial competence left them dependent on office-holding and the kings who made that possible. In the demonology of Holland House, Burke was pre-eminent;

> As to Burke's return from the Toryland I neither expect it nor wish it, I hope he may remain there and do his new friends as much harm by his extravagance as he is accustomed to do his old ones by violence and ill judgment.[43]

Pitt[44] and Wellington[45] ran a close second and third. At a

37. Add. MSS. 51738, f 1; Holland to Caroline Fox, 20 Jan. 1806.
38. *Parl. Deb.*, vol. XLV 585-90.
39. Holland, *Memoirs of the Whig Party during my Time*, p.94.
40. See Chapter Six.
41. Greville, *Diaries*, iii 151. 17 Nov. 1834.
42. Lady Holland to Henry Fox, 21 Nov. 1834; *Elizabeth, Lady Holland to her Son*, p.155. See also Add. MSS. 51754, f 3; Holland to Henry Fox, 9 Jan. 1835.
43. Add. MSS. 51731, ff 137-9; Holland to Caroline Fox, 1 Aug. 1793.
44. Add. MSS. 51795, f 77; Holland to Upper Ossory, 29 Jan. 1806.
45. Add. MSS. 51750, ff 182-3; Holland to Henry Fox, 1 Jan. 1828.

lower level, the Hollands shared all the prejudices brilliantly displayed by Macaulay in the famous third chapter of his *History of England*. Tories preferred the country to the town; they were religious bigots and hopelessly ignorant of foreign countries; there was nothing 'as selfish and as stingy as a landed gentleman'.[46] Even when they touched upon reform, Tories only did so because it was 'convenient and necessary',[47] and not because it was right. In office in the 1820s, Tory blindness brought the country near to revolution.[48] Out of office in the 1830s, the Tory tactic of using the House of Lords to block legislation brought the very existence of the second chamber into question.[49]

The antipathy was returned in full measure. For most Tories, Holland House represented cranky ideas and wild irresponsibility. One of the most intractable problems of 1827 was George IV's absolute refusal to have Holland in the Cabinet. He would in fact 'have no Minister who had insulted all the crowned heads of Europe'.[50] Herries, in discussing the same question, was equally firm:

> What really public object could it promote? It could not be supposed that Lord Holland would bring any useful addition of knowledge or ability to the Government in the management of our domestick concerns; and it will hardly be pretended that his principles and opinions as to our foreign policy and Continental affairs ... are of a nature to smooth the difficulties in which our foreign relations are at this time involved. It would not be impossible, I think, to prove the contrary.[51]

For Huskisson, Holland had 'too many wild notions, both of foreign and domestic policy'.[52] There was also another problem about Holland as far as the Tories were concerned. They were anxious to preserve the idea, in 1827, that Lord Liverpool's government had not given way to Whig but to

---

46. Add. MSS. 51740, f 196; Holland to Caroline Fox, 23 Sept. 1816.
47. Add. MSS. 51750, ff 192-3; Holland to Henry Fox, 3 March 1828.
48. Add. MSS. 51524, f 132; Sussex to Holland, 8 Jan. 1828.
49. Add. MSS. 51757, ff 84-5; Holland to Henry Fox, 23 Aug. 1839.
50. Creevey to Miss Ord, 18 Sept. 1827; *Creevey Diaries*, ii 128.
51. Herries to Bexley, 28 Dec. 1827; *Memoirs of J. Herries*, ii 44.
52. Huskisson to Granville, 8 Jan. 1828; *The Huskisson Papers*, p.277. See also Anglesey to Goderich, 6 Sept. 1827; *Pegleg*, p.176.

'mixed' administrations. The Canning and Goderich ministries must not be represented as Whig victories. In the Tory view, it would have been impossible to maintain this view of politics, if Holland had been a member of either of those governments. They were clear that his name and attitudes were such, that his entry into office would alone have been sufficient to turn a 'mixed' government into a Whig government.[53]

If English constitutionalism was principally threatened by kings and Tories, it was also harrassed by Radicals, who, in the first half of the nineteenth century, were increasingly tempted to move towards democratic remedies. As Holland noted, they were a constant irritant in politics.[54] Their views were visionary in the sense that the involvement of the bulk of the population in politics would sanctify ignorance rather than reinforce wisdom, for the reasons outlined above. Holland knew most of the Radical leaders and had an almost uniformly low opinion of them. Romilly[55] was a good man, but too taken up with 'the more grovelling and selfish maxims of his friend Bentham'. Cobbett was marked by 'such instability in principle and of such scurrility in controversy'[56] that any dealings with him were full of embarrassments. Stanhope was simply mad[57] and Horne Tooke erratic.[58] All of them were men of ability, but their readiness to call into politics opinion from outside the charmed world of Westminster was dangerous in the extreme. Even Samuel Whitbread, who was a reasonably regular diner at Holland House and someone whose claims the Hollands championed against the widespread suspicions held about him,[59] taught a son who eventually ruined himself in the idiocy of Queen Caroline's divorce.[60]

The only Radical leader who came to have a firm

53. Goderich to Lansdowne, 11 Aug. 1828; *Prosperity Robinson*, p.154.
54. Holland, *Further Memoirs of the Whig Party*, p.381.
55. ibid., p.264.
56. Add. MSS. 51871, f 860; Holland's Political Journal, 18 June 1835.
57. Holland, *Memoirs of the Whig Party during my Time*, pp. 35-6.
58. Fox to Holland, Feb. 1798; *Memorials and Correspondence of C.J. Fox*, iii 143.
59. T. Grenville to Lord Grenville, 27 Dec. 1809; H.M.C. *Fortescue* MSS. ix 437-8.
60. Add. MSS. 52173, J. Allen to Lady Holland, 7 June 1822.

relationship with Holland House was Sir Francis Burdett. He first appears in the Dinner Books in 1801, when he was invited as something of a curiosity. His early habit of saying unpleasant things about Whig heros, including Charles Fox himself, guaranteed that he would have to wait for full acceptance at Holland House.[61] This only came after 1817, when the Whigs' divorce from the Grenvillites forced them to take more seriously some opening in a Radical direction, and when, with age, Burdett had himself come to moderate his politics to some degree. The first extant letter from Burdett to Holland dates from 1818, and, a year later, there is the macabre spectacle of Fox's widow borrowing money from Burdett against the security of St Anne's Hill itself.[62] The mortgaging of this property almost made Burdett a member of the Fox family by proxy.[63] In the 1820s and 1830s, as Burdett moved steadily to the right in politics, there was more and more cooperation with Holland House, particularly on Catholic affairs.[64] By 1835, Lady Holland was asking him to nominate the Speaker.[65]

In all his dealings with the Radicals, Holland maintained a patrician aloofness which made it difficult for him to take them seriously. Even when Burdett was still in his Jacobin period, Holland remained unimpressed:

> However I may laugh at his absurdity I cannot feel or express any sort of indignation much less any alarm or apprehension of Sir F. Burdett's politics – Should Ministers take any steps whatever against him I think it due to public freedom and discussion to resist it most strenuously and not the less so because he and Horne Tooke are evidently actuated by as great or even greater hatred towards us than towards Ministry – the influence of the Court is the great evil and that is the only quarter from which any danger is to be apprehended.[66]

61. Add. MSS. 51738, f 22; Holland to Caroline Fox, 3 Nov. 1806.

62. Fox's private house in Surrey.

63. Mrs Fox to Coutts, 29 May 1819; Bodleian MSS. Eng. Lett. c 65 f 89 (Burdett MSS.).

64. Add. MSS. 51569, f 1; Sir F. Burdett to Holland, 1827.

65. Lady Holland to Burdett, Feb. 1835; Bodleian MSS. Eng. Lett. d 97, f 185 (Burdett MSS.).

66. Add. MSS. 51544, ff 44-6; Holland to Grey, 2 Nov. 1806.

To argue that the Radicals were not dangerous because the Court was evidently more dangerous is hardly logical, but it seems to represent Holland's opinion at most times. Separated by social distinctions, Holland could never become an expert on Radical thinking, but his dismissive attitude towards them was rather distinctive. The Hollands' obsession with executive power, the most durable of their family heirlooms, led to a blinkering effect with regard to threats to Whig principles coming from other directions. The one good thing about the strange notions of the Radicals was that, by implication, they harmed the Crown as well as other property holders:

> As to Jacobins and Burdettites I confess I think we employ a great deal too much of our time in speculating upon the effect of their doctrines and publications which after all have this merit, that they shake that great deference for power which has done so much mischief in this Country.[67]

Not surprisingly, Holland had very strong views on the question of a possible Whig/Radical understanding. In the first place, the Radicals needed the Whigs so badly that all the leverage in the negotiations was in the hands of Hollands' friends:

> It has happened more than once in the course of my life that the party called Jacobins, Levellers, or Radical Reformers, after reviling the Whigs and strengthening the High Church party by lowering their opponents, have sought in the hour of danger to shelter themselves under the party they have so traduced.[68]

Holland even believed that the Whigs could outflank the Radicals at their own game of mobilising 'opinion out of doors'. Not everyone who came to a public meeting was a voter, nor was everyone who signed a petition to Parliament, but Holland thought that the dangers involved in such activities were slight if the whole operation was managed with energy and skill. At Westminster, the Radicals were bound to

---

67. Add. MSS. 51544, f 189; Holland to Grey, 3 Jan. 1810.
68. Holland, *Further Memoirs of the Whig Party*, p.253.

be Whig pensioners. Outside Westminster, their power base was vulnerable, if the Whigs bestirred themselves.[69]

It was always the question of Parliamentary Reform which produced the greatest tension in Whig/Radical relations. Holland was always insistent that Whig distinctiveness on this issue must be maintained at all costs. On no account must it become the preserve of the Radicals or allowed to fall under their leadership:

> We cannot break too decidedly or too openly with the Radicals but we must in doing so have some clear line of distinction between us and those of their enemies whom we dislike and dread as much as we do them – This can only be done by devizing some measures of Concession to the people, and especially the disturbed and unrepresented districts ... with members in Parliament chosen by freeholders and inhabitants, and other devices of the same sort – not universal suffrage.[70]

It was the most sensitive of areas. The accusation that Grey used the expression 'cant of reform', in a speech in 1810, was enough to spark off a controversy lasting nine months.[71] Similarly, in 1820, Holland's description of Lambton's Motion on Reform as 'revolutionary, or, if carried, it would be as *bad* as a revolution' nearly produced schism.[72] On each occasion, Holland was unimpressed by Radicals parading hurt feelings. He was convinced that they needed the Whigs more than the Whigs needed them, and his long memory recalled the Radicals' own skill in abuse. The Whigs were too often themselves 'exasperated with the unjust and uncandid treatment they have received, and are everyday receiving, from the modern Reformers'.[73]

In the Holland House catechism therefore, the Tory defence of Crown influence was a real threat and the Radicals'

69. Add. MSS. 51577, ff 173-4; Morpeth to Holland, 7 Oct. 1813. See also Add. MSS. 51661, ff 117-18; Bedford to Holland, 7 Jan. 1818, and Holland to Brougham, 5 Oct. 1819; Brougham MSS. 48093.

70. Add. MSS. 41565, ff 57-60; Holland to Grey, 16 Oct. 1819.

71. Add. MSS. 51739, f 30; Holland to Caroline Fox, 10 Jan. 1810. See also Add. MSS. 51677, f 3, 5, 13; Lord John Russell to Holland, 7 Aug.-25 Sept. 1810.

72. Lambton to Grey, 10 Jan. 1820; *Life and Letters of Lord Durham*, i 131.

73. Holland to Brougham, April 1811; quoted in *The Creevey Diaries*, p. 144.

promotion of increasingly democratic ideas was a severe irritant. Holland's motivation for sympathising with a Parliamentary Reform of some kind stems from these assumptions. A Reform of the House of Commons was essential to make that body capable of fending off interference from the executive. It was equally necessary to ensure that, under Radical leadership, it did not become perverted into democratic paths. Both Charles Fox and his nephew responded to the question of Reform in these senses. There was no emotional involvement with the question on the part of either of them. Holland made no speech on the subject between 1821 and 1830, and said very little during the passage of the Reform Bill itself.[74]

For Lady Holland, it was 'that dreadful, overwhelming topick'.[75] For her husband, 'That cursed business of Reform of Parliament is always in one's way. With one great man nothing is good unless that be the principal object, and with another nothing must be done if a word of Reform is even glanced at in requisition, petition or discussion.'[76] The Hollands supported the idea, as their uncle had done, because the Whig responsibility of balancing politics against Tory and Radical demanded some measure of this kind.

The first motive in the Hollands' support for Parliamentary Reform was always its effectiveness in limiting Crown authority. Detail was unimportant to them as long as this overall objective was kept in sight. As Holland frankly told Grey;

> ... for myself to say what I think of an alteration in the representation – viz that of any which without changing the basis of the Constitution affords a prospect of diminishing the influence of [the] Crown I will vote.[77]

Reform was not a panacea for the malaise in government since 1784, but it would undoubtedly help.[78] His relaxed attitudes

74. See below, Chapter Six.
75. Lady Holland to Sir Charles Vaughan, 23 Jan. 1821; Vaughan MSS. c 67/7.
76. Holland to Creevey, 24 June 1817; *The Creevey Letters*, i 263-4.
77. Holland to Grey, 2 Jan. 1817; Grey MSS. Box 34.
78. Add. MSS. 51733, ff 166-7; Holland to Caroline Fox, 11 Jan. 1796 and Add. MSS. 51734, ff 89-90; Holland to Caroline Fox, Jan. 1797.

stemmed largely from his belief that the franchise was a trust inherent in the holding of property. Burke and his generation, believing that the franchise was itself property, feared all talk of Reform because an assault on property in one area was easily generalised to others. If, as Holland believed, the franchise was not property but a trust inherent in property, the problem failed to arise. Trusts, badly managed, must be revocable. Equally the franchise as a trust excluded the possibility of universal suffrage because potential electors had to show themselves worthy of that trust. The same qualifications of literacy and rational thinking could be applied. Substituting a theory of trust for those based purely and simply on property gave away nothing to the democrats and allowed the idea of a reform of Parliament which kept Whig consciences clear.

It followed from the above that Holland always saw universal suffrage as 'the wildest fancy that could possibly enter into the conception of any human being'.[79] Equally, he was entirely happy to support the disenfrancisement of any constituency which, by corruption or malpractice, abused the trust of representation. The attack on Stafford's behaviour, in 1836, for example was not an attack on property:

He never would allow that the franchise was property and the argument which maintained it to be property would be the greater inducement for the adoption of universal suffrage and vote by ballot.[80]

The franchise, seen as a trust inherent in property-holding, would become available to more and more people as new forms of property were discovered and developed. Holland was clear that the political world must not become exclusive. Everyone must be admitted who could fulfil the trust reasonably. Macaulay believed that the essence of Whiggery lay in a speech of Holland's from 1825, 'namely, that the British Constitution and large exclusions cannot subsist together; that the constitution must destroy them, or they will

79. *Parl. Deb.*, vol. LXXI 420-4; 18 Feb. 1817.
80. ibid., vol. CXXXIV 1070-1; 15 April 1836. See also Add. MSS. 51546, ff 21-2; Holland to Grey, 11 March 1819.

destroy the constitution'.[81] On these terms, Parliamentary Reform was a sensible suggestion, but Holland loathed investing the issue with too much significance. It would help to circumscribe Crown authority, but 'it would not pay the national debt, feed the hungry, nor prevent improvident wars'.[82] The natural increase of property-holding would work as effectively as imposed solutions by Act of Parliament.

If these attitudes formed the context of thinking for the mature statesman, they cannot be imposed neatly on his career as a whole. In shouldering the Parliamentary Reform aspect of the Foxite legacy, Holland proceeded by bursts of doubt and confidence. Not surprisingly, as a young man, his faith in the efficacy of Reform was stronger. In his maiden speech for example, an incautious remark about 'the voice of the people'[83] led him to be severely taken to task by Grenville as to the meaning of these words. By way of reply, Holland, through a fit of stammering, ventured the following;

> ... the genuine constitution of England ... was no longer in existence. What he wanted, and he had expressed himself in clear language, was to revise that constitution in its purity, and the means he proposed was, not by any innovatory course, but by restoring to the people a just representation in Parliament.[84]

This hardly answered Grenville's question, and it is clear that Holland had not thought through the implications of his words. Both Lord and Lady Holland were unrepentant about the violent tone of the speech,[85] and were only marginally shaken when a favourite uncle, Upper Ossory, and College friends wrote to protest.[86] As one of the latter had to admit, 'I am a little angry with him for his violence, but those who know him well had certainly no right to expect great moderation.'[87] For the first ten years or so of his active

81. *Edinburgh Review*, vol. LXXIII, p.506 seq; July 1841.
82. *Parl. Deb.*, vol. LXXI, 420-4; 18 Feb. 1817.
83. ibid., vol. XXXIII, 1278; 9 Jan. 1798.
84. *Parl. Deb.*, vol. XXXIII 1296; 9 Jan. 1798.
85. Add. MSS. 51735, ff 1-2; Holland to Caroline Fox, 10 Jan. 1798. Add. MSS. 51744, f 40; Lady Holland to Caroline Fox, 13 Jan. 1798.
86. Add. MSS. 51795, ff 12-13; Upper Ossory to Holland, 12 Jan. 1798.
87. Add. MSS. 48226, ff 37-8; Morpeth to Boringdon, 13 Jan. 1798.

political career, Holland did subscribe to the view that
Parliamentary Reform, if not a panacea, was a first priority of
Whig politics.[88]

After experiencing the failure of Bonaparte and the severe
economic troubles which beset England after 1815, Holland's
views steadily moderated. At the end of 1816, he was telling
Grey;

> Whatever lengths *you* go in favour of it (the fewer I think the better) I
> will follow with good grace though without the slightest zeal – unless
> indeed some in disclaiming the mischievous nonsense of Cobbett and
> Hunt – The nearer I look to Parliamentary reform the less I own I like
> it and even when I saw it at a great distance I was none of its most
> fervent admirers.[89]

Even so, much to Grey's concern, Holland insisted, in 1820,
when there was a chance of the Whigs coming into office, that
some measure of Parliamentary Refórm must be introduced, if
only for 'the advantage of enlisting the popular cry under the
banner of moderate practical and useful reform instead of
Universal Suffrage and such like nonsense'.[90] As this
quotation suggests, Holland felt obliged to vote for
Parliamentary Reform whenever the issue was agitated, 'on
whatever side of the House he might sit'.[91] By 1830, Holland
was firm again: 'Nothing but the adoption of the principle
could I believe save our Monarchy or any of our institutions
from destruction and confusion.'[92] Over the period of thirty
years, the degree of enthusiasm for Parliamentary Reform had
varied widely, but at no point had the commitment itself been
dropped.

There was then no clear Holland House line on
Parliamentary Reform, but this did not in itself impair the
claim to the Foxite bequest. Charles Fox himself had never
spoken in detail on the matter. He had never given any

---

88. F. Horner to J. Allen, 28 Dec. 1809; *The Letters of Francis Horner*, pp. 16-17.

89. Holland to Grey, 2 Dec. 1816; Grey MSS. See Also Holland to Ebrington, 11
Jan. 1817; Fortescue MSS. 1262 M/FC 75.

90. Add. MSS. 51546, f 131; Holland to Grey, 24 Nov. 1820.

91. Herries to Bexley, 1828; *The Holland House Circle*, p.49.

92. Add. MSS. 51531, f 42; Holland to Grenville, Nov. 1830.

indication, beyond supporting Bills prepared by other people, of how many seats should be redistributed, how many new voters should be called up, or on what principles. Indeed, the defining of a political viewpoint into an Act of Parliament had never been a Fox family interest. The small print was always for other people to arrange. What remained was the consistent pressure for some measure of Parliamentary Reform expressed, with varying degrees of enthusiasm, over a fifty-year period. For Charles Fox, the issue related to the controlling of Crown authority. For his nephew, that motive remained entirely valid, and could be reinforced by the knowledge that, in a society in social and economic movement, some adjustments would inevitably become necessary to keep politics abreast of other forms of change. Of all the great reform issues of the early nineteenth century, however, Parliamentary Reform could least be called a special subject in Holland House.

By contrast, the Hollands were very clear-minded about opposing the coercive powers of government, which had inevitably grown perceptibly during the long wars with France. The many suspensions of Habeas Corpus and similar guarantees beautifully illustrated the Fox family theme on executive power. There were, in Holland's view, certain inalienable rights vested in the individual, and any government wishing to infringe them must be made to show just cause. In discussing civil and religious rights, Holland concluded:

> They belonged naturally to all classes, and when withheld, the onus probandi lay not on those to whom they were denied, but on those by whom they were refused ... And, indeed, although he certainly thought that the discussion of abstract rights was generally to be avoided, yet there were occasions, and this was one of them, when an understanding and concurrence in fundamental principles was indispensably necessary ... Let the issue be searched for in the Bill of Rights, which gave the death blow to that famous doctrine, that the interests of the governed were secondary and subordinate to the interests of the governors.[93]

93. *Parl. Deb.*, vol. LVI 678; 18 June 1811.

Holland agreed that sedition must be dealt with firmly, but such occurrences should provoke introspection, not vindictiveness. In speaking of the Cato Street Conspiracy, Holland urged that the guilty should be pursued with 'unrelenting severity', but went on to say:

> ... examine if after waging war for twenty years with revolution & sedition you have not by your taxes, your laws and your sanction of all violence (including assassination) against your foreign enemies & against turbulent men at home, contributed to reconcile the minds of men to deeds of atrocity.[94]

The disturbances after 1815, in Holland's view, were as much the products of a changing society and an unimaginative government applying blunt remedies as they were the fruit of evil. Riot and sedition suggested a malaise which required investigation and cure, even if the immediate symptoms had to be dealt with firmly. The appearance of primitive Trade Unions 'frighten some folks',[95] but Holland always opposed attempts to suppress them, because 'the same revolution which conferred on the House of Brunswick the character of legitimacy sanctioned and canonized the principle of popular and authorized expressions of publick opinion and *one* cannot be shaken without shaking the foundation of the *other*'.[96] As has been mentioned above, Holland, for the same reason, was always ready to mobilise opinion by meetings and petitioning against the abrogation of basic rights.[97] The upholding of individual freedoms and the right of association, even in the form of trade unions, was the one firm guarantee that social and economic change could be contained without recourse to violent upheaval.

The corollary of the surrender of civil rights was the growth of executive power. As the one declined, the other inevitably grew. Assuming therefore, as the Hollands always did, that the Crown and government were the principal dangers to

94. Add. MSS. 51546, f 92; Holland to Grey, 28 Feb. 1820.
95. Add. MSS. 51753, ff 81-2; Holland to Henry Fox, 17 April 1834.
96. Holland to Grey, 24 Dec. 1832; Grey MSS Box 34.
97. Add. MSS. 51544, f 1; Grey to Holland, 22 Jan. 1798. See also Add. MSS. 51661, ff 153-4; Bedford to Holland, 6 April 1810.

liberty, it followed that popular licence was less so. The Peterloo Massacre was an example of the executive running amok rather than a demonstration of democratic potential. It excited the most lively indignation at Holland House. The Manchester magistrates were 'completely in the wrong from beginning to end'.[98] The most vigorous protests should be registered at all levels of politics.[99] Above all, the event must not be allowed to rebound to the benefit of government:

> ... as to regulating meetings, punishing itinerant and seditious orators, exacting qualifications or limiting numbers of people assembling etc etc etc I have upon mature deliberation satisfied myself that they are not only radically wrong in principle but foolish, & even worse than foolish, irritating and mischievous in their effects. And my opinion on this subject is much corroborated by my recollection of my Uncle's view of similar measures both in his own time & in other periods of history ... The danger does not really consist in large bodies meeting in publick but in the spirit which induces them to meet. How to put down riot if it occur, and how to correct the disposition to riot in the people are the two rational objects of a government at a moment like this.[100]

If the utmost vigilance were not maintained, the agents of government, as in Manchester, would be congratulated by the House of Commons 'for cutting mens throats before the real necessity or even the legal pretence for so doing was made out'.[101] Repression became particularly absurd when penalties became so great that juries refused to convict.[102]

To the great majority of Holland's contemporaries, such views were idiosyncratic to the point of being unbalanced. The dangers presented by a mob were so obviously more apparent than those offered by the soldiers and magistrates restoring order. With property and lives at risk, it seemed quixotic to insist that government was too strong or too interventionist. A major division of opinion in early nineteenth-century politics

98. Holland to Ebrington, 1819; Fortescue MSS 1262 M/FC77.
99. Add. MSS. 51584, ff 82-3; Tierney to Holland, 14 Sept. 1819.
100. Add. MSS. 51653, ff 83-8; Holland to Mackintosh, 10 Nov. 1819 See also Add. MSS. 51546, f 74; Holland to Grey, 14 Nov. 1819.
101. Add. MSS. 51643, f 80; Holland to Mackintosh, 13 Sept. 1819.
102. *Parl. Deb.*, vol. LXXV, 119-21; 27 Jan. 1819.

rested on the question of whether one took, as the starting point of politics, the pretensions of the executive or the democracy as the case to be answered. The French Revolution and its consequences resolved that problem in most people's minds. The mob was the greater threat. The Fox family insisted that the Whigs uphold the alternative view, based in the first instance on their discoveries and experiences before that Revolution actually broke out.

It is not surprising to find, therefore, that, whereas Holland's parliamentary performance on the Reform question was hesitant and intermittent, his opposition to the limitation of basic rights was enthusiastic and unremitting. His defence of his uncle's libertarian law on libel was, for example, a duty cheerfully undertaken.[103] It was, however, the guardianship of the Habeas Corpus principle that provoked his greatest efforts. There was virtually no suspension or infringement that Holland did not speak against in the Lords, quite often reinforcing vocal opposition with a formal Protest in the Journals of the House.[104] In retrospect, he allowed that the circumstances of 1794 might have justified the abrogation of Habeas Corpus, but there was, in his view, no other year which was remotely comparable. The suspensions of that guarantee in the late 1790s and immediately after the Napoleonic Wars were nothing but the actions of a predatory government. For obvious reasons Holland could not argue that there were no situations in which Habeas Corpus might be put into abeyance, but his conditions are so tight that it would be hard to imagine them ever being met. As Holland put it, the stakes were very high:

The personal liberty of the people was no concession. It was a right antecedent to any statute, and equal to the right of the lordships to vote in that House or to the right of the king to sit on the throne. He did not mean to say that there was an absolute limitation to the

103. *Parl. Deb.*, vol. LXXVI 973-4; 9 Dec. 1819.
104. ibid., vol. XXXIV 171; 4 Jan. 1799; vol. XXXV 752, 19 Dec. 1800 and vol. LXXII 1061-2; 19 June 1817. See also S. Smith to Holland, 13 March 1817, *The Letters of Sydney Smith*, i 274-5; and Holland to Cloncurry, 8 July 1817, *Personal Recollections of Lord Cloncurry*, pp 146-8.

power of parliament on this subject, when circumstances rendered
such a stretch of power indispensable, but he did say, that to suspend
this right of a people was an act of as great violence as to suspend the
prerogatives of the crown, and could only be justified by the clearest
evidence of the most overwhelming necessity.[105]

In this, as in all his general political attitudes, Holland
showed himself the devoted pupil of his uncle. The theme,
based on a crusade against executive power, had been
established by Charles Fox and was embellished and
developed by Holland. The political thinking of Holland
House was conditioned by it. Tories were malevolent because
they connived at the growth of prerogative power. Radicals
had to be considered as potential allies because they opposed
it. Parliamentary Reform had to be seen as a possible weapon
in the fight, and all the statutory defences of personal liberty
enacted since the Glorious Revolution had to be endlessly
reinforced. There was little that was detailed in all this and a
good deal that was defensive. For much of the time indeed,
Holland believed that he was engaged in a battle which he
would ultimately lose. His trusteeship of this major Foxite
theme was undertaken with no expectation of ever being
called into government. The consistency of the approach
allowed Holland to share in his uncle's political martyrdom.
For a hesitant and stammering man, the Foxite wail about the
power of the executive also provided a ready-made point of
reference against which all other decisions could be set.

Inevitably therefore, there was something eccentric, or even
old-fashioned, about Holland House. It was thought odd to
worry about governmental power when Political Unions were
raising the question of universal suffrage. There was perhaps
something strange in seeing the motivation for Parliamentary
Reform in a possible circumscription of royal authority rather
than as an arresting of popular pressure. In short, Holland
House ran the risk, in defending the Foxite faith, of
championing an eighteenth-century preoccupation in a
nineteenth-century context. Baldly stated, this charge would
be unfounded, in that Holland fully recognised the democratic

105. *Parl. Deb.*, vol. LXXIII 4-5; 27 Jan. 1818.

claims of the 1820s and 1830s as problems to be dealt with, and, in this sense, his vision was not entirely blinkered. However, in continuing to give priority to concern about the abuse of executive power, Holland House might reasonably be accused of clinging too closely to a set of beliefs which were established before the French Revolution totally changed the face of politics.

4

Slaves, Catholics and Dissenters

If a suspicion of kings was the first article of the Foxite faith, the second was a commitment to racial and religious toleration. It was, for one thing, so much more straightforward an issue. To agitate for the removal of impediments on personal freedom was so much easier than becoming involved in the thickets of Parliamentary Reform. The argument resolved itself into a discussion of first principles with which any educated man felt at home. One of the standard Pittite or Peelite complaints about Whigs was that they refused to involve themselves in the detail of government, notoriously in money matters, preferring to run politics on general principles which might or might not be relevant to the question in hand. Certainly, the inter-related issues of relief for all forms of religious dissent and for slaves were those which excited the most genuine enthusiasm in the Fox family. The monument over Fox's tomb in Westminster Abbey shows the body of the dying statesman being supported on each side by weeping negros.

The family tradition allowed Holland no choice whatever on these questions. He believed that the emancipation of the slaves was the issue most dear to his uncle's heart, and as he told the Lords in 1814, 'he would venture to assert, from his own knowledge, that ... the complete abolition of the Slave Trade was so much a matter of constant anxiety with Mr Fox, that not three hours in the day passed without the subject being uppermost in his mind'.[1] Wilberforce could always

1. *Parl. Deb.*, vol. LXIV 356-7; 28 June 1814.

appeal for his cooperation 'quasi Lord Holland and quasi nephew to Mr Fox'.[2] It was widely known that Fox regarded the abolition of the Slave Trade as the principal success of the Talents Ministry, and possibly of his whole career. The arguments he used were based firmly on theories of natural rights inherent in all men, which were not open to control by the state. Interestingly, he also dealt firmly with any claims to racial superiority based on differences in colour. In discussing the slave question, in 1792, Fox had spoken before the Commons as follows:

> There was an argument which had not been used, but which was the foundation of the whole business; he meant the difference in colour ... Such a custom could not now be tolerated; and as to the pretext, that what could be great cruelty to us, who profess strong feelings and cultivated minds, would not be injurious to those who are ignorant and uncivilized, it was, the height of arrogance, and the foundation of endless tyranny.[3]

In the Fox family catechism, personal freedom must be the first object of every human being; and it was a right, of which he who deprives a fellow creature is absolutely criminal in so depriving him.[4]

What was simple for Fox became complex for his nephew by his marriage to Elizabeth Vassall, in that the Vassall estates in Jamaica became an essential aspect of the Holland House economy. Brougham was not the only contemporary to point to the incongruity of one of the leading emancipators being also by marriage a major slave-owner, and even he had to allow the Hollands some credit for steadily putting a point of principle before their immediate financial interests.[5] In 1799, it was estimated that the Vassall plantations at Friendship and Sweet River, Jamaica were worth £800 p.a. and were worked by nearly five hundred negros.[6] When, as the price of the divorce, part of the revenues from these estates

2. Add. MSS. 51820, ff 38-9; W. Wilberforce to Holland, 23 Feb. 1823.
3. *The Speeches of Charles James Fox*, IV 377; 2 April 1792.
4. ibid., IV 182; 19 April 1791.
5. Brougham, *Statesmen of the Time of George III*, iii 330.
6. Add. MSS. 51819, f 1; Lady Holland to ? Plummer, 1797.

went to Sir Godfrey Webster, Holland took over the name Vassall himself to preserve a long-term title to the properties.[7] Thereafter, he always signed his name as 'Vassall Holland'. It is clear from surviving correspondence that the Hollands were humane and improving plantation owners. Churches and schools were built for example.[8] Even so, the uncompromising views enunciated by Charles Fox inevitably looked odd in the mouth of a slave-owner, even when that slave-owner was supporting measures to his own financial detriment.

Fears about impending poverty reverberate throughout the Holland House correspondence. In 1821, Lady Holland believed 'the most rigid economy necessary and hardly equal to our out-goings'.[9]

In 1830, Creevey found the situation worse;

> I was at Lord Holland's yesterday ... They both looked very ill. They are evidently most sorely pinched – he in his land, and she still more in her sugar and rum. So when I gave it as my opinion that, if things went on as they did, paper must ooze out again ... she said she wished to God the time was come, or anything else to save them.[10]

The period 1830-4 was particularly calamitous. The Swing Riots had so badly affected the Hollands' English estates that Holland found it hard to make any allowance for his son at all.[11] When the Grey ministry was ousted by William IV, in 1834, Holland regarded the loss of his job as Chancellor of the Duchy of Lancaster as provoking financial ruin.[12] Above all, after the emancipation of the slaves in 1833, the Jamaican estates ceased, to all intents and purposes, to make any contribution to Holland House at all, and the scale of the entertaining had to be cut down significantly after that date.[13]

Against this background, it was very hard for the Hollands

7. Add. MSS. 51734, f 78; Holland to Caroline Fox, 20 Dec. 1796.

8. Add. MSS. 51819, f 32; Rev. T. Stewart to Holland, 14 Nov. 1836.

9. Lady Holland to Henry Fox, 28 Feb. 1821; *Elizabeth, Lady Holland to her Son*, p.2.

10. Creevey to Miss Ord, 11 March 1830; *The Creevey Letters*, ii 209.

11. Add. MSS. 51752, ff 101-2; Holland to Henry Fox, 25 Dec. 1832.

12. Diary of Lord William Russell, 10 July 1834; *Lord William Russell and his Wife*, p.313. See also Lady Holland to Henry Fox, 11 July 1834, *Elizabeth, Lady Holland to her Son*, p.151.

13. *The Journal of Henry Edward Fox*, p.51.

to speak on West Indian affairs without keeping their own finances very much in view. In their correspondence, the two factors are always interconnected.[14] From 1824 onwards, Holland began to diversify capital by investing in the laying out of new streets and squares of residential property in the Holland Park area, but the venture was not immediately successful, and could only marginally relieve their dependence on the West Indies.[15] Embarrassing though it might be for a nephew of Fox, Holland was acknowledged to be a leading member of the West Indian lobby in Parliament, and it is not surprising that he took a much greater role in everything concerned with West Indian affairs than in the struggle for Parliamentary Reform. His dependence on his uncle and wife made his position on slavery potentially anomalous. It required great skill to fulfil both obligations adequately. The position he was forced to adopt from these circumstances was to make a distinction between the abolition of the Slave Trade and the abolition of slavery itself. On the first, he was absolutely his uncle's heir. On the second, he still followed Fox's basic lead, but with the reservations of a West Indian proprietor.

The abolition of the slave trade had been a cause close to the hearts of the Fox family for at least twenty years before it won success. Holland and his sister Caroline fully shared their uncle's prejudices on the subject. While still in her twenties, the latter had composed a vigorous anti-slave trade poem called 'The Negro's Complaint', which showed enthusiasm, if only a rude literary talent:

> Forc'd from Home and all its Pleasures
> Afric's Coast I left forlorne,
> To Encrease a Nation's Treasures
> O'er the raging Billows borne
> Men from England bought & sold me
> Paid my price in paltry Gold
> But tho' theirs they have enroll'd me
> Minds are never to be sold.[16]

14. Add. MSS. 51547, f 17; Holland to Grey, 10 Feb. 1824.
15. *The Chronicles of Holland House*, p.254.
16. Add. MSS. 51731, f 23; Caroline Fox to Holland, 11 Oct. 1789.

Her brother was equally firm. His Parliamentary opposition
to everything involved in the Slave Trade was unremitting. He
supported, by speeches and formal Protests, its limitation,
amelioration or abolition.[17] He rightly believed that, 'as a W.I.
proprietor my opinion in favour of the Ab. might have some
weight in forming an exception to the general apprehension of
those concerned'.[18] In his *Memoirs*, he looked back with
pleasure on the fact that the only time he ever sat on a
Parliamentary committee to frame a bill was on that
abolishing the Slave Trade, 'a measure which Mr Fox had so
earnestly promoted, and which put an end to one of the
greatest evils to which the human race has ever been
exposed'.[19] The issue was one of the strongest political ties
within the Fox family.

In publicly attacking the Trade, Holland rehearsed many of
his uncle's arguments and added some of his own. When one
of his friends was accused of having some negro blood,
Holland quickly retorted that, 'if so, he afforded practical
proof that the narrow theory which denies capacity to that
affectionate people is as erroneous as it is uncharitable'.[20] He
refused to believe that the force of prescription could apply to
the question of slavery or that the numbers of negros in the
West Indies could only be kept up by continuous
reinforcement from Africa.[21] Above all, he powerfully attacked
the notion that the whole British trading position in Spanish
America depended on the Trade:

> Fortunately, British manufactures were become of absolute necessity
> to the inhabitants of South America, and they would have them,
> though the slave importation trade, which, according to the
> statement of the noble lord, was used as a cover for a more important
> branch of commerce, were annihilated.[22]

17. *Parl. Deb.*, vol. XXXIV, 1117-8; 5 July 1799. See also Add. MSS. 51735, ff 113-14; Holland to Caroline Fox, 8 July 1799.
18. Add. MSS. 51737, ff 60-1; Holland to Caroline Fox, c June 1804.
19. Holland, *Memoirs of the Whig Party during my Time*, ii pp. 157-8.
20. Holland, *Further Memoirs of the Whig Party*, p.295.
21. *Parl. Deb.*, vol. XLIV 671-2; 5 Feb. 1807.
22. ibid., vol. XLIII 230-1; 16 May 1806.

There was no pseudo-scientific theory based on race, no moral theory based on philanthropy and no economic argument based on necessity that was not challenged at Holland House. The fact that the Slave Trade could be attacked on so many fronts by a West Indiaman was gravely embarrassing to the Trade's defenders.

Holland's main contribution to the destruction of the Slave Trade lay outside an English context altogether, however. As men like Wilberforce and Zachary Macaulay recognised, it was Holland's extensive foreign contacts that should be exploited. The first step towards the unlikely alliance of Holland House and the Saints of Clapham was taken in January 1807, when Wilberforce approached Holland with the suggestion that he should persuade the Spanish and the Portuguese liberals to follow England's lead in renouncing the Trade.[23] Until at least 1820, Holland acted as interpreter between Wilberforce and sympathetic Spaniards, and lost no opportunity himself of pointing out the natural connection between the abolition of the Trade and the triumph of liberalism in the Iberian Peninsula. Andres de la Vega was told, for example, that the constitution-making of 1812 in Spain would be incomplete without some statement against the Trade: 'Let Spain and Portugal concur with us, and there is an end of this disgraceful and revolting trade for ever. Africa will then be open to civilization, and the state of society in the West Indies susceptible to improvement.'[24] Holland's Spanish and Portuguese friends often had to suffer a moral battering on this subject.

While Wilberforce wanted Holland's help with the Spanish and Portuguese, Zachary Macaulay required his assistance with the Americans. Holland had been brought into close contact with America when, as Lord Privy Seal, in the Talents Ministry, he had been one of the principal negotiators about the status of neutral American shipping trading with

23. Add. MSS. 51820; William Wilberforce to Holland, especially folios 7, 9 and 21.

24. Add. MSS.51626, ff 68-9; Holland to Andres de la Vega, 12 Oct. 1812.

Napoleonic France. His advocacy of a conciliatory line towards the Americans was conditioned by a concern for the West Indies, for whom the American trade was crucial. Indeed, he believed that the West Indian plantations could not survive without it:

> He trusted that parliament would never again be led by the experiment which was productive of so much misery in our West-India colonies, in the period from 1784 to 1786, when their supply from America was cut off, and in consequence of which, in Jamaica alone, 15,000 negroes died from the famine which that regulation produced.[25]

In Holland's view, relations with America were crucial to the well-being of the West Indies and absolutely vital if the post-Slave Trade system was to be made to work. In addition, he urged the American government to take action against privateers, who, against its wishes, continued to operate in the Slave Trade.[26] For some years, Holland was in correspondence with the American abolitionist Thomas Clarkson on these questions,[27] with Zachary Macaulay attempting to co-ordinate the English and American campaigns. The United States always exercised considerable fascination for the Hollands, and their preoccupation with the West Indies contributed greatly to this inclination.

Predictably, though, it was with the French that Holland hoped to have the most influence. All his weight was thrown into the attempt to persuade the French to abandon the Slave Trade, and there were two occasions when English pressure might have proved successful. In 1814-15, Holland believed that, if the Allies had pushed hard enough for the abolition of the Slave Trade, the French would have capitulated. In his view, which was enshrined in a formal Protest in the Lords' Journal,[28] Castlereagh deliberately sabotaged the possibility of change:

25. *Parl. Deb.*, vol. XLII 596; 31 March 1806.
26. Add. MSS. 51820, ff 49-52; Z. Macaulay to Holland, 17 Feb. 1810.
27. Add. MSS. 51820, f 58; T. Clarkson to Holland, 22 March 1810.
28. *Parl. Deb.*, vol. LXIV 356; 28 June 1814.

I am sure that Castlereagh sacrificed the Abolition even more than I
imagined, there was less prejudice in favour of the trade in France
than we were told – the least earnestness would have carried the point
and certainly the smallest sacrifice would have bought & might now
buy it.[29]

The second opportunity came with the July Revolution of
1830, which wafted Holland's old friends Lafayette and Louis
Philippe back to power. Lafayette proposed an Anglo-French
assault on 'l'abominable traite des noirs',[30] and Holland
believed that both he and 'K. Philip were for such a measure
bona fide'.[31] The difficulty surrounding the abolitionist case in
French terms was the memory of the emancipation of the
slaves, which had taken place early in the French Revolution,
and which had resulted in a murderous rebellion in Santo
Domingo. For the French, an abolitionist was a Jacobin. As
Holland complained to Wilberforce, 'they make no difference
between you and me, or me and Tom Paine.'[32] Even so,
Holland tried hard to influence French opinion, and this kind
of activity was a fitting extension of the unstinting support he
had given his uncle in the English context.

On the question of the abolition of slavery itself, however,
the story is very different. Publicly, Holland always supported
the proposal, however qualified his approbation might be.
Privately, Holland House entertained grave doubts. Unlike
the issue of the Slave Trade, the abolition of slavery in the
West Indies was not simply a moral question. In Holland's
view, it invoked real practical difficulties, which would have to
be overcome if the whole enterprise was not to end in disaster.
By this, Holland meant more than the mere compensation of
landowners like himself for the loss of a species of property,
though he did regard this point as a problem. Rather, he was
preoccupied with the question of how former slaves could be
turned into wage labourers and landowners without the
appropriate preparation. The ignoring of this problem had

29. Holland to Grey, 14 Sept. 1815; Grey MSS Box 34.
30. Add. MSS. 51635, f 214; Lafayette to Holland, 11 June 1833.
31. Holland to Grey, 20 Dec. 1830; Grey MSS Box 34.
32. Holland to Wilberforce, 1814; *The Holland House Circle*, p.38.

led, in his opinion, to the rebellions and massacres in the French West Indies after 1790. When Wilberforce claimed Holland as 'an honest Abolitionist' because of 'your strong likeness to your warm hearted Uncle & his inextinguishable zeal in that good Cause',[33] he may have been unduly optimistic. Other letters in Holland's correspondence make it clear that he was an acknowledged leader of the West Indian lobby.[34] The Vassall marriage tempered Foxite abolitionism with more practical considerations.

Against this background, it is not surprising that Holland House was often accused of operating a double standard on this issue. Superficially, there was something odd in John Allen welcoming well-attended anti-slavery meetings,[35] while Holland made such equivocal speeches in the Lords on the same subject, that he could almost be considered neutral on the issue. There was in fact no ambivalence. Holland House was firmly abolitionist, but insisted that due preparations be made for enacting the measure. No one would suffer more from a precipitate emancipation than the slaves themselves. An unthought-out measure 'could only tend to their own injury'.[36] In discussing the slave revolt in Barbados, in 1816, Holland wanted a firm denial that emancipation was imminent, because thwarted expectations had been the primary cause of the disturbance. Emancipation, though desirable, was not imminent because the ground had not been prepared in advance. He professed himself 'well aware that it was one of the evils of the state of slavery, that it so degraded the human mind, that it was not possible there could be a sudden and rapid passage from that condition to the enjoyment of all the rights and privileges of the British Constitution'.[37] Critics could easily construe such remarks as the landowner's rationalisation of delay, but this is probably unfair. A more subtle critic might have suggested that the Hollands' close involvement with slavery for once mixed their

33. Add. MSS. 51820, f 45; Wilberforce to Holland, 4 Jan. 1832.
34. Add. MSS. 51819, f 15; J. Barham to Holland, 18 Feb. 1824.
35. Add. MSS. 52172, f 95; J. Allen to Lady Holland, 2 July 1824.
36. *Parl. Deb.*, vol. XLIV 682-3; 6 Feb. 1807.
37. *Parl. Deb.*, vol. LXX 1271-7; 27 June 1816.

high-flying idealism with a little commonsense.

Not surprisingly, Holland took a deep interest in the final campaigns of the Emancipators in 1832-3. The whole question became more poignant when it had to be resolved against the background of a major slave uprising in Jamaica itself. Holland was very well-informed about the rebellion, during which twenty plantations were ruined and two thousand slaves were killed.[38] The letters of his agents are full of indignation against the idealism of English Emancipators who had little idea about the realities of the situation.[39] Baptist missionaries were particularly singled out for condemnation as people who raised expectations without being able to fulfil them. In Cabinet, Holland gave general support to the measure, but insisted that 'it be accompanied with some practical means of maintaining the police and the relations between various orders of society without which property cannot subsist'.[40] The claim to an expertise in these matters by Holland House irritated rather than impressed his Cabinet colleagues. Howick, for example, protested that 'I can not allow that we are so ignorant as you seem to suppose of the state of society in the colonies'.[41] On this occasion, however, Holland was speaking from harsh experience.

In the event, Holland House expressed itself very pleased with the final form of the Emancipation Act. The safeguards built into it appeared strong enough to guarantee the plantation owners against ruin and 'there is every prospect now of our being completely successful – which be it wisdom or be it luck, considering the difficulties that beset that question, is really almost miraculous'.[42] The measure seemed to have come as close as possible to marrying the twin objectives of bringing the slave within the pale of Whig liberty and of defending property. The apprenticeship scheme, by which the negro would be gradually introduced to new freedoms, looked eminently sensible. Even so, Holland

38. Add. MSS. 51635, ff 58-9; Talleyrand to Holland, n.d.
39. Add. MSS. 51820, ff 89-90; James Lawson to Holland, 5 Aug. 1832.
40. Holland to Howick, 4 Jan. 1833, Grey MSS. Box 111.
41. Add. MSS. 51820, ff 100-1; Howick to Holland, Jan. [1833].
42. Holland to Sir Charles Vaughan, 28 Sept. 1833; Vaughan MSS. c 58/6.

remained a vocal spokesman for the West India lobby, and he became a founder member of the Society of West Indian Planters in 1837. He lobbied for government protection of the West Indians' share of the sugar and rum trade against East Indian encroachments, and for a close supervision of the terms of the 1833 Act.[43] This defensive posture sprang directly from the savage drop in West Indian revenues after 1833, but the incongruity of Fox's nephew mixing pleas for emancipation with apologies for plantation owners remained, and it is therefore crucial to evaluate the validity of his reservations.

Throughout the discussions on slavery, Holland insisted that the views of the colonial assemblies and local residents had to be taken into account. Indeed, for many years, he believed that the best way to secure emancipation was to persuade the colonial assemblies themselves to deal with the matter.[44] This suggestion brought a stinging rebuke from Wilberforce, who demanded to 'accost you in your other character of a West Indian proprietor':

> I own frankly that what I cannot at all understand is ... that your Lordship should think it possible that the Colonial Assemblies will ever honestly adopt measures with a view to effect the ultimate abolition of Slavery. Surely to think this, is to suppose that Men who tell you that the carrying of the point you aim at will be utter ruin to them and who differ from you as to the means no less than the End you have in view, will adopt those means & act on them with sincerity.[45]

In fact, Holland would probably have agreed. His doubts stemmed from the practical consideration that no emancipation passed in England could be implemented successfully without the goodwill of the local community. His own orders to his estates in Jamaica were frequently ignored or lost en route. The most pious speeches in the House of Commons, 'depending for execution on the rulers and white part of the community in the West Indies',[46] would produce

43. Add. MSS. 51819, ff 25-6; E. Bancroft to Holland, 6 Oct. 1834.
44. *Parl. Deb.*, vol. LXXIII 575; 23 Feb. 1818.
45. Add. MSS. 51820, ff 40-1; Wilberforce to Holland, 12 Oct. 1830.
46. Holland to Howick, 7 Dec. 1831; Grey MSS. Box 111.

disaster if the cooperation of that community were not assured.

This pragmatic concern for the local situation could be seen as a delaying tactic by a colonial proprietor, but this is not the case. Holland held on to the point after 1833, when the idea of local opinion came to encompass black views as well as white. He accepted immediately the necessity of bringing the negro within the pale of a constitution based on property holding;

> ... I will never be a party to any direct or indirect method of cheating the black people of their due weight in the legislature as long as a representative system is allowed to subsist in Jamaica. It is quite proper that land held & tilled by Negroes should be adequately represented as well as land belonging to planters or colonists, as long as the laws which both parties should equally obey are made by an assembly pretending to represent the whole community.[47]

This is impeccable Whiggism. Rights and duties evolve from the ownership of land, irrespective of the colour or religion of the landowner. It followed that, just as the effectiveness of law in England depended on the cooperation of represented opinion, the same must apply in the West Indies. The question of distance reinforced the argument but did not initiate it. Holland was very happy to consider the suspension of Jamaica's Assembly if black rights were infringed.[48]

Holland also recognised that the question of enforcement rested, to some degree, on the success with which a new relationship could be worked out between the negro and his former master. Holland had the gravest doubts about a Colonial Office theory, expressed in a paper of 1833, that the transition from slave to wage labourer could be immediate. This was, in his view, 'a new theory' and 'if it should be found on examination & trial to be an erroneous one the whole fabrick raised upon it will become unsafe'.[49] Stanley's idea for an 'apprenticeship' period of seven years before full manumission, to prepare the negro for a new economic and social status, came as a great relief, and Holland encouraged

47. Add. MSS. 51819, ff 136-7; Holland to ? Curry, 1839.
48. Add. MSS. 51819, f 128; Holland to Howick, 1839.
49. Add. MSS. 51820, ff 98-9, Howick to Holland, 7 Jan. 1833.

his fellow West Indians to accept the scheme.[50] During the 'apprenticeship' period, Holland House was alternately depressed by reports of the scheme working badly[51] and delighted by any indication that it was going well. Further, Holland was quite clear that, in those parts of the West Indies where 'apprenticeship' had proved to be a success, landowners would be well advised to manumit well in advance of the end of the seven-year period to avoid too great an upheaval all at once.[52] The 'apprenticeship' scheme at least gave landowner and negro time to work out a new relationship and every advantage should be taken from this opportunity.

Holland's hopes were not fulfilled. By 1839, the West Indies were in a state of crisis, and the Vassall estates were not exempt from the general confusion. Too many landowners refused to accept the new status of the negro as a wage labourer, and tried to cheat him of his new-found rights and to exploit the value of his labour. Too many negros, with high expectations after 1833, rejected the status of wage labourer and resorted to violence. As Holland had feared, the ending of slavery had left the negro more vulnerable than before, in that he had exchanged the minimum guarantees of servitude for theoretical rights which he could not enforce against the white proprietors. The recourse to violent protest was not therefore surprising. The response of Holland House to this situation is revealing in its dependence on the enforcement of a law produced by landowners, in theory black and white. The slaves had been freed, but they remained on a contractual basis with respect to property. The authentic voice of Whiggery can be heard in Holland's answer to a report that the Vassall tenants were proving difficult:

Nothing can be more false or foolish than their notion that they have any legal possession of their grounds without rent & that they had them before Lady Holland was born – Lady Holland & I are always pleased to hear that they are happy & contented & always disposed

50. Add. MSS. 51869, ff 580 & 608; Holland's Political Journal, 17 March & 9 June 1833.

51. Add. MSS. 51819, ff 64-5; W. Hankey to Holland, 2 March 1838.

52. Add. MSS. 51819, ff 73-4; W. Lascelles to Holland, 5 April 1838.

to contribute to that happiness as much as we can – but the only way to satisfy both us & them is to be *just* in our dealings – & that is that we should pay them wages for the labour on the estate & that they should pay us rent for the land they cultivate for their provisions or for their own profit – *This they will find is the Queen's law* & I hope the government *will expound & enforce it* – It is, however, my opinion that the most prudent course is to give as good wages as one can afford especially to those willing as well as able to work.[53]

Land could be held by black or white. Political representation could, as a consequence, fall to both groups. The law, however, which defended property and demanded a reciprocity between landowner and labourer, had to be enforced. Contractual legalism, basic to Whig thinking, here emerges in full force.

Throughout the emancipation debate, the Hollands appear in the unusual rôle of pragmatists moderating the aspirations of idealists. In the same guise, their most profound contempt was reserved for the large number of Nonconformist missionaries in the West Indies. These 'soi-disant friends'[54] of the slaves deliberately inflated stories of maltreatment before 1833 and raised unrealisable expectations after that date.[55] If the negros behaved well, it was in spite of the missions rather than just because of them. Holland commended one governor of Jamaica because 'he growls a little at Baptists – He is a sensible & good man'.[56] In response to this situation, Holland House, notoriously agnostic though it was, found itself arguing in favour of drafting Anglican curates to the West Indies in large numbers to counteract the baleful effects of Dissent. Holland built churches and schools on his own estates, and took a lively interest in the reorganisation of the parish system and the provision of adequate stipends.[57] The irony of the Fox family rushing to the support of Anglicanism as a safe vehicle for religious expression did not escape contemporaries. Such a policy produced frosty interludes

53. Add. MSS. 51819, f 84; Holland to ?, 15 Feb. 1839.
54. Add. MSS. 51743, f 56; Holland to Caroline Fox, 25 Sept. 1838.
55. Add. MSS. 51868, f 362; Holland's Political Journal, 21 Feb. 1832.
56. Add. MSS. 51743, f 134; Holland to Caroline Fox, 10 Aug. 1840.
57. *Parl. Deb.*, vol. LXXV, 848-52; 4 March 1819.

between Holland and Wilberforce's Saints, but it was at least in line with his overall insistence that the question of emancipation could only be dealt with pragmatically and not by the simple application of general principles.

Overall, it is possible to claim that, on the slave issue, Holland stayed true to the legacy of his uncle. He had supported him to the hilt when the slave trade itself was abolished, and, whenever the question of emancipation was moved publicly, Holland was found among its supporters. His involvement with the West Indies brought complications which Fox had not had to face, but they never clouded his views on colour or the notion that emancipation was anything but right and inevitable. As a proprietor in Jamaica, Holland had a concern for the proper implementation of a reform which was often lacking in other areas. From this concern came embarrassment, as pragmatism conflicted with other aspects of the Hollands' political posture, notably in religion. Holland House was always vulnerable to criticism on the slave issue, as Holland struggled to reconcile the rôle of Fox's nephew with that of a Jamaican planter. Throughout the emancipation campaign, however, Holland the planter only suggested amendments to Holland the Foxite. The main theme remained that of Fox family tradition.

If a Foxite concern with the plight of slaves survived at Holland House by filtering through self-interest, the Foxite belief in a maximum expression of religious freedom flowed unrestricted. The Hollands carried over into the early nineteenth century an Englightened scepticism which, at best deistic, on the whole preferred to ignore the claims of religion as irrelevant and unprofitable. As Greville noted, the Hollands were simply not moved by such matters:

> It was not, however, the custom at Holland House to discuss religious subjects, except rarely and incidentally. Everybody knew that the House was sceptical; none of them ever thought of going to church, and they went on as if there was no such thing as religion.[58]

In Holland's view, 'good sense is a greater security for a Man's good behaviour than any speculative opinion of Philosophers

58. *The Greville Diaries*, V 155-7, 14 April 1843.

or any fear of a future life'.[59] They loathed any expression of religious enthusiasm in that it was often accompanied by the desire to proselytise and persecute. Sydney Smith's brilliant sallies against Methodism in the *Edinburgh Review* were received with delight. Harriet Martineau's dabbling with mesmerism and clairvoyance was depressing, but was simply an extension of an initial gullibility in religious matters.[60] Like so many of their literary preferences, the philosophical context of Holland House remained firmly that of the Enlightenment. Charles Fox would have agreed. There was simply the 'very unpleasant truth that no opinion, however just & right, if pursued ultra quam satis est, is exempt from the infirmity which generates calumny & persection'.[61]

Not unnaturally, Holland House acquired its reputation for irreligion very easily. John Allen, 'Lady Holland's Atheist', would walk around London, muttering to himself 'No first cause, no first cause.'[62] Henry Fox for once agreed with his parents that 'Laws and Religion are necessary evils to keep society together'.[63] In Lady Holland, scepticism and freethinking went hand in hand with wild superstitions about thunderstorms and Fridays, and an abhorrence of the word 'death'. She always walked out of productions of *Hamlet* during the funeral scene, and she asked the Earl of Carlisle to level the mausoleum at Castle Howard because it 'made her too sad'.[64] As Sydney Smith found, such a combination of attitudes was easy to satirise:

> When the fire broke out at Lord Lilford's, Lady Holland woke up Allen, who, hearing the crackling of the flames, and smelling the Smoke and seeing Lady Holland, conceived he had slipt off in the Night to a very serious place at a high Temperature; he attempted to recollect a prayer, but utterly failed, and was fairly pulled out of bed by Lady H and the maids.[65]

59. Add. MSS. 51733, f 209; Holland to Caroline Fox, April 1796.

60. Lady Holland to Henry Fox, 10 Dec. 1844; *Elizabeth, Lady Holland to her Son*, p.220.

61. Holland to W. Shepherd, 5 March 1840; Shepherd MSS., vol. 8 f 1.

62. *The Diaries of Lord Glenbervie*, ii 71-3; 1 Oct. 1810.

63. *The Journal of Henry Edward Fox*, p.193.

64. F. Leveson Gower, *Bygone Years*, pp. 35-7.

65. S. Smith to Lady Grey, *The Letters of Sydney Smith*, ii 693.

In Lord Holland, a broad agnosticism was matched by a philosophical contempt for death in the best eighteenth-century manner. The dying words of his uncle had been 'It don't signify', and Holland could equal this detachment. Like so many of their generation, however, the Hollands were puzzled and trapped by the 'reformation of manners' and return to piety of the early nineteenth century. In Lady Holland's amazement at anyone wanting to close the London Parks on Sundays is the protest of one century against the absurdities of the next.[66]

The only interest shown by the Hollands in Church affairs centred on patronage. Holland was acutely aware of the sacrifices made by Whig clergymen during the long years of the Pittite and Liverpool governments. One of his principal duties as Chancellor of the Duchy of Lancaster after 1830 was to provide Grey with lists of Whig clergy who should be considered for promotion. He went out of his way to tap local knowledge about good Whigs, who had been 'actually starving because they have been unwilling to accept or seek for Tory preferment'.[67] In his more hopeful moments, he hoped to provide Grey with enough names for an ''Εκκλησια Εἴγγικα' [a Whig Church].[68] Holland's involvement in such Barchester politics was incongruous in view of his family's reputation, but it stemmed from politics rather than religion. Anyone who had shared the sacrifices associated with Foxite loyalties must now be rewarded, even if they were clergymen. It was a source of endless regret at Holland House that their efforts failed ultimately to secure Sydney Smith a place on the episcopal bench.[69] The cause of toleration and the claims of political loyalty could both be met in the advancement of Whig clerics.

Religious toleration, perhaps the most uncomplicated of Holland's crusades, was grounded in Holland House scepticism. It was wide-ranging and all-embracing. Lady

66. Lady Holland to Henry Fox, 11 March 1834; *Elizabeth, Lady Holland to her Son*, p.146.
67. Holland to E. Ellice, 18 Sept. 1833; Ellice MSS. f 130.
68. Holland to Ebrington, 6 Oct. 1837; Fortescue MSS 1262 M/FC92.
69. Lady Holland to Henry Fox, 17 Feb. 1838; *Elizabeth, Lady Holland to her Son*, p.167.

Holland reflected, after her husband's death, that 'toleration was his darling object. Peace, amity & indulgence to all mankind were the predominant feelings of his heart.'[70] Their fundamental point in favour of toleration was a refusal to believe that a political establishment depended on a religious establishment. In the Hollands' view, Dissenters and Roman Catholics were not by definition enemies to a constitutional settlement based on property rights. If Anglicanism had ever been the sole defence against Dissenting democrats and Catholic despots, its role had become redundant by the early nineteenth century.[71] The indivisibility of Church and State, involving mutual support and protection, was, according to the Hollands, a Tory notion, which at best had only a historical justification, and that too was now exploded. Relief for Dissenters in 1828 was a major event, not because of the scale of the measure, but because it demonstrated that bringing non-Anglicans into political life brought no danger to established political practices. Remaining exclusions were therefore anomalous:

> It is the greatest victory over the *principle* of persecution & exclusion yet obtained. Practically there have been greater such as the Toleration Act in W 3d's time & the Catholick bill of 1792. Practically too the Catholick Emancipation when it comes will be a far more important measure, more immediate & more extensive in its effects – but *in principle* this is the greatest of them all as it explodes the real Tory doctrine *that Church & State are indivisible.*[72]

Pluralism in religion could be proved to involve no political dangers.

Once this point could be established, it followed that the state had no right to meddle with or obstruct the free play of conscience, or to put up barriers based on religion. Holland was always a fervent supporter of an open entry to Oxford and Cambridge.[73] He even saw nothing wrong in allowing people

70. ibid., 5 June 1841; ibid., p.191.
71. Add. MSS. 51870, f 665; Holland's Political Journal, 29 July 1833.
72. Add. MSS. 51750, ff 198-9; Holland to Henry Fox, 10 April 1828. See also Holland to Anglesey, 13 May 1828; Anglesey MSS.
73. Add. MSS. 51871, f 889; Holland's Political Journal, 13 July 1835.

from any level of society to preach, even though there was an obvious argument that a man who could advise on such profound matters might be worthy of a vote. This dangerous hint of democracy was overridden by Holland's insistence that the state withdraw from the supervision of religious expression.[74] In his view, 'religious liberty could not subsist, unless it was perfect and secure. In the language of Locke, it was equal and impartial, and entire liberty, of which religion and religious men stood in need.'[75] The state had no right to enforce monopolies in education or public life which were based on religious exclusions. It simply had no standing in such matters, and should be neutral in everything pertaining to religion. The state was in all respects secular, neither God-given nor divinely protected.

Nor was Holland entirely happy with the argument that, even in the sixteenth and seventeenth centuries, there had been a proper mutual interdependence between Anglicanism and the avoidance of democratic or absolutist theories. Whigs never opted out of the historical dimension to an argument and Fox himself had been the historian of James II's reign. In arguing against the Test and Corporation Acts, Holland insisted that they had only been directed against Roman Catholics, not Dissenters, and then for only a limited period. They were intended to meet a particular emergency, and the point was proved by the fact that 'these vaunted acts, so wise, so expedient, so provident, have never been in actual force, never practically executed for more than three, or at most seven years during the whole hundred and fifty that they have remained on your Statute Book'.[76] Further, Holland was so anxious to divorce politics and religion, that he was even prepared to argue that the problems created by James II had had no connection with his Catholicism:

The connection of the Catholic religion and King James's cause was, I maintain, purely accidental; and our ancient and unprecedented rights (to use the words of the Bill itself) vindicated at the Revolution,

74. *Parl. Deb.*, vol. LV, 1132-3, 9 May 1811.
75. ibid., vol. LVI, 248, 21 May 1811.
76. *Speech of Lord Holland in the House of Lords on the Second Reading of the Bill for the Repeal of the Corporation and Test Acts* (London 1828), p.13.

were as much the rights of our Catholic ancestors, as they are ours; and would be as much our rights tomorrow, if we were reconciled to the errors of the Church of Rome, as they are today, when we renounce those errors ... The Protestant monopoly of seats in Parliament, and offices of trust and profit, is not there declared to be a fundamental law or an undoubted right of the people of England.[77]

This surprising historical judgment on seventeenth-century conditions reinforced the Holland House view that, if there ever had been a justification for the state's involvement in religion in the past, it had been of an entirely transitory nature. There was no real historical case for arguing the indivisibility of Church and State. This was poor history but a good attempt at consistent argument.

The basic objection to all forms of state interference was carried over into all aspects of Church government. Holland supported attempts to secure the fair apportionment of Queen Anne's Bounty,[78] but refused to countenance the idea of a minimum stipend for priests and curates because 'it was an improper legislative interference in the private concerns and contracts between man and man; for such he esteemed those between the curate and the incumbent to be'.[79] The state had no right to intervene in Church affairs even to regulate abuse or unfairness, and this applied to the Roman Church equally firmly. Holland voted for a proposal for state salaries for the Irish Catholic clergy, in 1825, but regretted his decision bitterly afterwards.[80] The same priorities held on the question of Church building. Given his background, Holland in no way shared the feeling of urgency about the reorganisation of parishes or the provision of new churches which was current after 1820, but his opposition to any suggestion of state subsidies for such purposes stemmed not from Foxite agnosticism but from the continued belief in the state's lack of standing in religious matters. Whether the question was debated in a historical or a contemporary dimension, the necessity to divorce Church and State was always the starting point of Holland's thinking.

77. *Parl. Deb.*, vol. LVIII, 699-703; 21 April 1812.
78. ibid., vol. LII, 830; 4 May 1810.
79. *Parl. Deb.*, vol. XLI 703-4; 1 July 1805.
80. Add. MSS. 51749, f 88; Holland to Henry Fox, 29 April 1825.

Not surprisingly therefore, Holland House was a refuge for Dissent. On the crucial days of the 1828 Toleration debates, for example, 'This house is filled in the morning with Jews and Dissenters; people of all persuasions, even up to the Archbishop of York, to whom I sent Mary in the Library to amuse him until Papa got off some of the Sectaries.'[81] Holland firmly believed that there was a natural affinity between Whig politics and Dissenting religion which allowed cooperation over wide areas of public life. Historically, it could be shown 'that disunion between them is little more or less than conferring a triumph on a party inimical to & intolerant of both'.[82] Within the Whig party, Holland was seen as something of an expert on Dissenting matters. He was nominated to the appropriate committees whenever the matter was under discussion,[83] and, in 1828, presented 861 petitions for the repeal of the Test and Corporation Acts in so far as they applied to Dissenters. It was perhaps the major speech of the debate, which appealed equally to the force of historical evidence and to 'the march of intellect', and which was the culmination of a longstanding commitment.[84] In 1808, Holland had assured Christopher Wyvill that 'politic or impolitic whenever I am in public called upon to give my opinion or vote on these subjects it shall be in favour of Toleration'.[85] The firmness of the line taken on relief for Dissenters contrasts poignantly with the doubts and long silences on the subject of Parliamentary Reform.

In Holland's view, the Dissenters had to be the first beneficiaries of the disjoining of Church and State because, unlike the Catholics, they were not related with an associated problem of the magnitude of Ireland. The Dissenters would therefore breach the principle first and then allow the Catholics through in their wake. It was peculiarly gratifying for Holland to see his Dissenting friends willingly assisting in

---

81. Lady Holland to Henry Fox, 28 April 1828; *Elizabeth, Lady Holland to her Son*, p.83.
82. Holland to William Shepherd, 18 Sept. [1835]; Shepherd MSS. vol. 7, f 83.
83. Add. MSS. 51677, ff 123-6; Lord John Russell to Holland, 17 Aug. 1834.
84. *Parl. Deb.*, vol. XCV 1450-1482; 17 April 1828.
85. Holland to Wyvill, 11 Feb. 1808; Whitbread MSS. 4272.

pro-Catholic movements. There are many examples of cooperation between Holland House and Dissent to this end. In 1813, Holland stopped an anti-Catholic petition emerging from a County meeting in Wiltshire, 'partly, we flattered ourselves, by argument, but chiefly by the assistance of the Protestant Dissenters and the Methodists'.[86] For some years, he had used the Methodist organisation to disseminate pro-Catholic propaganda. From 1817 to 1829, Holland annually took the chair 'at a strange, full meeting composed chiefly of dissenting Ministers & ladies who admire them' to petition Parliament for Catholic Emancipation. Holland found the experience 'really curious & if a knowledge of man's manners & minds is a rational study, instructive'.[87]

In the final struggle for Catholic Emancipation, in 1829, the Dissenters behaved splendidly:

> My friends the dissenters are acting admirably & I do not say this from mere predilection for them ... but from positive knowledge of their spontaneous ... activity in favour of *general* religious liberty, since the *particular* measure of it by which they are benefited has been accomplished. Many Churchmen conceive opposition to Catholicks is hopeless now the strong hold of the necessity of Conformity to the enjoyment of civil power is abandoned.[88]

As 'A Dissenter' informed Holland in a pamphlet addressed to him personally, they favoured the removal of all constraints on Catholicism, and looked forward to 'contending with it on the open field of fair argument and honourable warfare'.[89] Generous attitudes such as these convinced Holland that all his suppositions about divorcing Church and State had been correct, and that no danger was to be anticipated from such a move. There is no doubt that his close ties with Dissent encouraged him to take a full part in the campaign for Catholic Emancipation, for which his support might otherwise have been more muted.

---

86. Holland, *Further Memoirs of the Whig Party*, 1813.
87. Holland to Ebrington, 1 May 1829; Fortescue MSS. 1262M/FC85.
88. Add. MSS. 51750, f 207; Holland to Henry Fox, May 1828.
89. *A Letter to the Rt. Hon. Lord Holland occasioned by the Petition from the General Body of the Dissenting Ministers of London for the relief of the Roman Catholics* (London 1829), p.6.

Inevitably, it was on the Catholic question and the associated problem of Ireland's future that Holland's views on toleration were most keenly tested. Unlike the English Dissenter, whom Holland knew and liked, the Irish Catholic was a much more ambivalent figure in the Holland House world. Lady Holland described Grattan's brother-in-law as 'a narrow-minded, silly man – an Irishman of course'.[90] Even so, the Hollands regarded Catholic Emancipation as a peculiarly Foxite cause and therefore their own property. They prided themselves on the Fox family connections with Ireland, and, when the measure was finally passed, regarded themselves as vindicated even though it was Wellington and Peel who managed the proceedings. Lady Holland was delighted to find, in 1829, that 'the world are very just, & ascribe the merit entirely to Fox & Grattan & those worthies who first agitated the matter'.[91] Holland himself was slightly more generous to his opponents in making the same historical point:

> Indeed we old Whigs have no right to quarrel with those who join our Standard & to feel any mortification at not being the ostensible & Ministerial agents when we have been the consistent & in fact the real effective champions of the cause for 30 years. [It] would be so paltry that I trust all of us & I am one is incapable of it.[92]

In 1793, 1801 and 1829, Pitt and his heirs attempted to assist the Irish Catholics, but their motives were entirely prudential in the desire to avoid Irish disturbances. Foxites, by contrast, had championed the Catholic cause for fifty years by arguing from first principles.[93] It was a distinction that the Hollands were fond of making.

The Fox family involvement in Ireland had a long history. Henry Grattan had been a close friend of Charles James Fox,[94] and, most important, his aunt married the Duke of

90. Lady Holland to Henry Fox, 21 April 1829; *Elizabeth, Lady Holland to her Son*, p.103.

91. Lady Holland to Henry Fox, 10 April, 1829; *Elizabeth, Lady Holland to her Son*, p.101.

92. Add. MSS. 51750, f254; Holland to Henry Fox, 6 Feb. 1829.

93. The Le Marchant Diary, July 1833; *Three Early Nineteenth Century Diaries*, p.366.

94. Add. MSS. 51468, f18; Fox to ?, 17 Nov. 1783.

Leinster. Thereafter, this Fitzgerald connection formed the basis for Holland's Irish news and information. Inevitably, Fox had taken a keen interest in the Volunteer Movement of 1779 to 1782, in which both Grattan and Leinster were involved, and which ended in a Whig granting of legislative independence to a Dublin Parliament. The Irish question was always set in the contexts of the American and French Revolutions, as illustrating the disasters which naturally emerged from the denial of political and religious rights. Pittite duplicity on the subject of Ireland was indicative of a much wider malevolence, and the thwarting of Fitzwilliam's reforms as Lord Lieutenant in 1795 merely made it clear to Fox and his nephew that his old school-friend had been unwise to go to Ireland at Pitt's behest at all.[95] The only fair and sensible way of settling the Irish question was to approach it from principle and not from shuffling expediency.

Although Holland himself followed his uncle's Irish views faithfully through the early 1790s, it was the great Irish Rebellion of 1798 which determined his thinking on the subject. His first cousin, Lord Edward Fitzgerald, was one of its principal leaders, and was someone for whom Holland retained an unbounded respect. Writing in 1824, he noted that 'many of my political opinions are softened ... but my approbation of Lord Edward Fitzgerald's actions remains unaltered and unshaken. His country was bleeding under one of the hardest tyrannies that our times have witnessed.'[96] In his memoirs, Holland romanticised the circumstances of Fitzgerald's death outrageously, and from the brutal suppression of the Rebellion he acquired a lifelong loathing of Orangemen. At the time of Lord Edward's trial, both Charles Fox and Holland asked the Duke of Leinster if he would like them to go across to Dublin as character witnesses for their Fitzgerald cousin.[97] When this offer was declined, Holland

95. Fox to Holland, 6 March 1795; *The Memorials & Correspondence of C.J. Fox*, iii 100-1. Fitzwilliam had been a contemporary of Charles Fox at Eton. For a full account of his ill-fated Lord-Lieutenancy of Ireland, see E.A. Smith, *Whig Principles and Party Politics*.

96. Holland, *Memoirs of the Whig Party during my Time*, pp. 101-3.

97. Add. MSS. 51735, f 35; Holland to Caroline Fox, 26 May 1798. See also *The Life and Letters of Lady Sarah Lennox*, ii Appendix E.

supported Leinster's motion in the Lords for a Committee of Enquiry into the state of Ireland, and when this was refused, entered a formal protest in the Lords' Journals. In what was regarded as his first major speech, Holland set his face against coercion in Ireland:

> A noble lord ... has asked if any one will put his hand to his heart, and say that conciliation would produce the effect of tranquillizing that country? I ask, will any one put his hand to his heart, and say that coercion will produce it.[98]

Henceforth, the 1798 Rebellion became a point of reference for Holland's thinking.

If coercion was no answer to the Irish problem, nor, in Holland's view was the Act of Union, by which the Dublin Parliament was abolished and Ireland was returned to legislative dependence on Westminster. Fox himself, still seeing merit in the Whig secession from Parliament, attended none of the debates on this subject but was clearly anxious to use his nephew as a proxy for his views. The incident has importance because it produced one of Holland's rare rebellions against his uncle's wishes. Both men were opposed to the Act of Union, but Fox wanted Whig opposition to it to be grounded on the legalistic point that the Irish Parliament could not vote itself out of existence without sounding out the wishes of the electorate.[99] As Holland later recalled, 'he wished me to question the right and competency of Parliament. I was not myself satisfied of the soundness of that ground of opposition, and I avoided it.'[100] This unusual declaration of independence is interesting in itself, but is doubly important for bringing to the surface themes which Holland answered for himself.

In major speeches on the proposed Union, Holland developed two principal ideas. The first represented a return to an old preoccupation. The abolition of the Dublin

---

98. *Parl. Deb.*, XXXIII 1327-8; 21 March 1798. See also Add. MSS. 51734, f 42; Holland to Caroline Fox, 27 June 1798.

99. Fox to Holland, 19 Jan., 18 Feb., 23 Feb. 1799; *Memorials and Correspondence of C.J. Fox*, iii 150-60.

100. Holland, *Memoirs of the Whig Party during my Time*, p.143.

Parliament, with the consequent arrival at Westminster of Irish M.P.s and Irish representative peers meant a massive reinforcement for the executive. The closed boroughs in Ireland would be the new prop of royal influence, and this, according to Holland, was probably the major motive behind the measure.[101] Secondly, the Union project itself was futile. Only Catholic Emancipation could begin to contain Irish discontent: 'The emancipation of the Catholics was a measure absolutely necessary to tranquillize men's minds in Ireland, and prepare the way for the attainment of those benefits which were expected from the Union.[102] The fact that the Catholics had been given the vote in 1793 made their continued exclusion from Westminster ridiculous. In this double-headed assault, Holland neatly paired two family priorities. The Act of Union was objectionable because it was an inadequate alternative to toleration and because it reinforced the malevolent capabilities of executive power.

In retrospect, Holland never altered his opinion that the Act of Union had been a disaster. For twenty-nine years, 'it continued a hindrance rather than a help to all good government in Ireland'.[103] It became a point of great pride with him that he had been the first person formally to move the political emancipation of Roman Catholics:

> I perhaps indulge a little pardonable complacency in reminding my reader that the great measure, commonly called Catholic Emancipation, which so many of its inveterate opponents were driven to adopt in 1829, was first moved in the House of Lords by the writer of these pages.[104]

Once his views on coercion and the Act of Union were formed, it was no surprise to him that Ireland should continue to prove troublesome all through the French wars. The Emancipation question was all-important for, 'if decided as it should be [it] would be a better defence bill than the Levy en masse'.[105] In

101. *Parl. Deb.*, vol. XXXIV 706; 19 March 1799.
102. ibid., vol. XXXV; 30 April 1800.
103. Holland, *Memoirs of the Whig Party during my Time*, pp. 163-4.
104. ibid., p.164.
105. Add. MSS. 51736, f 293; Holland to Caroline Fox, 9 Dec. 1803.

this discussion, Holland never fell into disagreement with his uncle, but he was insistent that the debate should be carried on over a much wider area than Charles Fox thought politic.

In the tangled political situation which followed the resignation of the Younger Pitt in 1801, there was obviously the danger that Catholic Emancipation might be sacrificed as part of a pact or bargain that brought the Whigs to power in alliance with some other group. Holland never thought that such a treaty could be justified. The pre-eminence of Catholic claims was always uppermost in his mind. With the Grenville faction, Catholic Emancipation provided a point of contact. It was in fact 'the great publick question on which the component parts of Opposition could most consistently and most cordially concur'.[106] On the other hand, the matter was a stumbling block in negotiations with Addington's followers, and it was not one that Fox wished in any way to be removed. The possibility of enlisting Addington in an enduring alliance was always slim, but neither Charles Fox nor his nephew wished to increase the chances of such an alliance at the expense of the Catholics.[107] Within the Whig party, Holland was most persistently in favour of promoting the measure as a priority.

The greatest test to Foxite sincerity came with the formation of the Talents Ministry in 1806. George III was known to be an inveterate opponent of Catholic claims, and therefore the survival of the administration in terms of Court favour lay in the postponement of the issue for the time being. Both Grey and Grenville were prepared to accept this condition.[108] The Duke of Bedford, then Lord Lieutenant of Ireland, protested vigorously against any such retreat:

> What is to be done? It is impossible for you to oppose the question on the ground of the season being unfit for its discussion – If you give it a hollow and inefficient support, you place yourselves on a level with Pitt on the questions of the Slave Trade and parliamentary reform – If

106. Holland, *Memoirs of the Whig Party during my Time*, pp. 196-7. See also, Fox to Holland, 17 Dec. 1804; *Memorials and Correspondence of C.J. Fox*, iv 67-9.

107. Fox to Holland, 26 April and 2 May 1805; *Memorials and Correspondence of C.J. Fox*, iv 78-9.

108. Add. MSS. 51661, f 14; Bedford to Holland, 18 Dec. 1804.

you give it the firm and unequivocal support you ought to do the Question is carried, and then what becomes of you with the K[ing]? ... I have a dread of lapsing into the temporizing System of Pitt.[109]

When, early in 1807, the dilemma had to be faced squarely in response to a petition for relief from the Irish Catholics, Bedford tried to secure Holland's support by referring to 'your Uncle, whose principles still live, & flourish as the sacred inheritance of a large Portion of the Cabinet'.[110] Once the Catholic petition was presented to Parliament, the Whigs could either demonstrate their consistency by supporting it, in the sure knowledge that the King would then try to secure their overthrow, or stay in office at the expense of principle.

The Fox family reaction to this problem is instructive. Both uncle and nephew took the view that the first objective of the Talents Ministry had to be the securing of a peace with France. All other reform projects were conditional upon such an event. The Catholic petition was therefore inopportune, and Holland, in trying to stop it at source, hoped that the Irish Catholics 'might be apprized of the fatal tendency to their cause & to the power of their friends of any unseasonable application to Parliament'.[111] They could gain nothing from the fall of the Talents, and that was the likely outcome of a precipitate move. Even the abolition of the Slave Trade might have been jeopardised earlier. However, if the Catholics could not be dissuaded from proceeding with the petition, Holland had no hesitation in supporting it, whatever the consequences. Bedford was left in no doubt of this intention: 'The influence of government cannot be better employed than in giving them the benefit of laws to their full extent, in making common cause with them, and in pushing them wherever it can into Corporation's, places etc etc ... As to the petition my opinions remain unaltered, if it is presented and moved I shall support.'[112] In spite of the threat to a possible peace with

109. Add. MSS. 51661, ff 48-9; Bedford to Holland, 18 Dec. 1806.

110. ibid., f 72; ibid., 28 Feb. 1807.

111. Add. MSS. 51544, ff 68-9; Holland to Grey, 12 Feb. 1807.

112. Add. MSS. 51661, f 78; Holland to Bedford, 13 March 1807. See also Holland to Howick, 6 March 1807; H.M.C. *Fortescue* IX, pp. 67-8.

France and the other reforming ambitions of the Talents administration, the Catholic cause, if formally presented, allowed of no compromise.

As Holland had feared, the airing of Catholic claims prompted George III to round on the Grey/Grenville ministry by dissolving Parliament, and thereby throwing the Whigs into a general election campaign for which they were neither prepared nor equipped. It was an election in which for Holland 'the cry of intolerance' was matched against 'the friends of religious liberty',[113] and was victorious. In retrospect, Holland had few regrets about the fate of the Talents Ministry. The Catholic issue could not have been ducked indefinitely, and its thwarting by the expedient of a Parliamentary dissolution was a further proof of the power of the Crown and suggested a close analogy to the events of 1784. In Holland's view, George III 'allowed Lord Howick in 1807, as he had done Mr Fox in 1783, to proceed with a measure under the impression that he acquiesced in it, with a full determination to disarm him and to convert the transaction into a means of dismissing him'.[114] It had been right to support the Catholics, and their disappointment showed the nature and extent of executive power. It was a thesis which brought together many strands of Foxite thinking.

Throughout the long years of opposition, from 1807 to 1830, the Catholic question remained in the forefront of Holland's politics. It provided the principal link with the Grenvilles.[115] It was the sticking point in the occasional negotiations for a new type of coalition government.[116] During one such overture, Holland told Grey bluntly that

> I not only agree with you but conceive it to be a point of principle &
> not merely of expediency & therefore one from which those who think
> as we do cannot recede – I mean this – that the full powers of settling
> & settling immediately the Catholic claims should be a sine qua non

113. Holland, *Memoirs of the Whig Party during my Time*, ii 226-7.

114. Holland, *Memoirs of the Whig Party during my Time*, ii 194.

115. Add. MSS. 51530, f 98; Grenville to Holland, 5 Dec. 1808; see also T. Grenville to Lord Grenville, 24 Jan. 1814; H.M.C. *Fortescue*, X, 371.

116. Add. MSS. 51530, ff 149-54; Grenville to Holland, 27 Oct. 1809. See also Add. MSS. 51545, ff 22-4; Holland to Grey, 3 Nov. 1812.

to the acceptance of office. I have no hesitation to repeat to you what I said at the time to my uncle that the omission of such a stipulation at the formation of [the] last Administration was a *stain* on its character.[117]

Equally, through the 1820s, Holland's interest in Catholic Emancipation, if measured by public performance or private preoccupations, was always livelier than his concern for any other issue. So central a point was it that Holland expressed his willingness to cooperate with Wellesley, Canning or even Wellington himself, if any of them would announce himself a convert to the Catholic cause.[118]

By 1828 therefore, when the Catholic campaign entered its final phase, Holland's parliamentary advocacy of toleration had a thirty-year history. It had been argued from first principles rather than expediency, and stood in stark contrast to Pittite alternatives. Coercion had been proved ineffective and the annual re-enaction of penal legislation was 'abhorrent to the genius of our constitution and to the humanity of our age'.[119] In the hands of 'the Protestant magistracy',[120] these Acts became truly barbarous. In particular, it was absurd to try to smother the success of O'Connell's Catholic Association by legislation.[121] For a generation, coercion had not contributed in any way to a solution of the Irish troubles. Equally, the Union was destructive in its effects on Anglo-Irish relations. It had been passed by fraud and was maintained by corruption. Its existence posed a clear set of alternatives, 'either to admit the Irish people to a full participation of all the advantages of the British constitution; or to repeal the Act of Union, and restore them to the situation in which they were antecedently placed.'[122] No policy could work, in Holland's view which failed to take Catholic Emancipation as its starting point.

117. Add. MSS. 51544, f 197; Holland to Grey, 13 Jan. 1810.
118. Holland to Cloncurry, 7 March 1823; *Recollections of the Life and Times of Lord Cloncurry*, p.281; see also *The Journal of Mrs Arbuthnot*, i 384.
119. *Parl. Deb.*, LXXXVIII 1454-5; 18 June, 1824.
120. ibid., LXXXIII 196-206; 9 Feb. 1822.
121. ibid., LXXXVIII 868-72; 3 March 1825.
122. *Parl. Deb.*, LXXXIV 1078; 14 June 1822.

Further, Holland House assumed that such ideas were distinctively Whig, in spite of the fact that Canning and other members of the Liverpool government professed themselves to be supporters of the Catholic cause. According to Holland, Canning's behaviour[123] retarded rather than forwarded the campaign, for, as long as he remained associated with Liverpool, the Emancipation issue could not be presented as a clear-cut choice between government and opposition policies. The result was an unhelpful muddying of the water:

> There is a notion, a very foolish one I think, of putting off the Catholick question till after Easter – It is clear if we had the power of carrying it, it should not be delayed a month a week or a day, & if it is so right to pass it directly it cannot be wrong to propose it immediately – one of the many objections to the sort of half faced fellowship which Canning's system of neutrality in office creates in the supporters of this grand question is that he & the ministerial supporters are naturally & necessarily always for postponement.[124]

In spite of the Canningites confusing matters, Holland saw the Catholic question in party terms, and when, in 1827, the Tories 'for the first time these sixty years' found themselves out of power, he was forced to 'smile at their shallow artifice of representing the Catholick question as having no influence on their conduct'.[125] Whoever passed Catholic Emancipation, there was no doubt at Holland House that party consistency made that event a great Whig victory.

Liverpool's death, in 1827, was recognised by Holland as the event which opened up every possibility in politics, and not least 'in domestick questions connected with religious liberty'.[126] It was a decisive break in the clouds. Royal Dukes began publicly to support the idea of toleration,[127] and Holland House, much excited, took steps to prepare for the final campaign. Their new acquisition as a correspondent was the Marquess of Anglesey, who had just taken up the position

123. See below, Chapter Five.
124. Holland to Carlisle, 2 Feb. 1827; Castle Howard MSS, LB 139.
125. Holland to Carlisle, 14 Feb. 1827; Castle Howard MSS., LB 10.
126. Holland to Sir Charles Vaughan, 1 July 1827; Vaughan MSS. c 58/9.
127. Holland to Anglesey, 13 June 1828; Anglesey MSS.

of Lord Lieutenant of Ireland, and who, throughout 1828 and 1829, kept Holland House as well-informed about Irish affairs as the Wellington Cabinet. Within two months of Liverpool's death, Holland fired the first salvo in the new campaign by publishing a pamphlet in answer to an anti-Catholic tract written by the Warden of New College, Oxford. In his *Letter to the Rev. Dr Shuttleworth*, Holland regurgitated the historical point that concessions to Dissenters and the enfranchisement of Catholics in 1793 had brought no dangers to the state. Toleration was safe because Church and State were no longer interdependent in practical terms. More ingenuously, Holland insisted that the Irish Catholics objected only to the political monopoly of the Anglican Church in Ireland, and therefore represented no threat to its tithes or other temporalities, an unfortunate suggestion in view of the politics of the next ten years.[128]

As Wellington squared up to the question of Emancipation, Holland was prepared to help in any way possible: 'Let him epouse manfully the great question of Ireland & I put all my objections political & personal, old or of later date in my pocket & will for one work like a dray horse for him in the H. of Lords or out of it.[129] Yet assistance with the actual passing of the Bill could not restrain Holland from making the obvious points which followed from his belief in the essentially Whig nature of the measure. If Wellington and Peel were responsible for the final Emancipation, they were not moved by goodwill. They were responding only to the harsh necessity that the alternative for Ireland was chaos. The Duke had been forced 'to submit to necessity'.[130] There was nothing generous in his actions. The reform was prudential, rather than moral or intellectual in origin. There was no cause to moderate his views in any way on Tory shortcomings: 'Acquiescence in the measure of Cathk Emancipn would indeed cover a multitude of sins, but there are many to cover, & till we have the mantle for our pains I do not much approve of the present system of

128. Holland, *Letter to the Rev. Dr Shuttleworth* (London 1827).
129. Holland to Brougham, 28 Oct. 1828; Brougham MSS. 14,954.
130. Holland to Anglesey, 27 June 1828; Anglesey MSS.

concealment.'[131] Wellington had to be assisted to secure the Bill's passage but his motives were suspect. Catholic Emancipation was a Whig measure, because, in Holland's view, it could only properly be brought forward on the arguments that the Whigs had been promoting for a generation.

This insistence on seeing the Emancipation Bill in party terms had a blinkering effect on Holland's view of politics, the most surprising outcome of which was his complete inability to foresee any possibility that the Tories might split up on the issue. The violent dispute between Wellington and Peel on one side and the Ultra Tories on the other, which allowed the Whigs back into government in 1830, came as a complete surprise to Holland House. In December 1828, Holland was confident that the Ultras would, in the last resort, stay with the Duke.[132] It was even possible, in his opinion, that the Tories would emerge from the whole matter stronger than ever, in that, once Emancipation was on the statute book, one of the most important unifying influences in the Whig party would be removed, and, at the same time, one of the main reasons for the Canningites to manoeuvre in a Whig direction would have gone. For Holland, there was party satisfaction in watching Peel and Wellington legislating for the benefit of Irish Catholics, but he was completely unaware of what the consequences might be. The return to office in 1830 was as surprising as it was welcome. As Holland observed, as late as February 1829:

> Though conscious that the success of the measure as now brought forward closes yet more certainly than ever their access to place or power, they [the Whigs] have been as eager as zealous & as accommodating in the conduct of the business & in the support of Wellington against Court intrigue as if their friends not their enemies were to reap the profit.[133]

131. Add. MSS. 51750, ff 245-6; 27 Nov. 1828.
132. Holland to Anglesey, 30 Dec. 1828; Anglesey MSS. See also S. Rogers to D. Rogers, Feb. 1829; *Samuel Rogers and his Contemporaries*, ii 25.
133. Add. MSS. 51750, f 260; Holland to Henry Fox, 13 March 1829.

Predictably, Holland House followed the debates in the Lords and Commons with the greatest possible interest. Lady Holland gave her son an almost day-to-day account of the Bill's progress. Until the very last moment, the Hollands refused to believe that the Ultra Tories, or 'Brunswickers' as Holland House called them, would break with Wellington.[134] In spite of the fact that Holland's performance in the Lords was muted by another painful attack of gout, the whole proceeding was accompanied by a great deal of mutual self-congratulation among the Fox family:

> It is a delightful concession, & so surprizing that one feels in a dream. Peel is the only honest one. The great Duke is what one always thought, devoid of principle, gratitude, generosity ... The King has been circumvented, and he ought to be when great benefits are necessary for the country. Remember, your Papa was the *first* man who moved C. Emancipation in the House of Lords, when he was very young. It is a proud thing for him ... One is so absorbed in this wonderful event, that there is not time to think even of other things.[135]

Since it was not easy for Wellington to find an argument supporting his new attitude to Catholic Emancipation which had not already been used by the Whigs for half a century, there was some justification for Holland House's self-satisfaction.

Neither the Slave issue nor Catholic Emancipation ever became simple party issues. Wilberforce cooperated with Holland and valued his opinion, but remained firmly Pittite in his general politics. George Canning would have agreed with nearly everything that Holland House would preach about toleration, but almost always opposed his old College friend on other issues. Such complications irritated the Hollands but in no way deterred them. They continued to think of the defence of slaves and Roman Catholics as something distinctively Whig, indeed something distinctively Foxite.

134. Lady Holland to Henry Fox, 31 March 1829; *Elizabeth, Lady Holland to her Son*, p.100.
135. ibid., 6 Feb. 1829; ibid., pp. 94-5.

With occasional equivocations the family had been their unswerving guardians. Their political sacrifices, stretching over a fifty-year period, had been made for the sake of civil and religious toleration. As quoted earlier in this chapter, in Lady Holland's view, the passing of Catholic Emancipation was not the vindication of Wellington or Peel, but rather it represented the political apotheosis of her husband and his uncle Charles.

5

The Problem of the Lansdownes and George Canning

If the Holland House creed was hallowed by the blood of martyrs, it also had the dévot's exclusiveness. The Hollands saw politics in terms of black and white much more than most of their contemporaries. They were anxious to claim that the great reform issues were matters distinctively Foxite, or even matters personal to the Fox family. Such views were untenable, and two men in particular, Canning and Lansdowne, operated systems of politics which so disturbed the clear lines of argument that the distinctions Holland wished to draw proved impossible. The Lansdowne family was Whig in the sense that it was in opposition to the Younger Pitt and his heirs for most of Holland's lifetime. George Canning was a potential Whig in the sense that he had nothing in common with Eldonite Tories. The problem was that both found alliances with Tories as plausible a tactic as alliances with Whigs, and, by involving themselves with some of the reform programme, they made it impossible for the Hollands to claim it as their own. In short, from Holland's point of view, the Lansdownes and George Canning were thoroughgoing nuisances. His attitude towards them throws much light on Foxite prejudices.

The duel between the Fox and Lansdowne families was a battle waged between relations. The first Marquess, formerly the Earl of Shelburne, had taken as his second wife Lady Louisa Fitzpatrick, whose elder sister Mary had become the second Baroness Holland. William, first Marquess of Lansdowne (1737-1805) was therefore Holland's uncle, while John, second Marquess (1765-1809), and Henry, third Marquess (1780-1863), were his cousins. In addition, Caroline Fox had been taken in by the Lansdownes at Bowood after the death of her mother, and the third Marquess, as Lord Wycombe, had been Holland's travelling companion for his European tours in the early 1790s. In eighteenth-century terms, such a set of circumstances should have ended in a close political alliance, but this was not the case. The Lansdownes had risen to prominence as protégés of the Elder Pitt. Lansdowne himself had been responsible for giving the Younger Pitt his first experience of government. In return for this loyalty, the Marquisate had been created for the family in 1785. As far as the Hollands were concerned, such a record was the mark of Cain.

The problem raised was this. Lansdowne always called himself a Whig and based his claim on the fact that the Economical Reform of royal government and administration would severely reduce the number of placemen in the Commons, and thereby destroy executive power in an evolutionary way. The difficulty was that, by such a definition of the word Whig, Pitt himself could and did make the same claim. In Holland's view, there was no point in opposing Pitt's war measures, if Lansdowne insisted on retaining a reading of Whig principles which allowed Pitt a claim to them. Such an attitude was bound to excite suspicion. As Holland told his sister:

> You know I never was sanguine about an alliance between L. L & him [Fox]. I have to say the truth never wished for it, their opinions are directly the reverse, My Uncle is for acting in a party, & for increasing the power as well as the respectability of the House of Commons. Ld L—e is of a very different opinion & I really think in his heart loves the crown better than the Parliament though he may love the People better than either.[1]

It was taken for granted in the Fox family that Lansdowne had been primarily responsible, as a royal agent, for

---

1. Add. MSS. 51731, f 104; Holland to Caroline Fox, 5 Jan. 1793.

destroying the Rockingham/Shelburne government of 1782, and that his nicknames of 'Malagrida' and 'the Jesuit of Berkeley Square' had been well-earned. The irritating outcome was that, as long as Lansdowne retained an interest in the future of slaves and Catholics, while centering Whiggery on Economical reform, the Fox family's attempts to make those issues exclusively their own were necessarily impeded.

Doubts on these points took on political significance in the 1790s when logic dictated that the Lansdowne and Fox families should have acted together. Both took broadly sympathetic views of the French Revolution and both deplored Pitt's war policies at home and abroad. From 1793 onwards, there were a number of peace initiatives, usually initiated by Caroline Fox from Bowood, who saw herself as the obvious intermediary between her uncles Fox and Lansdowne. On each occasion, however, her brother reminded her of the contested definition of Whig and the harm that it generated:

> With regard to Lord Lansdowne & my Uncle Charles's arrangements, it is natural for you to wish it, & loving them both I cannot wonder that you should wish to see them friends, but as discussing their merits one with another, it seems to me not to be the question whether Ld L thinks my Uncle an Honest Man, or my Uncle him, but whether their opinions coincide & I am sure that if I understand either they are diametrically opposite as opinions can be, one attempting to force the Crown through the means of the Aristocracy to abandon its influence in parliament & to receive the Minister from parliament, the other hoping to destroy the Aristocracy by means of the crown & the public & to reform the parliament by means of an administration formed by the Court & not forced on it by the parliament – One to lessen the influence of the King through parliament, the other to reform the parliament through the medium of the King.[2]

The force of the last sentence had led to the traumatic experiences of 1782-3. Both families claimed to be interested ultimately in circumscribing Crown influence, but, according to Fox and his nephew there was only one true Whig creed, opposed to which all was heresy. Sheer pressure of events

2. Add. MSS. 51732, ff 192-3; Holland to Caroline Fox, 22 March 1795. See also same to same ff 141-2, 2 Dec. 1794 and f 159, 24 Jan. 1795.

might drive Fox and Lansdowne together in the 1790s, but it would be an unloving partnership.[3]

For Holland, the problem remained the same for the next thirty years. In 1809, 1812 and 1827, whenever in fact the question of coalition politics arose, Holland had to assess the reliability of the Lansdownes. Although he personally liked Henry, the third Marquess, he would never be sure that he would not follow family tradition and bolt into royal service. The crucial question to be asked was at what point, if any, had the Lansdownes surrendered the idea of securing reforms through the agency of the Crown, by coming to see kings as the major obstacles to all change. To present the same question in the terms of Holland House, at what point had the Lansdowne family become proper Whigs? As long as the ambiguity remained, Holland could not present the clear-cut choice between the heirs of Fox and the heirs of Pitt, as he would have wished. Lansdowne drew on both traditions and therefore confused the issue horribly. In practical terms, it made it difficult to demand that the Whigs enter government as a party when elements within it like the Lansdownes were, by inclination, so susceptible to ideas of coalition.

If the Lansdowne family was difficult, George Canning was worse. As contemporaries at Christ Church, Canning and Holland had become close friends. As Oxford 'Jacobins' and pupils of Dr Parr, they had acquired a joint notoriety. As Holland recalled, 'you may easily guess that the congeniality of our political sentiments was a great topick of conversation between us & of course was the occasion of our foreseeing in our minds at least many delightful prospects of future cooperation'.[4] Holland was simply amazed by Canning's decision to become a junior minister in Pitt's government. It ran counter to everything in his recent Oxford career. To resolve the mystery, Holland and Sheridan took Canning out for dinner to demand an explanation, whereupon 'Canning got excessively drunk and told me many facts in that state which I never was acquainted with before – but as this was in

3. Add. MSS. 51733, f 166; Holland to Caroline Fox, 11 Jan. 1796.
4. Add. MSS. 51731, ff 152-4; Holland to Caroline Fox, 31 Aug. 1793.

a state of intoxication I neither thought it proper nor generous for me to *open* the discussion again'. No further details were given except that Canning's reasons 'are not very complimentary either to Sns principles or reputation'.[5] Holland continued to express great regard for his College friend, but for many Whigs, Canning's shift from 'Jacobinism' to Pittitism within a year or two of leaving university was hard to forgive.

The problem was that Canning should have been a Whig. He admired Fox, felt sympathetic towards the slavery question, had welcomed the French Revolution in its early stages, and was thought to be positively enthusiastic about Catholic claims. The one insuperable barrier to Canning becoming a Whig, as Holland later recalled, was his detestation of the principles of aristocracy: 'Canning had always hated the aristocracy (a hatred which they certainly returned with interest).'[6] Canning's mother had been an actress, and therefore his position was dependent on ability rather than birth. In the Whig world, this put him on a par with Burke, Sheridan and Macaulay at the minor government-post level. A surname like Fox, Russell or Spencer was required to go higher. Canning simply refused to accept this aristocratic exclusiveness, and chose instead to follow a freebooting course in politics on his own account. The consequence of this, which the Whigs had to wrestle with for the next thirty years, was that, as long as Canning remained in largely Pittite governments, the Whigs could not claim the slave or Catholic issues as their own, and doubt might even be thrown on the Whigs' exclusive rights to Parliamentary reform. Canning's behaviour muddied waters that should have become clear.

Not surprisingly therefore, Canning was able to provoke the strongest emotions in Whig circles, and he had no more consistent enemy than Lady Holland, even if the prospect of office could sometimes moderate its impact.[7] Their mutual

---

5. Add. MSS. 51731, ff 152-4; Holland to Caroline Fox, 31 Aug. 1793.
6. *The Greville Diaries*, iii 138-9.
7. Brougham to Grey, 3 Oct. 1809; *The Life and Times of Lord Brougham*, i 461-3.

antipathy was one of the basic assumptions of social and political life.[8] As Lady Holland candidly remarked:

> ... to Mr Canning the Whig Party owe their compactness much more than to the merit & conciliating talents of their Leaders, for those who were half inclined to drop off & follow a more active Chief, were restrained by the unsteady & feeble line, not to say more, he has generally taken upon all great issues ... My stomach will bear hot water, my stomach will bear cold water, but my stomach absolutely rejects lukewarm water, so Mr Canning makes me sick.[9]

She bitterly resented Canning's early friendship with her husband, and was irritated by the lingering influence he retained over Holland's mind. John Allen faithfully supported his mistress in this opinion. He was delighted when Canning 'met with another rebuff from the Aristocracy',[10] and insistent that 'no man seems to trust him'.[11]

More seriously, the Whig grandees had issued an anathema. Bedford vetoed any prospect of an alliance with Canning in 1812,[12] and Grey declared that he 'could not now bring myself either in or out of office to act with him'.[13] Canning's crimes of obscuring party divisions and propping up Pittite governments were just too great.

Under these pressures, Holland's attitudes remained ambivalent. He was genuinely depressed when a Holland House protégé joined Canning's entourage,[14] and, whenever Grey cracked the Foxite whip, Holland hastened to fall into line:

> You cannot be more averse than I am to any thing savouring of a coalition with any of the No Popery Ministry & so far from Canning being an exception recent events have proved that of all of them his temper & mode of activity render him the least safe & agreeable associate in or out of office.[15]

8. Lady C. Lamb to Lady Bessborough, 21 Aug. 1808; *Lady Bessborough and Her Family Circle*, pp. 170-1.

9. Lady Holland to Sir Charles Vaughan, 30 June 1813; Vaughan MSS. c 61/8.

10. ibid., 25 Nov. 1812; Vaughan MSS. c 68/3.

11. J. Allen to Sir Charles Vaughan, 12 Aug. 1812; Vaughan MSS. c 9/6.

12. Grey to Grenville, 17 Nov. 1812; HMC. 30 *Fortescue* x, 313.

13. Grey to Holland, 5 Oct. 1809; Grey MSS. Box 35.

14. Add. MSS. 51739, f 93; Holland to Caroline Fox, 25 Dec. 1812.

15. Add. MSS. 51544, f 179; Holland to Grey, 9 Oct. 1809.

1. Lady Holland: 'Lady Webster as a Virgin of the Sun' by
George Romney

2. Whig statesmen by W. Lane

At the same time, Holland could not shake off a great respect for his intelligence and abilities, and retained 'too much personal good will to him to be a fair or impartial judge of the propriety of attacking him'.[16] For him, there was just 'so much mystery in that quarter',[17] that a clear line of response was difficult. Holland's ambivalence in the crisis of 1827, when some firm answer to the prospect of a Whig/Canningite ministry was absolutely required, is prefigured in his letters of twenty years earlier. In his view, there was so much in Canning's political make-up that ought to have been Whig, that Holland found it bewildering that it was not so. The real problem was that Holland House tried so hard to draw firm lines between Whig and Tory that the type of cross-currents in politics that Canning followed left them irritated or puzzled.

In the 1820s, the 'mystery' surrounding George Canning deepened. In terms of foreign policy, the Whigs had to admit a positive gain.[18] The substitution of Canning for Castlereagh would lead to a more relaxed English attitude towards Greece, Portugal, Spain and other causes close to Whig hearts. As Holland himself reported from Paris, such a liberalisation in foreign policy was likely because it was now European Ultras who were making those disparaging remarks about Canning's ancestry that always stung him into the sharpest of responses:

> Canning is not likely to bear the personal insinuations against him by Russians & Ultras so tamely as Castlereagh would have done. They are not sparing & call him un aventurier, a parvenu and what not. The cause of liberty may for once derive a benefit from his sauciness & smart temper which have so often made him hostile to it.[19]

Just as Canning could not be a Whig because his social origins denied him the possibility of holding the highest office in such circles, so he could not feel comfortable among the ambassadors and diplomats of the Vienna powers. As a result, in the Whig view, he became the patron of European liberalism.

16. Holland to Brougham, 9 Jan. 1810; Brougham MSS. 34193.
17. Add. MSS. 51741, f 200; Holland to Caroline Fox, 30 Dec. 1822.
18. Add. MSS. 52175, f 103; Henry Fox to John Allen, 18 Sept. 1822.
19. Add. MSS. 51546, f 203; Holland to Grey, 3 Dec. 1822.

There was also no doubt, as the trial of Queen Caroline for adultery suggested, that, whenever George Canning chose to attack Liverpool, he was the most effective irritant for Tory skins that could be imagined. In this sense, if no other, he was a potential ally of the Whigs. A whole volume of the Holland House manuscripts is given over to the Queen's trial and demonstrates the close interest that the Hollands took in the matter.[20] During the Talents Ministry, the Whigs themselves had become embroiled in the Queen's adventures, and endless comparisons are made with what Holland called 'the first Caroline affaire'. Lady Holland, whose own early life made her moralising less than convincing, thought that Caroline's behaviour had been wholly reprehensible, and was not surprised therefore to discover that another of her pet aversions, George Canning, had become the Queen's champion.[21] The importance of the Queen's trial became a real point of difference at Holland House. While Lady Holland wished only to score moral points, her husband could not resist extracting humour from the situation. When, for example, it was alleged that Caroline's adultery had taken place under the canopy of a Venetian gondola, Holland sent the following comment to his son at Christ Church:

> If crime must both act & intention suppose
> No bill can be put & no penalty meant
> For now, as allowed by her bitterest foes
> All that's proved 'gainst the Queen can be only *in Tent*.[22]

The truth was that Holland too found the whole episode mildly distasteful, not least for the hypocrisy on the part of George IV in bringing such an action against his wife.[23] It was unwise, however, simply to ignore the issue because it was clear that great political profit could be derived from it. Liverpool's relationship with George IV was unlikely to

20. Add. MSS. 51521.

21. Creevey to Miss Ord, 19 Jan. 1821; *The Creevey Papers*, ii 3.

22. Add. MSS. 51748, ff 124-5; Holland to Henry Fox, 29 Aug. 1820.

23. Add. MSS. 51877, f 34; Carlisle to Holland, n.d. See also Add. MSS. 51748, f 78; Holland to Henry Fox, 16 Feb. 1820.

withstand the strain of the trial unimpaired, and that fact
alone must justify, in Holland's view, continued Whig activity.
Caroline of Brunswick was an unattractive object for a Whig
crusade, but she was able to embarrass a Tory government
and that was enough. When she was finally acquitted,
Holland saw the verdict as a political victory: 'Hurrah,
Hurrah, Hurrah – Liverpool has been compelled to give up
the bill – on the third reading we voted 99 against & 108 for
the bill & Liverpool then said that ... he felt that so small a
majority & the sense of the country were sufficient motives for
giving it up.[24] Above all, Canning's defence of the Queen had
once again proved his usefulness as a Tory-baiter, and as a
result his stock with Lord Holland rose. For the same reason,
even Brougham was spoken of with more charity. By contrast,
Lady Holland remained implacably hostile to both men, but
undismayed by his wife's views, Holland found it even more
strange that a man like Canning, who could inflict such
wounds on Tory attitudes in domestic and foreign politics,
could not settle for a Whig name.

It was on the issue of Catholic Emancipation that the
problem became chronic. On the one hand, Canning's
enthusiasm for the Catholic cause had been often and publicly
expressed. It was also the case, as Holland pointed out to
Grey, that, if the measure were ever to meet with success,
Canningite votes would be needed: 'But yet after all, though
he takes Pitt & not you or my Uncle as his model ... yet I
believe his object as far as the Catholic question is concerned
is the same with ours & I am sure that whether it be or no,
that object can never be attained unless in the course of the
pursuit we for a season at least keep company with him.'[25] On
the other hand, by entering the Liverpool administration,
Canning had divided the cause of Catholic Emancipation
between government and opposition, and thereby made its
realisation unlikely. The Whigs could not regard the Catholics
as a monopoly interest nor could there be a straight fight
between Tory and Whig on the subject.

24. Add. MSS. 51748, f 124; Holland to Henry Fox, 10 Nov. 1820.
25. Add. MSS. 51547, f 114; Holland to Grey, 16 March 1827.

The decision to be made therefore was between applauding
Canning for bringing a touch of liberalism to a dark Cabinet,
particularly in foreign policy, or to condemn him for
ultimately retarding Catholic relief. Holland took the second
view:

> As to home politicks I think he is just now giving the C. question as
> much assistance, as consistently with the awkward situation, in
> which *he has voluntarily & at the risk of that very measure placed himself*, he
> can do – but I cannot agree with you that by entering a divided
> Cabinet which you pleasantly term 'moderating' a Cabinet he has
> served the cause as well as those who have steadily pursued it, & have
> sacrificed, surrendered & refused power unless they attained that
> object, which you as whimsically call 'blustering & talking'. Few I
> think have blustered & talked more than himself but I cannot think
> his manoeuvering & 'serpentine' line of politics would ever have
> brought the question so near to a final & favourable issue as I hope it
> is now, unless some others had shewn a stouter & more
> uncompromising spirit in its support.[26]

For the Hollands, George Canning was the Prodigal Son in
the campaign for Catholic Emancipation. Without making
any personal sacrifices in its defence in a true Whig manner,
he wished to acquire political capital by claiming to be its
supporter. In fact, in the Hollands' view, his selfish power-
seeking had had the effect of putting off the issue for many
years. It was George Canning's greatest crime.

The Hollands followed Canning's 'serpentine' course
through the shoals of Catholic Emancipation with the greatest
possible interest. In April 1822, they were delighted that a bill
favouring the Catholics passed the Commons, and joyfully
acknowledged that its success owed much to a speech by
Canning.[27] Even Lady Holland was seen applauding in the
Ladies Gallery.[28] Three years later, they were appalled when
Canning lent his name and support to coercive measures
against O'Connell's Association. All the Holland House
suspicion burst out again:

26. Add. MSS. 51749, ff 79-82; Holland to Henry Fox, 25 March 1825.
27. Add. MSS. 51748, f 162; Holland to Henry Fox, 26 April 1822.
28. *The Journal of Henry Edward Fox*, p.114, 30 April 1822.

Canning with his usual good judgment saucily upbraided them [the Whigs] with their conduct 35 years ago & at the moment that he is expecting stern inflexible adherence to principles in his support from them, vacillating, hesitating and changing his measures himself. I confess I shall grow quite out of patience with my friends if they continue much longer to submit to such treatment when they know they have it in their power to make their enemies smart for their insolence.[29]

Whatever period of Canning's career was studied, the record was the same. Canning simply could not run straight. His willingness to coerce the Irish was the final example of his readiness to compromise any principle for the sake of remaining in power. As Holland put it: 'The whole has an air of compromise by which he has abandoned the Catholicks to the Tories & they have given up restrictions on trade & Sth America to him.'[30]

At the time of Liverpool's death in 1827, which raised the possibility of a government led by Canning himself, the Hollands had had the opportunity of assessing his reliability over a long period. Both agreed that he was the major obstacle to their presentation of politics as Foxite white against Pittite black. By being potentially a government partner of both Liverpool and the Whigs, Canning blurred issues horribly. One consequence of this was that Catholic claims were retarded rather than advanced, because their sympathisers could never be found on the same side of the political fence. The second result of Canning's behaviour, even more heinous than the first, was to make the conducting of politics along strict party lines impossible, and in such a situation kings could manoeuvre the full weight of executive influence. As Holland lectured his son, party was the constraint kings could not escape, and Canning refused to work through parties:

... the effect of his home policy is hitherto to place more power than ever where it is as much his interest as other men's that there should be very little – The reign of party is over – & the consequence is the

29. Add. MSS. 51749, f 181; Holland to Henry Fox, 6 March 1826.
30. ibid., f 69; ibid., 7 Feb. 1825.

Court does what it likes except when the clamour of the mob, & the
manoeuvres of some Demagogue frightens it into compliance.[31]

Holland's early liking for Canning and respect for his ability
therefore gave way ultimately to the realisation that Canning,
by his behaviour, had retarded the vindication of the Catholics
and assisted the growth of executive power. No Foxite could
see such a record as anything but dismal.

The most hopeful aspect of Canning's behaviour, as far as
the Whigs were concerned, was that it seemed to annoy the
Ultra Tories as well. The Hollands were aware of the tensions
in the Liverpool Cabinet between Canning and the Ultras,
and, long before 1827, they took the view that a return to a
Foxite system of government on party lines was not
impossible. As Holland told his son, in 1825:

> My opinion *entre nous* is that whenever a New Parliament does meet
> some great change in parties & possibly in Government will ensue &
> the Eliptic serpentine line, as Canning calls it, which divides the
> political world at present become as strait & simple again as an
> Equator. As things stand, Ministerial & Opposition are very
> arbitrary terms indeed & hardly designate any particular principles
> or opinions, nothing in short but the position of the individual.[32]

This straightening of the dividing line in politics would either
come about through Wellington manoeuvring Canning out of
office,[33] or through Canning turning the tables on the Duke.[34]
If the first, Canning could have no future political home but
the Whig party; if the second, Canning would need Whig
votes to stay in power. On both reckonings, if the Whigs held
firm, Canning's capacity to operate between parties was at an
end. He would have to become an honest man of party at
last.[35]

If all these speculations led Holland to the notion that

31. Add. MSS. 51750, f 59; Holland to Henry Fox, 27 March 1827.
32. Add. MSS. 51749, f 113; Holland to Henry Fox, 19 Aug. 1825.
33. Add. MSS. 51750, f 16; Holland to Henry Fox, 20 Jan. 1827.
34. Add. MSS. 51547, f 87; Holland to Grey, 20 Nov. 1826.
35. These hopes were of course dashed by Canning's death in 1827. Huskisson, the
new leader of the Canningite group, was implacably hostile to the Whigs. The Tory
divisions of 1829-30 were not foreseen; see above, Chapter Three.

Canning's political buccaneering days must soon be brought to an end, he was also aware of the possible flaw in the argument. All his assumptions were based on the idea that, when Liverpool's Cabinet broke up into 'a jumble of men', the Whigs would stay united and only accept Canning's friendship on their terms. As Holland was forced to admit, this was a large assumption. It was also the point at which the Canning and Lansdowne problems dovetailed. As early as 1825, Holland was alive to the fear that, if Canning attempted to divide the Whigs, it would be Lansdowne who would be most susceptible to such offers: 'On Trade, on Sth America & I suppose on Corn bills he is in opinion, if not nearer, at least warmer with Huskisson etc. etc than you or I who do not care about or perhaps understand such matters so much.'[36] Through three generations, the Lansdownes had retained an interest in financial and departmental reform, which made it a family speciality. Holland House almost literally had no views on such topics. Canning and Huskisson, by contrast, gave intellectual leadership to them. Add to this temptation the second-hand Whig credentials of the Lansdowne family, and the ghosts of 1782 began to walk again in front of Holland's eyes. The first Marquess had contributed to the defeat of Charles Fox. Holland prophetically feared that his son would compromise the Whigs again and give Canning his chance.

Long before Liverpool's death produced the point of crisis, therefore, Holland had squared up to the likely political choices. If the Whigs would not hold as a united group, some form of alliance was likely with Canning as leader or joint-leader. In this situation, Holland had to decide whether it was better to accept Catholic Emancipation at the hands of George Canning, who had hitherto been seen as the main force retarding its progress, or to refuse Canning's cooperation and thereby postpone the measure even further. It was not an attractive set of alternatives. On neither option could the Whigs act honourably in party formation. The only safe line of action in Holland's view was to judge all options with the passing of Catholic Emancipation as a first priority. The

36. Add. MSS. 51547, f 68; Holland to Grey, 2 Sept. 1825.

unreliability of some Whigs might still give Canning scope for mischief-making, but his behaviour on this issue must be firm, for 'if not he can hardly expect that men who look to it as the one thing needful can have confidence in a system of professed neutrality which has hitherto retarded it, & in which they never acquiesced'.[37]

On 17 February 1827, Lord Liverpool suffered a paralytic stroke, and, although it was some weeks before it was clear that there would be no recovery, all the points about which Holland had speculated for two or three years now acquired immediate relevance. The battle between Canning and Wellington for dominance over members of the old administration gave the Whigs and reformers their best opportunity of influencing politics for many years. It was also a matter of pure joy to the Hollands that the Tories were likely to be out of office. On the other hand, the 'mystery' of George Canning had never been deeper. If he emerged at the head of a new Ministry, the Whigs had to be sure of the terms of his understanding with George IV before committing themselves to his support. On 27 February, Holland restated the old dilemma for his son:

> In the meanwhile the general notion is that Canning is to be Premier & Robinson Minister in the Lords. This I should hope must mean the Catholic question & then we are all or at least I am for one a Ministerialist. But there are disagreeable whispers that the office & patronage is to be Canning's but that he submits to leaving the great question in the state it has hitherto been & to be *the Minister* without enforcing the measure he deems necessary to the happiness of the country for fear his Colleagues may have the spirit, which he himself has not, of quitting their office than be parties to a system of policy they disapprove. I hope for the cause & for Canning's fair name this may not prove true, if it does he makes a pitiful figure.[38]

Grey and Lady Holland had no doubts in the matter. Canning would sacrifice any principle or ideal for office and the only victor of the new situation in 1827 would be George IV. As Lady Holland insisted, 'this confounded division of the

37. Holland to Carlisle, n.d., Castle Howard MSS. LB 139.
38. Add. MSS. 51750, f 38; Holland to Henry Fox, 27 Feb. 1827.

country into Protestant and Catholic makes the King as powerful as ever Henry VIII was'.[39] Holland fully shared these doubts about the terms on which Canning became Prime Minister, but balanced them in his mind with other practical considerations. In his view, it was simply impossible to pass Catholic Emancipation without Canning. Whig friability made their bargaining position weak, and Canningite votes might make the difference between success and failure. This argument at its fullest extension led to the horrifying conclusion that, by refusing to treat with Canning, the Whigs themselves might come to bear some of the responsibility for a further postponement of Catholic claims. Holland disliked the 1827 situation thoroughly, but felt that Grey's impassiveness had to be answered:

> I agree with you yet more of what you say of Canning & his conduct, but yet you must not deceive yourself on one point. It being as you think impossible to carry the Catholick question without a Catholick ministry & it being necessary to the safety of the country that one should be carried & the other formed, it is clear to me that neither the one can be carried nor the other formed without Canning being the Minister & Leader in the Commons – therefore a determination to oppose him personally is almost synonymous with a determination to throw obstacles in forming such a Ministry as we think alone can save the country.[40]

It was in fact a moot point whether the Whigs held the fate of Canning in their hands or whether he could dictate terms.

In the six months between the death of Liverpool and the death of Canning, these basic positions remained unaltered. Only Lady Holland sufficiently modified her views to allow a desire to see her husband in office to overcome her loathing of Canning.[41] It was an undignified position to adopt and one which caused Holland severe embarrassment. At one dinner party, Holland requested his wife 'to leave him alone, and not give advice either one way or the other. This is very strong

39. Lady Holland to Lord John Russell, 1827; *The Holland House Circle*, p.48.
40. Add. MSS. 51547, f 111; Holland to Grey, 9 March 1827.
41. Lady Holland to Henry Fox, 25 May 1827; *Elizabeth, Lady Holland to her Son*, p.63.

language from the mildest of men and the most submissive of husbands.[42] His aunt asked Henry Fox whether he could 'by any means persuade your Mama to put a padlock on her tongue'. Clearly Holland was in an unhappy and sensitive situation and had lost his normal calm sense and judgment. The existence of a Canning ministry demanded a response of some sort, and Lady Holland's solution was anything but helpful.

Just as serious was the fact that the problem of Canning was inflicting terrible damage on Holland's oldest political friendships. His correspondence with Grey is interrupted abruptly in April 1827 after thirty years of the most intimate exchanges. Holland, who had a very sentimental attachment to old friends, found the whole experience very wounding. As he reported to his son, 'some few of our old friends (The Duke of Bedford & Grey alas! alas!) agree too earnestly in their distrust of Canning & hatred of the new junction'.[43] Everyone seemed anxious to supply Holland with good reasons why outright opposition to Canning was the only honourable course.[44] His own son opposed his father's position and reproved him for 'kneeling under' to Canning 'so disgracefully'.[45] Even social life was disrupted. The Duke of Bedford stormed out of a dinner party at Holland House in June 1827, and, on hearing that one of his sons was inclined to support Holland in trusting Canning, retorted: 'You say you have tied yourself to the tail of that great fish, Lord Holland. I wish you joy! He will swim you into foul waters. I have always loved Lord Holland for his *private* virtues, his good heart and social qualities, but as a politician, I have long thought him shabby and dirty, and always void of that essential quality in a statesman – judgement.'[46]

Grey and Bedford, who had been Holland's closest political associates for a generation, were 'hurt to the quick' and 'quite

42. *The Chronicles of Holland House*, pp. 80-1.
43. Add. MSS. 51750, f 112; Holland to Henry Fox, c 20 June 1827.
44. *The Formation of Canning's Ministry*, pp. 75, 114, 212-14.
45. Add. MSS. 51750, f 132; Holland to Henry Fox, July 1827.
46. Bedford to Lord W. Russell, 22 June 1827; *Lord William Russell and his Wife*, p.144.

broken hearted'[47] at their separation from Holland. Their
views on Canning, however, remained unchanged. His whole
career, in their view, bred distrust. He had shown no
willingness to stand up to the scruples of George IV on the
question of Catholic Emancipation as a member of the
Cabinet, and would not now do so as prime minister. Both
men believed firmly that Canning's association with Liverpool
had in fact retarded the measure by dividing its sympathisers
between government and opposition. His overtures to the
Whigs since Liverpool's death had been dictated by nothing
except necessity. The Whigs, who had always 'stood on high
ground', were in danger of being compromised: 'You say this
junction is an "Experiment" – It is so indeed, and I earnestly
hope and pray that the Whigs may come as safely out of it.'[48]
In sum, Bedford and Grey presented a case that was difficult
to answer, if only because Holland was forced to admit that so
much of the evidence for it was true. His own disappointments
and frustrations about Canning's behaviour were of thirty
years standing. The strength of feeling about Canning was
such that Holland was even inclined to believe rumours that
Grey and Bedford, in order to destroy their bête noir, were
seriously countenancing an alliance with the Ultras against
him.[49] Canning had totally baffled the heirs of Fox.

As Holland had predicted, the problem with regard to his
cousin Lansdowne was somewhat different. The latter had
been almost immediately approached by Canning as the most
likely of the Whigs to join him in a coalition. This simple fact
allowed Grey and Bedford to raise the spectre of 1782, thereby
confirming their opinions of both Canning and Lansdowne. In
the last two weeks of April 1827, many letters passed between
Holland and Lansdowne on the prospect of coalition. Buffeted
by the stern advice of his family and friends, Holland was not
in a position to offer firm advice. He limited himself to saying
that 'he would join no Ministry which did not distinctly
espouse the Catholic cause, but I would oppose none which

47. Add. MSS. 51662, f 106; Bedford to Holland, 20 May 1827.
48. Add. MSS. 51662, f 101; Bedford to Holland, 5 May 1827.
49. Add. MSS. 51750, ff 118-125; Holland to Henry Fox, 3 & 13 July 1827.

was formed without the Tory faction, and support any that was formed against it. But with all the manoeuvres and indirect methods of Canning, of which I cannot quite acquit him, I suspect his adversaries are as capable of them as himself.'[50] Just as Holland could not quite disagree with Grey and Bedford in their belief that Canning was untrustworthy, so he also allowed Lansdowne's point that all the alternatives were worse.

Holland finally tried to impose some pattern on to his disordered thoughts by transforming Lansdowne's bargain into a test case. Insisting that, in historical terms, it was easier for a Petty than a Fox to break the Whig ranks, Holland tried to argue that Lansdowne's presence in the Ministry guaranteed that the Catholic question would receive priority. As his son noted, his father's 'intention therefore is to support the Ministry, and to consider himself, though without office, a ministerial man, if Lord Lansdowne is part of the Ministry and takes the lead in the House of Lords. If not, he shall always feel disposed to countenance and support any Ministry that keeps out of power the enemies of liberty abroad and of toleration at home.'[51] The apotheosis of Lansdowne as the guarantee was not very satisfactory, even though it gave Holland a viable political standpoint. As he himself admitted, the whole affair was 'hazardous and doubtful, and perhaps scarcely right.'[52]

Holland's position was greatly enhanced when, in addition to the Leadership of the House of Lords, Lansdowne became Home Secretary. It was now more plausible to see his cousin as the guarantee of Catholic claims. After hearing the news, Holland told Henry Fox that 'our confidence in Lansdowne should be unqualified – On the whole I trust & believe he has decided for the best – & some sacrifices are well made to give full trial to an experiment of keeping out of power the enemies of liberty abroad and toleration at home ... In justice to

50. Holland to Lansdowne, 13 April 1827; *The Formation of Canning's Ministry*, p.73.

51. Political Memorandum by Charles Richard Fox, 20 April 1827; *The Chronicles of Holland House*, p.77.

52. Holland to Tierney, 23 April 1827; *The Formation of Canning's Ministry*, pp. 159-62.

Canning I must say however that I see nothing in *his* proceedings with Lansdowne but what is fair honourable & conciliatory.'[53] Trusting Lansdowne, a great Irish landowner and a committed Catholic sympathiser, was, superficially, a neat method of overcoming the problem that the Petty family had always presented. As Home Secretary, Lansdowne's integrity on the Catholic cause would be publicly vindicated or destroyed. Such a pinning down of Lansdowne solved the problem of his family's fickleness and contributed something to the formulation of Holland's own views.

Predictably, the Lansdowne problem widened the breach which Canning had opened up between Holland on one side and Grey and Bedford on the other. As far as the latter were concerned, Lansdowne's entering the Canning Cabinet altered nothing. If Lansdowne was a Catholic sympathiser, Canning would have claimed the same title. On too many occasions, the principle had been surrendered as the price of holding office. At no stage in the negotiations had there been any suggestion that George IV's views on the issue had changed, and therefore, as Holland himself had to admit,[54] Emancipation remained a perilous undertaking for any minister or set of ministers. According to Grey, Canning, Lansdowne and, by implication, Holland had once again split the Catholic cause between ministerialist and opposition voters. It was a mistake, in their view, to think that the King's mind could be changed by anything except a concerted opposition attack. They were not surprised to find Holland 'full of crochets',[55] and when he announced that 'he will sit behind L. in the House and follow his leading as implicitly as he would have done his uncle's', the spectacle was merely disgusting. At the very least, there was something incongruous about Fox's nephew swearing fealty to Shelburne's son.

At the centre of this buffeting, Holland found a rock on which to build his politics. It was quite simply to give priority to the Catholic question. This, in turn, required him to work

53. Add. MSS. 51742, f 32; Holland to Caroline Fox, 30 April 1827.
54. Add. MSS. 51742, f 32; Holland to Caroline Fox, 30 April 1827.
55. Lady Cowper to Frederick Lamb, 24 April 1827; *The Formation of the Canning Ministry*, p.176.

for the exclusion from office of the Ultra Tories, even if such a
course meant trusting Canning. Referring to Canning's
Cabinet, Holland told the Lords that 'the consequences of its
being overturned must of necessity be the establishment in full
power, of that very party and those principles which he had
spent his whole political life opposing.'[56] To his son he was
even more explicit:

> As for politicks, I know not where to begin & still less where to end –
> The die is cast – We are Ministerial – If I had some reluctance or
> doubts about the propriety of our new line of conduct the language of
> the Exministers & New Opposition completely dissipates them.
> Their reasons for quitting & resigning, however fair & honourable,
> are quite sufficient to make our junction so too. They lament that the
> Composition of the Ministry, however neutral in intention, is so
> Catholic in its teaching that no Anti-Catholick can honestly support
> it – If that be so we must at least support it sufficiently to prevent that
> character being changed.[57]

The Canning arrangement was the most proCatholic
government possible in the circumstances. The alternative
was not a Whig Cabinet but a return to Wellington and the
Ultras. Distrust of Canning had therefore to be set aside.
'Politicks like all human affairs are too often a choice of
evils.'[58]

Holland had not, however, gone over completely to the
Lansdowne point of view. His support for Canning must be
placed alongside his decision to offer that support from
outside the Government. George IV's veto on Holland as a
potential Cabinet minister, of which Holland House was very
much aware, was not the only reason for the exclusion. It is
very likely that, even if an offer had been made, it would have
been firmly rejected. Much to his wife's annoyance,[59] the
decision by Holland to support Canning was a corollary of his
decision to stay out of government. It was simply
inconceivable for the nephew of Fox to join any ministry on

56. *Parl. Deb.*, vol. XCIV 858–866; 17 May 1827.
57. Add. MSS. 51750, f 88; Holland to Henry Fox, 4 May 1827.
58. ibid.
59. Add. MSS. 51750, f 95; ibid., 25 May 1827.

imprecise terms. Everyone recognised the symbolism of the Fox name. As soon as the Ministry was formed, Canning was under pressure to make the Whig element in government credible by taking Holland in. Such a move would, as Lady Cowper pointed out, 'conciliate the old Whigs, many of whom don't like and even cannot *understand* the whole proceeding; it's so unlike the year '84.'[60] Even if George IV could have been persuaded to take such a step, Holland would probably have refused to agree.

The problem George Canning presented to Holland House could be overcome to the extent of giving disinterested support only for the long-term benefit of Irish Catholics. Any greater degree of commitment grated against the Fox family sense of caste. Holland saw himself as the patron of a clientele and the guardian of an ideal. No ministry led by Canning could satisfy either responsibility. On the patronage point, there was no likelihood of a situation 'enabling me to secure the permanent confidence & support of many attached to my Uncle's memory & myself as his representative, & that can only be accomplished by some marked distribution of patronage & titles on the Whigs'.[61] More important, the terms of Canning's relationship with the King were too imprecise to satisfy Foxite requirements: 'Canning has I am quite satisfied behaved fairly openly and cordially to us all – but his power is not equal to his inclination – & he has more confidence in the efficacy of management & more dread of the consequences of a little force or intimidation in certain quarters, than suit our Whig theories of the English Government.'[62] Canning had never squared up to the question of containing executive power, and it was clear that there had been no resolution of the problem in 1827. If Holland thought Lansdowne right to give the Catholics a chance, he fully shared the Foxite doubts of Grey and Bedford on the origins and nature of Canning's ministry.

Canning's death in August 1827 and his replacement by Goderich changed attitudes very little. The acrimony between

60. Lady Cowper to Frederick Lamb, 12 June 1827; *The Formation of Canning's Ministry*, p.241.
61. Add. MSS. 51750, f 113; Holland to Henry Fox, 22 June 1827.
62. Add. MSS. 51750, f 106; Holland to Henry Fox, 5 June 1827.

Holland, Grey and Bedford was if anything sharpened along the same lines of argument. According to Bedford, the new arrangement was even less Whiggish than the old:

> I think you have made out no case whatever for Lansdowne remaining in office ... What amuses me, is that you all talk of keeping the *Tories out*, as if the exministers are Tories *par excellence* – what say you to Goderich, Herries, Bexley, Lyndhurst, Anglesey etc etc? I see no advantage in keeping out one set of Tories to support another set – I have always one comfort which is Canning is gone – had he lived, he would have done infinite mischief.[63]

Holland could only defend himself once again by insisting that harsh choices had to be made:

> The question resolved itself as political questions generally do, into a choice between those in power & those who would be in on a change i.e. Peel and the Exclusionists on one side – Huskisson & a mixed Government composed of a majority of friends to toleration on the other. I prefer the latter. I think it an improvement on any we have had for the last 20 years & I own I do not understand why it should excite more active hostility even in you who disagree with me, than those which have recently preceded it.[64]

According to Holland, if Catholic Emancipation remained the priority, the options were the same. Throughout the 1827 negotiations, the Canning and Lansdowne problems exerted, at full force, an irritating influence on politics which separated Whig from Tory neatly and precisely. George Canning and the Lansdowne family refused to follow this model. For different reasons, the one social the other historical, both rejected Foxite exclusiveness. Unfortunately, neither could be ignored. Canning's pre-eminence in debate gave him the leadership of the House of Commons, an area in which the Whigs were notoriously weak throughout the early nineteenth century. The Lansdownes, by historical title, had just enough Whig credentials to establish an alternative to the Foxite faith, and thereby confuse matters. If a Lansdowne found himself in government, it was arguable whether this represented a Whig

63. Add. MSS. 51662, f 108; Bedford to Holland, 9 Sept. 1827.
64. Add. MSS. 51547, f 128; Holland to Grey, 12 Sept. 1827.

presence or not. Both men subscribed to certain articles of the
Foxite faith, and thereby, much to the Hollands' irritation,
removed them from an exclusively Foxite context. By thus
shading the blacks and whites of politics into a bewildering
grey, they were responsible, in Foxite eyes, for retarding the
implementation of all major reform.

The embarrassments in the 1827 situation were obvious.
The political world had been so thoroughly upset that
Holland no longer knew where he should sit in the House of
Lords. His old place near Grey and Bedford was not feasible,
but it was not easy to think of an alternative.[65] In this
confusion, Grey's and Bedford's refusal to make concessions is
readily comprehensible. Canning had transgressed too often
to be forgiven. It was a pure and consistent response to harsh
experiences. The difficulty with such a line, as Holland
pointed out, was that, since the Whigs simply lacked the
numbers to form a government exclusively their own,
alliances with other groups were unavoidable. Otherwise,
reform would remain an unrealisable ideal. In condescending
to treat with Canning, the Whigs were stooping to conquer in
the battle for one of their most cherished objectives, Catholic
Emancipation. From his College days, Holland had been
baffled by Canning's behaviour. He had always been too
clever to trust or ignore. Holland's solitary position in 1827
with regard to his family and closest friends, was the price of
this long acquaintance. It must have been some consolation
when, in 1830, Grey himself became Prime Minister and was
forced to allow Canning's heirs, Melbourne and Palmerston,
into his Cabinet.

65. Add. MSS. 51742, f 42; Holland to Caroline Fox, May 1827.

6

Lord Holland in Government, 1830-1840

In January 1832, Holland recorded in his diary the fact that 'the only complete year from 1st of January to 31st of December in which the Whigs have been in office for near seventy years is elapsed'.[1] For his generation, a promised land had been reached. The Whig success in the general election of 1830 had owed as much to the Tory divisions over Catholic Emancipation as to their own prowess, but the gods were now smiling. Even George IV's death appeared providential. Holland entered the Cabinet as Chancellor of the Duchy of Lancaster, a post he was to retain until his death ten years later. Gout[2] and continued doubts about his judgment precluded any more important office. He became the Cabinet's diarist,[3] and not infrequently its host. In the next few years, it was not unusual to find the whole Cabinet dining at Holland House and warding off Lady Holland's enquiries, before adjourning to another room to settle a point of business. Holland's rôle in the Grey and Melbourne Cabinets was clear. He represented the Foxite conscience of the party. Not surprisingly, his disagreements in Cabinet were with men like Palmerston who came from other political backgrounds.

1. Add. MSS. 51868, f 279; Holland's Political Journal, 1 Jan. 1832.
2. Durham to Lady Durham, 16 Nov. 1830; *The Life and Letters of Lord Durham*, i 215-16.
3. See A. Kriegel, *The Holland House Diaries, 1831-1840* (London 1977).

In Holland's view, the vindication of Charles Fox had begun with Catholic Emancipation and must now be pressed home. The martyrs of the 1790s had established obligations over time that could not be gainsaid.

Above all, the perennial question of Parliamentary Reform brooded over the Grey government like the threat of plague. Holland's views in 1830 had not changed substantially from those of his youth. He had never had an emotional involvement with the issue, as he frankly explained to his son: 'For my part, I was never a very keen reformer, but I think reform now absolutely inevitable, and I am sure, if it be so, the sooner it is done the better.'[4] The Fox family had always seen Reform as a means of containing executive power, and were happy, if not enthusiastic, about change because they saw the franchise as a trust inherent in property-holding, revocable in certain circumstances, rather than as a species of property in itself.[5] As they had grown older, both he and Grey had become increasingly sceptical about the whole question, but these old men were completely trapped by the past. They, the Foxites of the 1790s, were at last in power. Charles Grey had introduced Reform Bills in 1792 and 1797 which were more radical than those he was to sponsor in 1831 and 1832. Holland and Grey had 'sacrificed' their political careers in the defence of principle. Their position would have been meaningless if, once in power, they had not taken action on principles they had defended for forty years. Reformers they had been and Reformers they just had to remain. The word Foxite chained them to their past.

To this traditional motive the situation of 1830-2 added fear. Holland's estates had suffered in the 'Captain Swing' disturbances, and his correspondence from the summer of 1831 onwards is full of foreboding.[6] Reform of some kind becomes the alternative to upheaval or even revolution. He favoured the recalling of Parliament a month early in November 1831, because it was too dangerous to leave the

4. Holland to Henry Fox, 1830; *The Chronicles of Holland House*, p.136.
5. See above, Chapter Three.
6. Lady Holland to Henry Fox, 30 Aug. 1831; *Elizabeth, Lady Holland to her Son*, p.114.

country 'for another month without a Parliament'.[7] The success of Grey's ministry was crucial: 'I am convinced Grey's resignation or removal would be the signal for such confusion as this country has not seen for a century and a half.'[8] It is important to note, however, that the Hollands' fear is centred on middle-class aspirations and not on mobs. Lady Holland, drawing on her wide knowledge of France, was not alarmed by the burning of Nottingham Castle, but was terrified by reports of a National Guard being formed and a run on the banks.[9] Her husband agreed. He told Grey that 'if the great mass of the middle class are bent upon that method of enforcing their views, there is not in the nature of society any real force that can prevent them'.[10] The Political Unions were dangerous as visible expressions of 'middle class' discontent, 'and would not and could not be extinguished until the cause of them, impatience at the rejection of reform was removed'.[11] For a generation the Crown had blocked all change. Above all it had engineered the exclusion from the franchise of many who could perfectly well exercise that trust responsibly. Executive power had produced the dangers of 1830 and had left the Whigs few options on the matter.

Even so, following the pattern of his whole career, Holland spoke very infrequently in the Lords on the question of Reform, and this timidity can only partially be explained by repeated attacks of gout. His first major speech was given on 29 September 1831. In it, he declared that 'that House ... was called upon to consider what would be the effect on all deliberating minds if they rejected a measure adapted to the character of the times, in harmony with the wishes of the people, and essentially calculated to leave the Constitution of the empire improved and confirmed'.[12] Every clause of this statement picks up a major Whig theme. 'The character of the

7. Add. MSS. 51868, ff 216-17; Holland's Political Journal, 19 Nov. 1831.

8. Add. MSS. 51751, f 100; Holland to Henry Fox, 20 Oct. 1831. See also Creevey to Miss Ord, 16 Sept. 1831; *The Creevey Diaries*, ii 236.

9. Lady Holland to Henry Fox, 18 May 1832; *Elizabeth, Lady Holland to her Son*, p.137.

10. Holland to Grey, 5 Nov. 1831; J. Cannon, *Parliamentary Reform 1640-1832*.

11. Holland to Anglesey, 7 Dec. 1831; Anglesey MSS.

12. *Parl. Deb.*, vol. CIX 782-3; 29 Sept. 1831.

times' points to a Whig appreciation of changing circumstances to which politics must respond. 'The wishes of the people', defined as usual as those with a claim to be within the political pale, were the ultimate justification of all action. The aspiration to leave 'the Constitution of the empire improved and confirmed' emphasises Holland's belief that the Bill was less an innovation than a cleansing of old practice. The prudential argument for Reform based on a fear of revolution only enters Holland's repertoire in a brief speech given in the Lords on 5 October 1831.[13]

Holland made no further public pronouncement until May 1832. Once again he emphasised the bringing of old principles up to date rather than the formulation of new ones. The Bill, he believed, had two objectives: 'One of them was of a temporary character, and yet of great urgency and importance, for it was nothing less than the reconciliation of the people to the ancient and noble institutions of their country. The other was the revision, correction, and improvement of the ancient principle and practice of the Constitution, by rendering it the true conservative body of the rights and liberties of the people.'[14] If such a measure could be passed and accompanied by the reorganisation of local government, it would 'set us all right in spite of Cholera, burnings and Hunt'.[15] None of these points are worked out more fully, and, although it is possible to put flesh on these bare assertions by reference to Holland's past career, his public performance on the Reform Bill was thin, vague and almost embarrassed. To the last the Fox family could not discover any real enthusiasm for the idea. It was tepid work at best.

If it was difficult to sympathise with those who made large claims for the Reform Bill, Holland found it easier to pillory the Tories as opponents of the idea. From the beginning the Tory problem centred on the legislative veto of the House of Lords, where, in the course of his seventeen-year ministry, Pitt

13. *Parl. Deb.*, vol. CIX 1327-30; 5 Oct. 1831.
14. ibid., vol. CXIV 699-709; 7 May 1832.
15. Add. MSS. 51522, f 112; Holland to William IV, 16 Nov. 1831; The 'Hunt' referred to here is Orator Hunt, the Radical leader.

had ensconced a huge anti-Whig majority. Until almost the last moment, the Hollands were not sure that the Lords would actually surrender,[16] and, in the meanwhile, sniping at Tory stupidity was a congenial way of contributing to the Bill's success. Wellington's early declaration against Reform 'displeases every body',[17] and intemperate conduct of this kind confirmed Holland's low opinion of the Duke. Peel acted with more subtlety, but only by a whisker.[18] Both men embraced the tactic of trying to defeat Reform by associating it with revolution in Europe, thereby promoting the double disaster of civil war in England and an anti-French crusade.[19] Obstructionism of this kind, which seriously raised the stakes of the game, bewildered the Hollands who noted that 'there is no knowing how far passion & intemperate party feeling may carry men'.[20] It was simply astonishing that Peel and Wellington could not see the constitutional disease and its remedy. In the Whig view, so much depended on the Bill's success that the Tories' lack of awareness was marvellous to behold. Instead of accepting change and adaptation as natural, Wellington 'brought up many to take their seats who were considered dormant & done for, Ld. Scarsdale & some of that temper'.[21] The House of Lords debates began to resemble a meeting by the pool of Bethesda.

If the Ultra Tory blindness to the force of events left the Hollands almost speechless, the Waverers under Harrowby and Wharncliffe, who held out the hope that the Bill might clear the Lords by their abstentions, were little better. Lady Holland found it both comic and tragic 'that such a man as Ld. Harrowby should influence the destinies of Europe'.[22] As for Wharncliffe, he was too inclined to make speeches that

16. W. Holmes to Mrs Arbuthnot, 19 Sept. 1831; *The Correspondence of Charles Arbuthnot*, p.145.
17. Add. MSS. 51751, f 46; Holland to Henry Fox, 5 Nov. 1830.
18. Holland to Anglesey, 11 July 1831; Anglesey MSS.
19. Add. MSS. 51751, f 71; Holland to Henry Fox, 17 Aug. 1831.
20. Lady Holland to Henry Fox, 9 Sept. 1831; *Elizabeth, Lady Holland to her Son*, p.115.
21. Lady Holland to Henry Fox, 6 Sept. 1831; *Elizabeth, Lady Holland to her Son*, p.115.
22. ibid., 4 Oct. 1831; ibid., p.119.

were 'one loud rant rather than cant, with a great deal of God almighty & bidding both lay and Spiritual Lords to do their duty to God'.[23] Throughout the negotiations with the Waverers, Holland was much less inclined than Grey to put any trust in Harrowby's and Wharncliffe's promises.[24] The alternative tactic of passing the Bill by a mass creation of peers, though offensive to constitutional practice and Whig sensibilities, had to be ready the minute the Waverers proved unable or unwilling to keep their part of the bargain. As late as February 1832, Holland was clear that 'there have occurred incidents to confirm your suspicions of several of Harrowby's followers and I own I suspect that without callings up or creations we cannot make ourselves safe'.[25]

Above all, Holland was quite clear that no concessions should be made either to Wellington's intransigence or to the Waverers' supposed pliability. If some Tories wished to appease their consciences by allowing the Bill through the Lords by abstaining on the crucial votes, that would be acceptable. Otherwise Holland aligned himself in the Cabinet with Brougham and Durham in demanding a mass creation of Whig peers. One way or the other, the unamended Bill must pass. In Holland's view, by the end of 1831, the totality of the Bill had acquired a symbolism in the public mind that made any attempt to alter its provisions extremely dangerous: 'Good Whig principles at home & peace & honour abroad all depend on our success on the Reform Bill – He who would alter one iota or grumbles at the tendences or consequences of any clauses does pro tanto all in his power to ruin us & replace things in the state we have always condemned & deprecated. He is in short tainted with Toryism if not a Tory.'[26] No species of Tory had any choice in the matter. They could allow the Bill through by any means they chose, or turn the Whigs out and face the consequences. Such Tory discomfiture, as described by Holland, was arguably the most attractive aspect of Parliamentary Reform for Holland House. There was no

23. Add. MSS. 51570, f 61; Holland to Lady Holland, 1831.
24. Holland to Carlisle, c March 1832; Castle Howard MSS. LB 139.
25. Holland to Anglesey, 22 Feb. 1832; Anglesey MSS.
26. Add. MSS. 51751, f 228; Holland to Henry Fox, 20 March 1832.

pity for Tory feelings. When the Bill had finally cleared the Lords, Holland simply noted that 'all's well that ends well. Wellington has slunk off to Strathfieldsaye, so let him go.'[27]

If Tory behaviour was one imponderable in the Reform Bill situation, another was William IV himself. In the Hollands' correspondence he appears as an amiable, if slow-witted cart-horse, being driven one way by Grey and his own inclinations and then turned back again by his Tory Queen and his Tory brothers. Related by illegitimacy to the Hollands,[28] William was thought to be full of good intentions if only they could be realised. In the first year of his reign, he dined frequently at Holland House,[29] and, for the first time in many years, a member of the Fox family found something favourable to say about a king;

> Never was there such a king – he not only acquiesces in but espouses the measures deemed necessary by his ministers, however disagreeable they must in their nature be to Royal Palates. Our Reform (and I promise you it is not maukish milk and water stuff) is taken without a wry face and even retrenchment is more bitter to some (at least to me) who administer it than to the royal patient who takes it.[30]

William's long years in the navy had left him with several unregal characteristics, not least of which was a complete innocence of constitutional procedure. Allied to a lack of real party feeling, this naiveté involved Grey and Holland in countering the Queen's influence with long tutorials on what should be done about Reform and why.

The honeymoon period between William and the Whigs lasted just over a year. On 8 October 1831, the first attempt at Reform was defeated in the Lords by 41 votes. The King asked the Whigs to stay on and expressed sympathy, but, as the Hollands were quick to notice, he was also very reluctant to

27. Holland to Anglesey, 18 May 1832; Anglesey MSS.
28. See above, Chapter Three.
29. Add. MSS. 51751, f 33; Holland to Henry Fox, 31 Aug. 1830.
30. Holland to Anglesey, 2 Feb. 1831; Anglesey MSS.

give them any overt signs of royal favour.[31] It is also significant that communication between William and the Hollands now took the form of formal interviews, or trickled through the screening hands of the King's secretary, Sir Herbert Taylor. As the latter was forced to point out, William was thoroughly alarmed by the appearance of the Political Unions, but he could not see that a Reform Bill would solve the problem.[32] Above all, to create peers as 'an Exercise of Prerogative' for 'the gratification of the People's Wishes'[33] suggested precedents for both the use of the prerogative and the pressures to which it could be subjected, which might reasonably cause even the Whigs to hesitate. As Holland gloomily recorded, the defeat of the first Reform Bill had allowed William to revert to his family's normal practice:

The King reasonably enough thinks riots & publick meetings less permanently dangerous to legitimate authority than the self constituted Unions & National Guards, but is not sufficiently impressed with the undeniable truth that the delay, postponement or uncertainty in passing the measure of reform, is the real cause of those Unions & that they can only be prevented or put down by removing the inclination in the middling classes of society to form them.[34]

Throughout the first, nerve-racking months of 1832, there was to be no final resolution of this uncertainty. The King was friendly and willing to listen to Grey's and Holland's lectures,[35] but still held back from giving them the promise of full powers. The constitutional crisis only ten days before the Bill finally passed its second reading seemed to suggest that William was ultimately George III's son. On the very day before the Bill became finally safe, Holland was reporting that the King had decided to accept the Whigs' resignation rather

31. Add. MSS. 51867, f 176; Holland's Political Journal, 9 Oct. 1831.
32. Add. MSS. 51522, f 105; Sir H. Taylor to Holland, 1 Nov. 1831.
33. Add. MSS. 51523, ff 1-4; Sir H. Taylor to Holland, 7 Jan. 1832.
34. Add. MSS. 51868, f 196; Holland's Political Journal, 4 Nov. 1831.
35. Lady Holland to Henry Fox, Jan. 1832; *Elizabeth, Lady Holland to her Son*, p.126.

than allow them full powers in the matter of the creation of peers. Only on the 18 May itself, the day of the debate, was Holland finally clear that all would come right: 'All's safe and restored. The King agrees to give us full powers – and the Tories in the midst of their railing, seem to me to intend waiving their opposition and letting us go on without any immediate or violent exercise of power.'[36] In Holland's view, however, the battle to direct William's mind into proper channels had been a close-run thing.

In November 1831, Holland told his son that 'what is to be done with the Lords? is a question in every body's mouth – can we convert them? Ought we to intimidate them?'[37] Intimidation meant swamping the natural Tory majority in the Lords with a massive creation of Whig peers. Holland, as readily as the radical Earl of Durham himself, was clear that this must be done if all other expedients failed. Such a move, if seriously threatened, solved the dilemmas surrounding Tory and royal intentions. It presented the Tory with a clear option and it would demonstrate William's good faith. If Holland made little public contribution to the Reform Bill debate, he more than compensated for this in other areas. He was an eager canvasser of votes,[38] and, above all, he made the question of the new peers something of a personal interest. Throughout 1831-2, Grey was bombarded with lists of candidates for peerages drawn up by Holland himself, which were clearly the product of much sifting and analysis.[39] It was worth the effort, for too much was at stake. It had to be shown that it was not true 'that a knot of Lords and Commons, one half manifestly and corruptly interested in the question, can resist a measure just in principle and recommended by prudence and policy amounting almost to necessity'.[40]

Once again, Holland found himself prodding Grey. The latter had always been more inclined to trust the Waverers and more unhappy about coercing the King than Holland.

---

36. Holland to Anglesey, 15 May 1832; Anglesey MSS.
37. Add. MSS. 51751, f 131; Holland to Henry Fox, 7 Nov. 1831.
38. Anglesey to Holland, 2 May 1831; Anglesey MSS.
39. Grey MSS, Box 34.
40. Holland to Anglesey, 17 March 1831; Anglesey MSS.

Now the idea of a mass creation of peers troubled him greatly, both because it would be difficult to manoeuvre William towards such an objective and because the idea itself was offensive. Holland fully shared in Grey's distaste for so ruthlessly enlarging the aristocracy. The élitist sense of caste, central to all Whig ideas, was bound to be affronted. The Younger Pitt had been much criticised for the number of his creations. Quite simply, however, there was nothing else to do:

> The loss of this bill is civil war & revolution & above all the loss of the Lords to which our Aristocracy is so strongly attached – It seems an odd effect of love for that institution to risk its existence merely to prevent its increase & thus to prefer a large Hse of Lords to having none at all.[41]

As early as September 1831, Holland had decided to support a hard line on this issue, and there was no modification of his attitude over the next nine months. As he noted, 'unless we are prepared to overwhelm the majority by creations I do not understand how we can remain in office an hour after we are beaten'.[42]

The Hollands' campaign for new creations began in the autumn of 1831. On 5 September, Holland was outvoted in Cabinet on the issue of how many new peerages should be created on the occasion of William's coronation. The Hollands wanted at least thirty.[43] As Lady Holland observed, 'I hope our Ministerial friends will not be squeamish as to numbers. They ought not; for those who cry out against numbers will only laugh, if they do not make enough to compass the job.[44] After the first draft of the Reform Bill had been defeated, the Hollands' campaign against Grey intensified. Calling himself 'the most intrepid of peermakers', Holland passed on to Grey a paper by John Allen, which argued simply that conservative peers would have to be

41. Add. MSS. 51868, f 269; Holland's Political Journal, 27 Dec. 1831.

42. Add. MSS. 51867, f 112; ibid., 2 Sept. 1831.

43. ibid., f 123; ibid., 5 Sept. 1831.

44. Lady Holland to Henry Fox, 2 Sept. 1831; *Elizabeth, Lady Holland to her Son*, p.114.

converted or intimidated before reform could go through. The urgency of the situation ruled out the first, and therefore an immediate creation of fifty or sixty peers was unavoidable.[45] In the most ruthless manner, Holland was prepared to enter into an auction with the Tory peers and to push the bidding in terms of new peerages as high as was necessary: 'Our dukes and marquesses are scared at a fresh herd of barons ... It is a strange quirk to prefer the danger of having no House of Lords to a temporary enlargement of it. For my part, I am for a game of tennis, where one reckons fifteen, thirty, forty – game.'[46]

Between January and May 1832, as Grey partnered William IV in a stately dance of mutual hesitation and doubt, Holland's hardline views never varied. Each prevarication in Cabinet is recorded in Holland's Journal with scorn and indignation.[47] When Durham stormed out of the Cabinet on 7 March, in protest against continued delay, he had Holland's full sympathy.[48] He never trusted the Waverers to behave honourably, unless the threat of coercion was made real to them. Equally, the slow moving mind of the King had to be brought to a decision. To delay was too dangerous. When Anglesey wrote from Ireland to express the hope that the letters patent creating the new peers were already drawn up, Holland could only reply that 'I wish both the King and Grey saw your wise and emphatick words "*Spare not parchment*" written in letters of gold on their bed curtains every morning when they woke'.[49]

Holland House believed that the vindication of its hardline attitude on the question of new peerages lay in the awful doubts and uncertainties of the first weeks of May 1832.[50] The refusal to take decisive action on the peerage question allowed the Tories to hope until the very last minute that William would finally declare in their favour. Equally, the King's

45. Holland to Grey, 8 Nov. 1831; Grey MSS. Box 34.
46. Holland to Brougham, 31 Dec. 1831; *The Life and Times of Lord Brougham*, p.454.
47. Add. MSS. 51868, f 286 & f 318; Holland's Political Journal, 2 & 30 Jan. 1832.
48. Add. MSS. 51868, f 394; Holland's Political Journal, 7 March 1832.
49. Holland to Anglesey, 14 Feb. 1832; Anglesey MSS.
50. For a full discussion of the May crisis, see M. Brock, *The Great Reform Act*, pp. 282-310.

acceptance of the Whigs' resignations on 9 May demonstrated his basic unreliability. Although he was forced to reinstate them six days later, the result of this crisis was, in Holland's view, the most serious prospect of revolution that existed in his entire political career.[51] On 11 May, he told his son: 'You see we are out – victims of a great conspiracy – forced to resign – I am so dreadfully alarmed at the consequences at home & abroad of disturbance & war both of which I believe will occur that that fear absorbs all other considerations.'[52] The Whigs' reluctance to force the issue earlier had had the most dire results. Grey the Foxite should never have put any real trust in princes or their natural Tory allies. The danger passed, but, by allowing the Bill to pass on the strength of large Tory abstentions, the Reform Bill's success demonstrated 'the embarrassment' of continued Tory power as well as Whig endeavour. In the view of Holland House, the Reform Bill issue had been so badly mishandled that it had almost precipitated all the results it was designed to avoid.

The final success of the Reform Bill was not the end of the matter as far as Holland was concerned. The behaviour of the Lords throughout the crisis and their continued obstruction of Whig measures throughout the 1830s led him to take the keenest interest in proposals to reform the Upper House as a corollary to the 1832 Bill. Holland House indignantly rebutted the charge that the Whigs saw the Bill as a 'final' statement on the subject. Holland insisted that Lord John Russell was 'misunderstood to say that the reform bill was "final" ... The word "finality", which he *never used*, was repeatedly quoted against him and he was occasionally taunted with it for full two years.'[53] No political institution was static or immune to evolutionary processes. Rough handling of major institutions was always dangerous, but the historical sense of the Whigs made them aware of the realities of change. In particular, Holland made this point with regard to the House of Lords itself:

51. Add. MSS. 51869, f 478; Holland's Political Journal, 8 May 1832.
52. Add. MSS. 51752, f 25; Holland to Henry Fox, 11 May 1832.
53. Add. MSS. 51872, f 1057; Holland's Political Journal, 28 Dec. 1837.

I subscribe to every letter about the Lords – think the advantage of an organick change very questionable & an attempt at it now very hazardous & perhaps pernicious to the cause of liberty, but on the other hand Resistence to it on the high supertitious & foolish ground of inviolability, immutability & essential character of the institution is yet more dangerous & should be equally repudiated by those who wish to continue & those who wish to reform or suppress an hereditary legislature. The majority of the Lords of Parliament in Henry 7th's time were Bishops and Mitred Abbots – in the last Parliament of Charles I & the 1st of Charles 2d there were no Spiritual Lords at all, till the Union with Scotland no elective ones, & in 1801 when the Union Parliament meet the Majority sat by election, creation or nomination & *not* by Hereditary right. How then can it be said to be an unchangeable institution?[54]

The crucial point was that, with or without a reforming hand laid upon it, the Upper House must come to accept that the 1832 Bill had confirmed the Whig view about the ultimate primacy of the Commons, which had been a Foxite attitude since 1784. As Le Marchant noted in his diary: 'Lord Holland observed that one effect of the Reform Bill would be to throw the Government of the country into the House of Commons.'[55] The Lords must recognise this development in Holland's view, or face the consequences. Clashes between the two Houses were always likely, but, after the Whig victory in the 1832 elections, Holland hoped that the Upper House would fall into step.[56] If not, the disagreeable idea of another reform bill might have to be contemplated. Like his uncle before him, however, Holland placed such trust in the overpowering weight of a large majority in the Commons that he found it hard to believe that it would be constitutionally challenged: 'I cannot but believe that in England at all times and more especially since the Reform, the majority of the Commons backed by the Majority of the people, are the *gros bataillons* which secure the favour of the *bon Dieu*.[57]

This confidence was quickly shaken. Throughout the 1833

54. Holland to Ebrington, 28 Nov. 1836; Fortescue MSS. 1262 M/FC 92.
55. The Diary of Denis Le Marchant, July 1833; *Three Early Nineteenth Century Diaries*, p.366.
56. Add. MSS. 51752, f 94; Holland to Henry Fox, 14 Dec. 1832.
57. Add. MSS. 51754, f 116; ibid., 14 July 1835.

Session of Parliament, Grey's measures were mauled in the Lords in a way that suggested that they had forgiven and forgotten nothing. Large majorities in the Commons failed to impress them. Holland was genuinely surprised by the Lords' temerity: 'Really one should think My Lords the Bishops were acting the old Proverb of Quos deus vult perdere prius dementat.'[58] During the constitutional crisis of 1834-5,[59] Tory peers encouraged William IV to believe that it was a legitimate exercise of the prerogative to expel a Ministry from office which enjoyed the confidence of the Commons. Against this background, Holland, in 1835, only gave the Melbourne government an even chance of survival.[60] Not surprisingly, 1835 was the year in which a reform of the Lords was most seriously discussed, with ideas ranging from life peerages to the expulsion of the bishops being freely canvassed.[61] Holland remained very open-minded on the matter. Instinctively he distrusted sudden structural changes in the constitution, which was an organic rather than a mechanical entity in his mind. On the other hand, if the Lords refused to accept the full implications of 1832, then the natural corollary of that Bill would itself have to take legislative form:

> Certain it is that notions of reforms & remodelling of the Hse of Lds. are spoken of in private & in publick too, in a way that six months ago would have excited the ridicule of some & the horror of those who now listen with great composure to the discussion of them. However some new hare may be started before that time & I think it will be lucky for the Lords if there be.[62]

The accession of a young Queen with Whiggish sympathies solved the problem temporarily, much to Holland's relief.

Beyond a continuing interest in the implications of the Reform Bill, Holland showed astonishingly little concern for the domestic politics of the Grey and Melbourne governments. For a Foxite, the issues that had dominated political life since

---

58. Add. MSS. 51753, f 5; Holland to Henry Fox, 14 June 1833.
59. See below
60. Add. MSS. 51754, f 71; Holland to Henry Fox, 5 May 1835.
61. Add. MSS. 51753, f 9; ibid., 25 June 1833.
62. Add. MSS. 51754, f 57; Holland to Henry Fox, 8 Sept. 1835.

1789 had disappeared. Slavery had been abolished, the Catholics had won emancipation and the House of Commons had been purified. For a particular generation their work was done. Accordingly, after 1832, Holland transferred his whole attention to foreign politics[63] where, in his view, Foxite beliefs still had relevance. When a younger member of the government complained about the lack of content in the 1834 King's Speech, he met with very little sympathy: 'Lord Holland cared for nothing but foreign politics; he observed that he had obtained the introduction of the compliment to France, which perhaps was the only liberal portion of the Speech.'[64] He supported the Poor Law of 1834, assessing it as, 'with the Emancipation of the Negroes, the greatest work the Whig Ministries have achieved'.[65] Otherwise, Holland had nothing to say on economic or social issues. Bentham, Ricardo and Chadwick made no imprint on the Fox family tradition. Their world was London and Paris rather than Leeds and Manchester.

Although there are occasional references in the Political Journal which suggest a degree of irritation with Grey's aversion 'to the agitation of great questions',[66] Holland was basically delighted that the Whigs should now concentrate on foreign affairs. In 1833, Holland described a situation to his son in which the Whigs had never been more popular at Court[67] or in the country at large. The Reform Bill in short had guaranteed many years of Whig government: 'You may with truth as well as pleasure tell your foreign friends & enemies that the Whig Ministers are stronger than ever, & still more peremptorily & decidedly that there is no possibility of the Tories returning to power, or at least retaining it if they do, long enough to change one iota of our foreign policy.'[68] In turning away from activist politics, Holland believed that he

---

63. See below, Chapter Eleven.
64. Diary of Denis Le Marchant, 27 March 1834; *Three Early Nineteenth Century Diaries*, pp. 377-8.
65. Holland to H.S. Fox, 28 Feb. 1838; Bodleian MSS. eng.lett. c 234, f 105.
66. Add. MSS. 51869, f 581; Holland's Political Journal, 17 May 1833.
67. Holland to Ellice, 6 Sept. 1833; Ellice MSS, f 122.
68. Add. MSS. 51753, ff 36-7; Holland to Henry Fox, 16 Aug. 1833.

3. Lord Holland (1795) by F. Fabre

4. Lord Holland by Sir George Hayter

was echoing a national mood. The Radicals had been tamed by it.[69] As for the Tories, since relations between William IV and Grey remained excellent, there could be no danger from that quarter.[70] Later, Holland saw the Tamworth Manifesto less as a new Tory departure in policy than as an admission of defeat: 'What Howick says of Peel's Manifesto is most true, there is nothing specifick but devolution to [the] Irish Church. What shall we say of a book remarked Windham to me of Burke's reflexions of which the best argued & most finely written part is a Vindication of convents.'[71]

In two major areas, this assessment of politics proved hopelessly wrong. Just as the ending of slavery had brought new problems to the West Indies, so Parliamentary Reform and Catholic Emancipation led on to new problems. For a Foxite, this was strange and mildly irritating. These measures had been designed to solve problems rather than engender new ones. In fact, the Irish question, still much influenced by O'Connell's behaviour, assumed new contours. Provoking though this was, the Whigs were dangerously dependent on Irish votes in the House of Commons and therefore could not ignore their new claims. Similarly, the Whigs had seriously misread the King's mind. William IV had very much disliked many aspects of the politics surrounding the Reform Bill. He had been frightened and bullied on behalf of a measure for which he had had little enthusiasm. The constitutional crisis of 1834-5, which raised the whole gallery of Foxite ghosts, stemmed from that experience. William was not a Whig king after all. His countenancing of Reform had been the product of bewildered apprehension only. Try as he might, therefore, to move on from domestic affairs, Holland could not avoid the fact that Foxite reforms apparently cast a long shadow.

The Hollands followed the Irish question after 1832 with a mixture of boredom and irritation. In the deistic atmosphere of Holland House, the very idea that a problem could centre on religious differences was barely credible. For Lady

69. Add. MSS. 51742, f 109; Holland to Caroline Fox, 14 Jan. 1835.
70. Add. MSS. 51752, ff 49-50; Holland to Henry Fox, 12 Oct. 1832.
71. Holland to Grey, 19 Jan. 1835; Grey MSS. Box 34.

Holland, the Irish debate was conducted in anachronistic language: 'the Ministry are supposed to be in a moment de crise as the Lords are half mad with theology and topics of ecclesiastical policy more like the polemics of other ages than of this.'[72] To spend long hours in commitee discussing the endowment of the Irish Church or tithe commutation was tedious to minds that were sceptical about the whole religious dimension in life. Holland complained that he was 'so bored with it'.[73] It was a 'difficult & tiresome subject'.[74] Worst of all, the Irish had had a most unfortunate impact on English politics by using their bloc votes to blackmail governments. At one point, Holland believed that the Reform Bill itself would be thwarted by either the Catholics or the Orangemen. As he bluntly pointed out to Lord Cloncurry, the Irish were inclined to demand too much too soon:

> Your being in good humour is a good sign; and I really think you have no grounds to be otherwise, nor even to imagine that Irish interests would be sacrificed to forward English measures. You must always recollect that by attempting any Irish measures that are strongly reprobated by public opinion in England, we should not forward the interests of one or the other.[75]

It was saddening that the Foxite contention that Irish discontent would melt away after Catholic Emancipation had been proved wrong.

Throughout the Irish debates, Holland approached the problem with the commonsense of eighteenth-century rationalism. There was little understanding of O'Connell's assertiveness or Stanley's tender Anglican conscience. For Holland, it was absurd that the Anglican Church in Ireland, representing perhaps a tenth of the population, should enjoy the benefits of being the Established Church.[76] In particular,

72. Lady Holland to Lord W. Russell, 24 July 1835; *Lord William Russell and his Wife*, p.337.
73. Add. MSS. 51753, ff 28-30; Holland to Henry Fox, 23 July 1833.
74. Add. MSS. 51871, f 846; Holland's Political Journal, 29 May 1835.
75. Holland to Cloncurry, 8 Jan. (1835); *Personal Recollections of the Life and Times of Lord Cloncurry*, p.363.
76. Anglesey to Holland, 29 Jan. 1831; Anglesey MSS.

it was unjust that tithes should be paid to it by members of other denominations.[77] It was proper in such circumstances to take charge of Church revenue and redirect it to other purposes, both lay and clerical.[78] When this had been done, the Whigs would have removed the 'greatest practical grievances your peasantry have to complain of; and, above all, allay that perpetual conflict of interests between Protestant and Catholic, which is the greatest curse of your country.'[79] There was logic in this position if not much evidence of a genuine appreciation of Irish conditions. Holland's bewilderment about the endless dilemma of Ireland is contained in the admission that even with major Church reform, the Whigs might still find themselves 'baffled'.[80]

Predictably, this rationalist approach to Ireland pleased no one. For the Orangeman and Anglicans like Stanley, Holland represented the betrayal of true religion to Popery. For O'Connell, Holland's attitude was nothing more than traditional, English temporising. A pamphlet appeared in 1836 which devoted itself to an exposé of the embarrassment of Holland House on Irish matters.[81] It not unreasonably pointed out how strange it was to hear a leading Whig arguing for the expropriation of property by the state. In a major speech in the Lords, Holland had argued that tithe and glebe were 'two very singular properties', whose tenure was 'variable at the will of the state', because both were held conditionally upon the performance 'of certain duties prescribed by Parliament'. As the pamphleteer pointed out, it was possible to draw a distinction between Church property and other forms of property in these terms, but one so fine that all Whig consciences should have baulked at the idea. When Holland went on to quote Philip the Fair's confiscation of Templar property and Henry VIII's assault on monastic lands

77. Holland to Cloncurry, 26 Feb. 1834; *Personal Recollections of the Life and Times of Lord Cloncurry*, pp. 357-9.

78. ibid., 17 June 1834; ibid., pp. 463-4.

79. ibid., 18 July 1835; ibid., p.360.

80. Holland to Grey, c July 1832; Grey MSS., Box 34.

81. A Pupil of Canning, *The Irish Church. A Letter to the Rt. Hon. Lord Holland* (London 1836).

as precedents, the pamphleteer's doubts about his Whig credentials grew deeper. The difficulty of manipulating one form of property without endangering others was a problem Holland recognised. It was just one more embarrassment in what looked like an interminable debate, in which unreason dominated both sides of the argument.

Daniel O'Connell, the Irish 'Liberator', had been introduced to Holland House by the Lord Lieutenant Anglesey in the most unflattering terms: '... he is a coward, and may be more practicable whilst he is in a difficulty than when he is kicking the world before him.'[82] Upon acquaintance, the Hollands thought this description substantially correct. He lived on his nuisance value, and by provoking government, pushed it into the extreme course of coercion. Holland House found it impossible to accept religious belief as a motive for action, and was always ready to follow alternative explanations: 'I do not deny his talents nor am I insensible to his powers of pleasing but after all his chief if not sole importance is derived from the connexion which enables him to give pain.'[83] It was possible to see the Irish troubles as either the product of specific grievances upon which a handful of demagogues capitalised, or as the expression of a wider and broader religious and political mood. Holland believed that it was the first, whereas O'Connell's career was built on the fact of the second.

Although for much of the 1830s Irish votes were essential to the survival of Whig government, Holland always found the alliance less than satisfactory. In November 1835, in a long résumé of English politics, Holland observed that 'the only nail that drives at all against us ... is the *Connection* as they call it with O'Connell ... if he would but abstain from the vulgar & disgusting scurrility against Individuals, his powerful & valuable assistance, from whatever motive afforded us, would cease to be a reproach to us even in England'.[84] If the Liberator behaved somewhat better after the attempted Tory

82. Anglesey to Holland, 23 Jan. 1831; Anglesey MSS.
83. Add. MSS. 51753, ff 112-3; Holland to Henry Fox, 1 July 1834.
84. Holland to Edward Ellice, 3 Nov. 1835; Ellice MSS. f 154.

'coup' of 1834-5, the Hollands were only too aware that this improvement stemmed entirely from a fear of Wellington and Peel than from a genuine friendship with Whigs.[85] The Hollands, although intimately acquainted with much of Western Europe, never visited Ireland. For them, it was a country so riddled with superstition and other forms of mental vice that little sense could be made of it. They disliked O'Connell personally, and were quite incapable of attributing to him any generous motive or intention.

On the other side of the question, Stanley's Anglican conscience was equally difficult to come to terms with, the only difference being that the Hollands held him in high personal regard.[86] To their eighteenth-century, deistic minds, it was maddening that a man of Stanley's abilities should feel so strongly about points of religion that he could threaten the resignation of a useful career. As Holland told Anglesey, 'the different views taken by you and Stanley of this cursed Church measure etc etc etc weakens the authority of your government both here and in Ireland'.[87] Holland sympathised with younger Whigs who felt that Grey's Irish policy was being compromised by too many concessions to Stanley's sensibilities,[88] but tried to point out the man's value and his importance to the Cabinet as a whole. For his pains, he was reprimanded by his protégés. Lord John Russell accused him of 'surrendering the principles of a Whig & a Foxite',[89] and asked 'Why not preach to Stanley? Why not endeavour to convince him? Why try to make me act in a way contrary to your opinions & my own? ... none of you *dare* to urge him to change his opinions.'[90]

Holland's consideration for Stanley stemmed entirely from an appreciation of his ability. At no time could Holland House

85. Add. MSS. 51754, f 198; Holland to Henry Fox, 30 Oct. 1835.

86. Anglesey to Holland, 27 Oct. 1832; Anglesey MSS. See also Lady Holland to Henry Fox, 10 June 1834; *Elizabeth, Lady Holland to her Son*, p.149.

87. Holland to Anglesey, 14 Jan. 1833; Anglesey MSS.

88. Diary of Denis Le Marchant, 22 June 1833; *Three Early Nineteenth Century Diaries*, p.339.

89. Add. MSS. 51677, f 118; Lord J. Russell to Holland, 15 Oct. 1833.

90. ibid., f 106; ibid., 15 Feb. 1833.

sympathise with a religious prompting for political action. In this sense, discussions about Ireland seemed to revive seventeenth-century attitudes rather than to generate views appropriate to the nineteenth century. When Stanley, Sir James Graham and two others finally resigned from Grey's Cabinet on the question of the Irish Church, Holland's reaction was blunt. It had been right to try to retain Stanley's abilities within the Cabinet. Equally, it was now right to let him go. His Anglicanism suggested a latent Toryism, and 'a suspicion of Tory propensities even in its most mitigated shape is fatal to any influence in the Hse of Commons – & by what power but by that of the Commons can a Minister since the Reform Bill retain or obtain his power'.[91] The Stanley resignation and the troubled alliance with O'Connell demonstrated the extent to which Catholic Emancipation had failed to make the Irish problem tidy. Holland, by temperament and upbringing, was badly qualified to understand the new situation.

A parallel situation arose out of the success of Parliamentary Reform. According to Foxite lore, one of the strongest motives for Reform had always been its capacity to settle once and for all the question of executive power. Unfortunately, William IV failed to appreciate this fact. The bullying and cajoling to which he had been subjected suggested the worst characteristics of party government. For some time, the idea of a 'broadbottom', less partisan, ministry must have appeared very attractive. When Melbourne, the ex-Canningite, succeeded Grey as Prime Minister, in July 1834, it was in a sense a step away from pure Whiggery towards the centre. Even a month before this event, the Hollands had been alive to the possibility of the King attempting political violence: 'there is the general feeling of apprehension especially among our timid friends that the administration will be overthrown at the end of the session.'[92] There was general relief that the transfer from Grey's leadership to Melbourne's had passed off without allowing the King an

91. Add. MSS. 15753, f 87; Holland to Henry Fox, 29 May, 1834.
92. Add. MSS. 51746, f 196; Lady Holland to Caroline Fox, c June 1834.

opportunity to recall the Tories, and thereby deprive Holland of a much needed salary.[93] The troubles of the summer of 1834 revived all the Fox family fear of executive power and brought into question yet again their assumption that, after the Reform Bill had passed, the constitutional supremacy of the House of Commons had been secured.

The blow fell on 4 November 1834.[94] William dismissed the Whig Ministry and asked Peel to take over, in spite of the fact that there remained an anti-Tory majority in the Commons. As a confrontation between legislature and executive the analogy with 1783-4 was exact. For the Hollands, this was an appalling experience. It demonstrated the extent to which the King and the leading Tories failed to understand the implications of 1832. As a grossly provocative act, it promised to resurrect all the anger and disturbances which had so recently been allayed. Above all, it brought back to power, however briefly, men who laboured under the 'very false & unphilosophical notion that Kings Princes & Ministers do really as well as nominally govern'.[95] Even before the results of the January 1835 election confirmed the Whigs in office, Holland House refused to believe that William's coup could succeed in the post-Reform Bill world.[96] His action inspired less anger than pity. In the Hollands' view, William was a befuddled old man who had failed to realise that it was no longer possible to act as his father had done.

Peel, in undertaking William's work, was by contrast fully aware of the new situation in politics. According to the French ambassador, 'il immole la prerogative royale et la Chambre des Pairs et il ne reconnait de force et d'influence qu'à la Chambre des Communes'.[97] As he and the Hollands realised, his only hope of surviving was either to attract Stanley, Graham and other disgruntled Whigs into some kind of

93. *Memoirs of the Duchesse de Dino*, i 119.

94. For a full discussion of the November crisis, see P. Ziegler, *King William IV*, p.253 seq.

95. Add. MSS. 51753, f 203; Holland to Henry Fox, 18 Nov, 1834.

96. ibid., f 219; ibid., 21 Nov. 1834.

97. Sébastiani to Mme Adelaide, 15 May 1834; Bibliothèque Nationale n.a. fr. 12219 f 23.

alliance[98] or to persuade Melbourne, Palmerston and other ex-Canningites to reconstruct the type of administration that Liverpool had led in the 1820s.[99] Both proved impossible, and therefore the Whigs returned to office in April 1835. The November 1834 to April 1835 crisis had vindicated the Hollands' view that, since the Reform Bill passed, all things were new. The Whigs had finally achieved the Foxite objective of circumscribing executive power:

> The effect & intention of the Reform Bill was to give to the people practically (what they had before theoretically) the virtual tho' not actual appointment of their rulers – & if the majority of their representatives, chosen on an appeal on this very point, are averse to the Ministry, can they justify themselves to their constituents if they allow old animosities or personal estrangences & suspicions to prevent giving them the benefit of a Ministry elected by them.[100]

Peel must be hounded out of office, in order to vindicate the settlement of 1832.

Peel's failure to translate William's 'coup' into a lasting political system 'recoiled to the advantage of Whig power'.[101] Holland delightedly returned to the point that the Reform Bill guaranteed Whig predominance:

> They have radicalized many an old Whig & Whiggified many an active Radical & habit & reciprocal assistance & support have greatly cemented that union. The Power of the Reformers is not so showy nor, to be timid, so formidable as it was in 33 but it is deeper rooted and more solid than ever ... that neither the demise of the Crown, the changes of Ministers or the change of wishes in either or both can materially alter the policy at home & abroad of the English Government. None but Reformers ... can hold power in England.[101]

Many factors led to the assumption that the Whigs were about to enjoy a long period in office. The country at large was disposed '*to be quiet*', from 'a conviction that another change would lead to dissolutions at home, absolute confusion in

98. Add. MSS. 51754, f 39; Holland to Henry Fox, 6 March 1835.
99. Holland to Melbourne, 22 Jan. 1835; *Lord Melbourne's Papers*, p.232.
100. Holland to Grey, 6 March 1835; Grey MSS, Box 34.
101. Add. MSS. 51754, ff 134-6; Holland to Henry Fox, 7 April 1835.

Ireland & perhaps war abroad'.[102] The prospect of a new Peel government constrained the Radicals to behave well,[103] and served to convince the Dissenters that the Whigs were their natural representatives.[104] Even O'Connell and the Irish had been frightened into responsible behaviour. By 1837, the 'Liberator' had become a regular guest at Holland House, where his manners were thought 'perfectly well bred and easy'.[105] The royal 'coup' left anti-Tory opinion little option but to follow the Whig lead.

From the accession of Victoria in 1837 until his death, Holland concentrated almost entirely on foreign affairs. He was aware of the difficulties which the Melbourne government increasingly laboured under, but remained basically convinced that the Reform Bill had made the return of a Tory government unlikely.[106] As has been said, he put no faith in the reconstructed Toryism heralded by the Tamworth Manifesto. The Hollands shared the alarms at the Chartist movements of 1837 and 1839,[107] but concluded that their failure had been guaranteed by the Whig revival of strict constitutionalism in 1832:

> To have quieted ... so widespread a discontent as the clamour against the poor laws & the political associations of the lower orders instigated by fanaticks ... without any effusion of blood & without any inroad even by temporary legislation on our general maxim of free government is an atchievement of which we may be justly proud.[108]

Above all, the continued rumblings of Chartism proved that a return to Toryism would be disastrous, as some of their more rational leaders saw.[109] As for the majority of the Tories, they

102. Add. MSS. 51754, f 81; Holland to Henry Fox, 26 May 1835.
103. Bulwer Lytton to Durham, (Jan.) 1835; *The Life of Edward Bulwer, 1st Lord Lytton*, p.468. See also Add. MSS. 51754; f 33. Holland to Henry Fox, 3 March 1835.
104. Add. MSS. 51870, f 792; Holland's Political Journal, 15 April 1835.
105. Lady Holland to Henry Fox, Feb. 1837; *The Chronicles of Holland House*, p.236.
106. Add. MSS. 51757, f 37; Holland to Henry Fox, 17 April 1839.
107. Lady Holland to Henry Fox, 2 April 1839; *Elizabeth, Lady Holland to Her Son*, p.174.
108. Add. MSS. 51757, f 113; Holland to Henry Fox, 1 Nov. 1839.
109. ibid., f 75; ibid., 16 July 1839.

would simply have to learn 'the inapplicability of their principles to the temper of the times'.[110]

The implementation of the Foxite programme had involved political events which the Hollands had never anticipated. The Catholics had been emancipated by Tories, not Whigs, and the measure had not solved the problems presented by Ireland. It is hard to guess what Fox would have thought of O'Connell. The slaves had been freed, but, as a result, as the Hollands knew well, the West Indian plantations were threatened with political and economic disaster. Only Parliamentary Reform had come fully up to expectations. The last flicker of the old system of politics in 1834-5 had been unpleasant to witness, but its failure demonstrated how well the Reform Bill had done its work. The power of the executive, which had broken the career of Holland's uncle, could never again be wielded with such effect. Under the pressure of these events, the Tory party splintered, and would, in Holland's view, take a generation to recover. He consistently underestimated the Peelite recovery after 1832. Within a year of Holland's death, the Tories were once again in power.

The years 1829-33 saw the clearing from the agenda of those issues which had dominated Holland's life and on which his uncle had lectured. When they brought new problems in their wake, Holland largely failed to adjust to them. For most of the 1830s, he preferred to concentrate on foreign affairs where he believed Charles Fox's teaching to be still relevant. The defeat of the dragon of executive power was at least accomplished, and the accession of the young Victoria pushed George III and his tiresome sons into history. As a good Whig, Holland normally regarded Coronations as 'pernicious both to Prince & to People'. In 1838, he was determined to enjoy Victoria's.

> It has shewn many who wanted such a lesson the real strength free institutions confer on a government, it has proved to Tories at home & to Ultras abroad that we are more firmly seated & above all that liberal principles are more cherished than they supposed.[111]

110. ibid., f 152; ibid., 13 Dec. 1839.
111. Add. MSS. 51756, f 170; Holland to Henry Fox, 27 July 1838.

The fulfilment of Holland's trusteeship of Foxite principles had had many unexpected and untidy aspects, but at least its broad intentions had been met.

7

Scots, Literature and Patronage

By birthright the Hollands were a family given over to politics, but this was not the full extent of their intellectual range. Just as Parliament sat for only five or six hours a day in the late eighteenth century, so politics was only a part of life. The drums, routs and balls of the London Season, when added to the more permanent features of club life, did something to fill up a day which in polite society started late and finished late. This was not the pattern of Holland House, however. Holland himself was not a very enthusiastic clubman, and his wife disliked crowded social events. They both preferred small lunch and dinner parties. Holland House offered hospitality for almost the whole day. People came for breakfast as much as for dinner. Its proximity to London made it the obvious refuge for anyone wishing to escape the pressures of the capital, among which might be numbered wives, literary critics and creditors. Not surprisingly therefore, literary distinction was as important an element in the salon at Holland House as political eminence. Sheridan came in the 1790s. Dickens and Disraeli appeared in the 1830s.

The Hollands prided themselves on their literary capabilities. As will be argued later in this chapter, the line between literary and political values in the early nineteenth century was thin, and it is by no means clear that Holland recognised it at all. As he himself remarked, the one imperceptibly influenced the other. At the end of his *Further Memoirs of the Whig Party*, he felt constrained to give some account of 'those who have without immediate connection with politics, acquired or deserved celebrity for genius or talent, learning or wit, in science, in art, in poetry, in literature, or in conversation. With some such I have been intimate, with many others familiarly acquainted. All have, no doubt, had directly or indirectly more or less influence on the task, temper, and opinions of society. The indirect manner in which it was exerted would not, indeed, justify the introduction of their names in any narrative of party events; but some traits of their characters and lives may not be misplaced on the distant ground of the picture I have attempted to trace.'[1] Any entertainment at Holland House would involve some of the semi-resident conversationalists like Richard Sharp and 'Poodle' Byng who constituted a literary staff. They were reinforced by Byron and the Macaulays who came by invitation, and who made explicit the connection between literature and politics in their own careers.

In thus following the example of European salons, in which literary men always had a place, the Hollands were also following their own inclinations. Literature and the world of ideas was their preferred form of recreation. By contrast, they both loathed the countryside and all its traditional attractions. Holland only shot his first pheasant in 1821, and the event seems to have brought on endless remorse.[2] Sydney Smith, like Ovid in exile in his Yorkshire parsonage, likened a visit by the Hollands to 'the march of Alexander or Bacchus over India, and will be as long remembered in the traditions of the innocent natives'.[3] On another occasion, he simply enjoined his patroness: 'never venture into the country, dear Lady Holland, it does not suit you.'[4] Intelligence, in every sense of that word, was to be found in London. Relaxation for the Hollands was metropolitan, cerebral and largely sedentary.

These attitudes had political importance in that, for the Hollands, they represented a point of difference between Whig and Tory. When Macaulay, in the celebrated third chapter of his *History of England*, described the Tory squire as a muddle-

---

1. Holland, *Further Memoirs of the Whig Party*, p.307.
2. Add. MSS. 51730, f 41; Holland to Lady Holland, 21 Nov. 1821.
3. S. Smith to Lady Holland, 7 Jan. 1823; *The Letters of Sydney Smith*, i 232.
4. ibid., 4 Oct. 1823; ibid., ii 402.

brained, bigoted rustic, he was speaking the language of Holland House. Holland peddled an image of the Tory party as an alliance of 'bobby Lords & squires, who saddled us with all the taxes & war & whose notions of prosperity are cheating their creditors & starving their labourers'.[5] It was as though the Enlightenment itself had not radiated beyond Kensington. Even Tories like Peel, who were obviously men of some ability, chose to direct their minds towards impenetrable subjects like the bullion question or political economy rather than to literary or philosophical speculation. A dinner in 1826 was ruined because 'political economy and bullion were discussed at terrible length'.[6] Just as Fox had found Pitt's obsession with figures to be a sure sign of an arid soul, so Holland found Peel forbiddingly cold and insensitive. Holland could not understand why the new science of political economy was held in 'stupid veneration' by 'the younger politicians'.[7]

This attempt to characterise Whig and Tory in terms of London against an unsophisticated countryside, or as literature and history against the insensitive laws of political economy, was in some sense reciprocated by their opponents. Pitt and Peel were clear that the Hollands were ignorant of the mechanics and techniques of government, and found this fact alarming. It seemed to indicate less the promptings of a sensitive intelligence than a wilful unwillingness to meet the demands of government in the early nineteenth century. Corn laws and trade regulations were the new stuff of politics. Holland approached these topics with an eighteenth-century disdain: 'I do not pretend to understand any thing about these matters ... Allen once made me comprehend the question between gold & silver as a standard, & though I have in some measure forgotten the reasons I still retain the conviction that silver should in all prudence be our standard.'[8] As in so many other aspects, the Hollands carried over the intellectual preoccupations of the eighteenth century into the nineteenth,

5. Add. MSS. 51742; f 1; Holland to Caroline Fox, 26 May 1826.
6. *The Journal of Henry Edward Fox*, p.98.
7. Add. MSS. 51749, f 216; Holland to Henry Fox, 30 Nov. 1826.
8. Add. MSS. 51547, f 70; Holland to Grey, 13 Feb. 1826.

and chose to make this preference a point of difference between Whig and Tory.

The presence of novelists and essayists at Holland House, beyond reflecting the tastes of its owners, also illustrated another inescapable fact of London life in the post-1789 world. The French Revolution had so challenged the assumptions on which society had hitherto been constituted that no aspect of life escaped its influence. Every school of thought in literature became a political party by definition. In ways which will be described, the form and content of a novel or poem became political declarations. Certainly, the Hollands saw no difference between the patronage of a young politician and the fostering of a young poet. In particular, the writing of history was highly controversial. Holland reproved his son for liking Gibbon's work for reasons that were entirely drawn from contemporary politics:

> I am reading Ferguson's Roman republick & though I cannot compare him with Gibbon as an historian, I must say I think his subject a much better one — & do not quite relish your taste for Tacitus, Suetonius & Gibbon for I should think a young one might be more interested in the growth of a small state to a great empire than in the crumbling decrepitude of corrupt & extensive despotism.[9]

An active involvement in literature was merely an extension of Whig politics. In someone like Macaulay, they were one and the same thing.

Not surprisingly, therefore, the patronage of literary talent was a permanent feature of Holland House. The discovery and promotion of able young men was identified by Brougham as something characteristic of the Fox family: 'Like his uncle, he [Holland] was always desirous of bringing forward the "young ones", and the whispering against any one did not at all weigh upon him any more than on his uncle.'[10] Interestingly, Holland himself could easily fall into using his uncle's exact phraseology. Delighted by one of

9. Add. MSS. 51748, f 58; Holland to Henry Fox, 25 May 1819.
10. *The Life and Times of Lord Brougham*, iii 461-2.

Macaulay's speeches, he reported the event to a friend with the words, 'Macaulay was, they say, magnificent last night. He is clearly of the young ones the most remarkable and most rising man. I wish he had a high office. It is true he should.'[11] Even so, the initiation into Holland House society was often uncomfortable. Even Sydney Smith occasionally found the experience somewhat overwhelming.[12] Leigh Hunt refused to go at all for fear of falling under a kind of tutelage: 'The more I admired and loved the character of Lord Holland, the less I dared to become personally acquainted with him; that being a far weaker person than he gave me credit for being, it would be difficult for me to eat the mutton and drink the claret of such a man, without falling into any opinion into which his conscience might induce him to lead me.[13] Such reticence was rare. Most young men of talent braved an invitation to Holland House. It became an avenue of promotion. In this, it fulfilled the Hollands' expectations.

In and out of office, the Hollands indulged in the dispensation of literary patronage. They secured Sydney Smith his living at Foston,[14] and they established Wishaw, the Edinburgh Reviewer, in the Public Accounts.[15] They tried to make a Master of the Rolls[16] and in no way disdained to interest themselves in a position in the Mint.[17] For Reginald Heber there was a rare redition of Camoens.[18] John Allen himself represented the most successful example of the Holland system in action. He had been presented to the Hollands by Sydney Smith in 1802 as someone who was well-qualified to accompany them on their intended Spanish tour. Within a few years, he had become 'my own dear Jack', as

11. Holland to Anglesey, 17 Dec. 1831; Anglesey MSS.

12. Add. MSS. 51653, f 9; S. Smith to Sir J. Mackintosh, 1 Oct. 1805.

13. *The Autobiography of Leigh Hunt*, pp. 202-3.

14. J. Wishaw to Brougham, 19 Sept. 1806; *The Life and Times of Lord Brougham*, i 374.

15. Add. MSS. 52180, f 163; J. Wishaw to J. Allen, 5 Sept. 1814.

16. *The Life and Times of Lord Brougham*, iii 424-5.

17. Caroline Fox to Mrs Valssy, 12 Jan. 1836; Bodleian MSS. Eng. Lett. c 198, f 105.

18. Lady Holland to R. Heber, n.d; Bodleian MSS. Eng. Lett. d 214, f 148.

librarian, talent scout and research assistant.[19] In 1811, again through Holland influence, he took up a position in Dulwich College and eventually became its Warden. Peremptorily he was told that he must give up all thoughts of staying in Scotland. As Lady Holland observed: 'It has been our wish to secure your residence in London.'[20] For Allen, Holland House came to represent a self-sufficient environment. His was an extreme case, but he symbolised a crucial aspect of the House's function.

The price of Holland patronage was high. Protégés were required to acknowledge indebtedness by a faithful attendance at dinners and by a full subscription to the Foxite system. John Allen accepted both requirements. Henry Brougham found it more difficult to come to heel. Allen had introduced him to Holland House in 1805, as yet another of the promising Scots associated with the early editions of the *Edinburgh Review*.[21] Through Holland influence, he was introduced to politics as an electoral agent in the 1807 election, and through the same patronage, he was brought into Parliament for the Duke of Bedford's borough of Camelford in 1810.[22] In spite of these acts of kindness, Brougham could never bring himself to submit to the Hollands' code, with his motives being variously ascribed to petulance or a spirited independence. He spoke of the Foxite tradition as someone who stood outside it.[23] More particularly he refused to accept Lady Holland's personal imperialism. As Lady Harriet Cavendish noted:

> I think I should like Mr Brougham very much. George Lamb says he always leaves Holland House the minute she begins ordering and giving herself airs, and one night that George asked him why he went early, he answered – 'because I see the fetch and carry work is beginning.' I think it is such a good expression.[24]

19. Add. MSS. 52173, f 51; Lady Holland to J. Allen, 1822.
20. Add. MSS. 52172, ff 53-4; ibid., 29 Aug. 1811.
21. Holland, *Memoirs of the Whig Party*, ii 227.
22. Bedford to Brougham, 2 Jan. 1810; *The Life and Times of Lord Brougham*, i 498.
23. Brougham to Rosslyn, 1 Dec. 1807; *The Life and Times of Lord Brougham*, i 391.
24. Lady Harriet Cavendish to Lady G. Morpeth, 2 Dec. 1807; *The Letters of Lady*

Brougham was to become the major rebel against Holland House, and, to the Hollands' irritation, the rebellion in no way impaired his steady success in politics.

No sooner was Brougham ensconced in the Commons, in 1810, than he broke off all relations with the Hollands. Lord Holland was deeply wounded: 'For full six years I had no political or private intercourse with a man whom I had been so anxious to place and so successful in placing in the House of Commons, and who never assigned, nor, I believe, could assign any motive for dropping all habits and connection with me.'[25] Brougham's own explanation for the breach was hardly more illuminating. He told Grey that 'I am morally certain that, if you knew the facts, you would say I had no choice. Quarrel there was none nor anything like it; but I was compelled no longer to frequent Holland House, and I ceased going there silently, without saying one word to any human being.'[26] The estrangement was between Brougham and Lady Holland rather than her husband, and it may have followed an occasion, perhaps apocryphal, when Brougham's mother refused to have her son's patroness in her house because the shadow of the Webster divorce still followed her. A reconciliation of a kind was worked out in 1816, which involved Lady Holland taking up 'a line of civility and sweetness', but Brougham was never again an habitué of the Hollands' circle.[27]

In recognition of Brougham's talent, Holland rescued his political career once more, in 1830, by persuading the Duke of Devonshire to bring him in for Knaresborough. Six months later, at the general election, he abandoned the seat and his new patron in a welter of recrimination.[28] Holland was

---

Harriet Cavendish, p.263. See also Brougham to Creevey, 14 Jan. 1816; *The Creevey Letters*, i 249.

25. Holland, *Further Memoirs of the Whig Party*, pp. 44-5.

26. Brougham to Grey, 5 Jan. 1814; *The Life and Times of Lord Brougham*, ii 99-101.

27. Lady H. Granville to Lady G. Morpeth, Feb. 1816; *The Letters of Lady Harriet Granville*, i 85.

28. Lady Holland to Henry Fox, 15 Jan. 1836; *Elizabeth, Lady Holland to her Son*, p.160.

bewildered by every aspect of Brougham's behaviour, and he attempted to describe his feelings in verse:

> There's a wild man at large doth roam,
> A giant wit! – they call him Brougham
>   And well methinks they may;
> He deals, whene'er he speaks and acts,
> With friends and foes and laws and facts
>   In such a sweeping way.[29]

To the end of his career, Brougham remained an irritant and an enigma. The Hollands could not understund why a man of such great talents found it impossible to work within the established conventions of a system based on patronage. The duties were relatively trivial and the rewards immense. To that extent, the problems presented by Brougham and George Canning were the same.

Beyond direct patronage and less distinct, was the Hollands' genuine interest in literature and its development. They always displayed an almost frantic desire to meet and challenge the latest playwright or novelist. The contradiction in this behaviour was that it seemed to deny their own literary preferences. Both the Hollands had had their judgments formed in the eighteenth century. For them, the Augustan age represented a pinnacle of English letters from which there had been a steady degeneration. Their tutorials with young writers were in a sense a desperate search for someone who could disprove this pessimistic theory. The flow was endless. Walter Scott and Bulwer Lytton were reasonably regular dinner guests at certain points in their career, and the latter dedicated one of his novels to Holland in 1823.[30] Fenimore Cooper disliked his interview with the Hollands,[31] while Washington Irving rather enjoyed the experience.[32] Dickens was found to be 'unobtrusive yet not shy, intelligent in

29. A. Aspinall, *Brougham*, p.21.
30. Holland to Lytton, 11 May 1823; Lytton MSS.
31. *The Journal of Fenimore Cooper*, i 357.
32. Lady Holland to Henry Fox, 17 May 1842; *Elizabeth, Lady Holland to her Son*, p.202.

countenance, and altogether prepossessing'.[33] He possibly seemed to represent some hope for the future. Disraeli's work, on the other hand, was 'full of talent; the most impudent, brilliant & tedious I ever read. Macaulay calls it "Young England written by old Jewry": well said.'[34] With these people formal patronage was impossible, but Lady Holland's interfering spirit was never quiet. In 1845, she attempted to stop Dickens's projected tour of America by saying 'go down to Bristol and see some of the third or fourth class people, and they'll do just as well.'[35]

In spite of this determined enquiry for talent and originality, the Hollands never really moved away from the opinion, first expressed in 1807, that literature 'both in France and England ... seems to me to be much upon the decline'.[36] Jane Austin's novels were disliked. There is no evidence that the Brontës were even read. Not surprisingly therefore, the Hollands came to believe that the real progress in the world of letters was being made in historical and philosophical writing. The essayist maintained the tradition of good writing, quintessentially in the new review form of which the *Edinburgh Review* was the prototype. In the Hollands' view, literary development lay more with men like Macaulay, historian, essayist and politician, than with the poet and novelist. Coming to the Hollands' notice as 'a clever writer in E. Review',[37] Macaulay was almost literally filched by Lady Holland away from Lansdowne patronage, under which he had first come to prominence.[38] Within four days of his introduction, he was attending his first dinner. He thereafter became a willing favourite.[39] When, in 1834, he decided to take up an appointment in India, Lady Holland 'became quite

33. *The Chronicles of Holland House*, pp. 240-1.

34. Lady Holland to Henry Fox, 4 June 1844; *Elizabeth, Lady Holland to her Son*, p.216.

35. *The Diary of Benjamin Haydon*, ii 797.

36. Add. MSS. 51653, ff 23-4; Holland to Sir J. Mackintosh, 1807.

37. Lady Holland to Henry Fox, 9 Feb. 1830; *Elizabeth, Lady Holland to her Son*, p.108.

38. *The Chronicles of Holland House*, p.137.

39. Macaulay to Hannah Macaulay, 30 May 1831; *The Life & Letters of T.B. Macaulay*, pp. 150-1.

hysterical', and was rebuked by her husband with the words: 'Can we tell a gentleman who has a claim upon us, that he must lose his only chance of getting an independence in order that he may come and talk to you in the evening.'[40] The difficulty was that, in the Hollands' view, there were few people in Macaulay's generation who could act as substitutes.

There was, however, one great exception to this generally pessimistic view of nineteenth-century literature. Byron was thought to be a poet of real genius, and his tempestuous career excited something like real compassion in the Hollands. His notoriety was itself a qualification for attention. Indeed, it was impossible to ignore him. In 1807, Brougham had dealt severely with a volume of Byron's poems in the pages of the *Edinburgh Review*. Byron's revenge was terrible. In *English Bards and Scotch Reviewers*, he systematically lampooned everyone connected with the *Review*. Francis Jeffrey, its editor, became a 'literary Anthrophagus',[41] and the *Review* itself 'a hydra'.[42] Unfortunately, even at this early stage in its career, the *Review* and its principal writers were already so intimately connected with the Hollands, that Byron assumed that the attack on him had been mounted as part of an editorial policy worked out at Holland House. According to Byron, the Reviewers 'defeat their object by indiscriminate abuse, and they never praise except the partisans of Ld Holland & co'.[43]

Accordingly, as part of his counter-attack, Byron penned lines which he was forever after to regret:

> Illustrious Holland! hard would be his lot
> His hirelings mentioned, and himself forgot!
> Holland, with Henry Petty at his back,
> The whipper-in and huntsman of the pack.
> Blest be the banquets spread at Holland House,
> Where Scotchmen feed, and Critics may carouse!
> Long, long beneath that hospitable roof.
> Shall Grub-street dine, while duns are kept aloof.

40. *The Chronicles of Holland House*, pp. 168-9.
41. *English Bards and Scotch Reviewers*, postscript, second edition (London 1811).
42. ibid., preface, first edition (London 1809).
43. Byron to the Rev. J. Becker, 26 Feb. 1808; *Byron's Letters and Journals*, i 157.

Dunedin! view thy children with delight,
They write for food, and feed because they write:
And lest when heated with the unusual grape,
Some glowing thoughts should to the press escape,
And tinge with red the female reader's cheek,
My lady skims the cream of each critique;
Breathes o'er the page her purity of soul,
Reforms each error and refines the whole.[44]

In view of Lady Holland's early career, the irony contained in
these lines was drawn in wide and unmistakable terms. Byron
had not yet met the Hollands, and the production of these
verses ensured that such a meeting would be much delayed.[44]

Only in 1811 was formal contact attempted, with the
initiative coming from Holland's side. In November of that
year, Byron noted that he had 'received indirectly a kind of
pacific overture from Ld. Holland, so you see, people are very
civil when one don't deserve it'.[45] Early in 1812, Byron
responded by asking for Holland's assistance in the
preparation of his maiden speech. The subject matter was to
be the distress of the frame-knitters of Nottinghamshire,
Byron's county, and Holland, as Recorder of Nottingham,
might be expected to be in a position to offer advice.[46] In
March, the two men met for the first time through the agency
of Samuel Rogers. Byron presented Holland with a copy of
Childe Harold as an explicit peace-offering for the insults
contained in his earlier work.[47] In September, Holland asked
Byron to enter for the poetry competition that was to be held
in conjunction with the opening of the new Drury Lane
theatre.[48] A month later, their understanding was complete.
Holland then assured Rogers: 'You cannot imagine how I
grow to like Lord Byron in my critical intercourse with him.'[49]
Thereafter they remained friends, but Byron's introduction

44. *English Bards and Scotch Reviewers* (London 1809), p.31.
45. Byron to J. Hobhouse, 9 Nov. 1811; ed. L. Marchand, *Byron's Letters and Journals*, ii 128.
46. Byron to Holland, 25 Feb. 1812; ibid., ii 165-6.
47. ibid., 5 March 1812; ibid., ii 168.
48. Holland to Byron, Sept. 1812; ibid., ii 190-221.
49. Holland to S. Rogers, 12 Oct. 1812; *Samuel Rogers and his Contemporaries*, i 89.

into Holland House society had been the most tentative and
protracted of all.

The motives for this rapprochement are not hard to find. By
1811, Byron's reputation as a literary figure carried some
weight. In addition, his liaison with Lady Caroline Lamb,
with whose mother, Lady Bessborough, Lady Holland had
shared her Italian adventures in the 1790s, was becoming a
major talking point. Here therefore were two good reasons
why he should be known. True to their new friendship, the
Hollands attributed most of the blame to Lady Caroline, who
'though she keeps other people in a fever ... is well enough
herself'.[50] Byron for his part was grateful for their support and
encouragement. From 1812 onwards, he made strenuous
efforts to suppress any republication of *English Bards and Scotch
Reviewers*, making a considerable financial loss by so doing. He
told his publisher John Murray, in 1817, that 'with regard to a
future large edition, you may print all, or anything, except
English Bards, to the republication of which at *no* time will I
consent ... I don't think them good for much even in point of
poetry; and, as to other things, you are to recollect that I gave
up the publication on account of the Hollands, and I do not
think that any time or circumstance can neutralize my
suppression.'[51] *The Corsair* was to be dedicated to Holland, to
whom Byron increasingly submitted new work before
publication for comment and criticism.[52] The Hollands'
contacts with Byron between 1812 and his leaving England for
good represent their nearest approaches to imaginative
literature.

While it is almost impossible to evaluate the interaction
between literature and politics with regard to the novel and
poetry, as Holland himself appreciated in his *Memoirs*,[53] the
problem becomes easier in the context of other forms of
writing. As has been pointed out, the Hollands preferred

50. Add. MSS. 51739, ff 148-9; Holland to Caroline Fox, 23 Oct. 1813.

51. Byron to J. Murray, 23 Oct. 1817; ed. Prothero, *The Letters and Journals of Lord Byron*, iv 176-7.

52. Byron to John Murray, 2 Jan. 1814; ed. L. Marchand, *Byron's Letters and Journals*, iv 14.

53. See above, p.1.

essayists and historians to any other kind of literary company, and, not surprisingly therefore, they became closely involved with the new Reviews. When the *Edinburgh Review* appeared in 1802, it established a new style of writing which was quickly followed by the *Quarterly, Blackwoods* and many more. The intention was didactic and informative. They were designed, as Walter Bagehot put it, to provide 'suitable views for sensible people'.[54] Whig, Tory and Radical Reviews dealt with books of immediate political, social and economic interest, and provided the essayist with a new forum for his skill and a larger audience for his views than had ever been possible before. Interaction between literary and political men was unavoidable. Brougham and Macaulay saw this kind of writing as a bridge between politics and *belles-lettres*. To the Hollands the possibilities opened up looked irresistible. The Review was the perfect vehicle for a dovetailing of literary and political interests. For the young Reviewers the patronage of Holland House guaranteed an audience. Each would influence the other.

The Hollands' involvement with the *Edinburgh Review* had one crucial long-term result. The Foxite creed, which had been static in terms of a restatement of the politics of the 1790s, now also began to be defended as a reflection of a society in motion. In 1835, the diarist Greville recorded the following conversation at Holland House;

> I asked, 'Then is there anything you think worse than advancing the movement?' 'Yes', cried out Lord Holland, 'making the movement stand still.' 'And do you mean that you believe there is any danger of that, and that the movement (the progress of improvement) ever can stand still?' 'Yes, I do believe it etc ... Such a miserable apology for their insane violence puts argument and reasoning out of the question.[55]

Holland's defence of 'movement', defined as 'the progress of improvement' was new. It had not been brought forward as an argument by Charles Fox. Yet, relief for Roman Catholics or

---

54. W. Bagehot, *Literary Studies* (London 1911), i 5.
55. The Greville Diaries, iii 197-8.

the claims of the Parliamentary Reformers could now be based on the idea of a movement in society which could be scientifically demonstrated, as well as on traditional Foxite views.

This idea was brought into Holland House from Scotland. The universities of Edinburgh and Glasgow had always enjoyed a high reputation in the eighteenth century, but, when the outbreak of the French wars in 1793 closed Europe to young Englishmen, they began to receive a flood of new pupils. Lord John Russell and Melbourne were educated in Scotland, as were Jeffrey, Brougham, Horner and most of the early Edinburgh Reviewers. They were taught by a remarkable set of tutors, among whom Dugald Stewart and John Millar were outstanding. These men preached a doctrine called 'sociological evolutionism'.[56] Reduced to its simplest form, this idea was based on a demonstration that the development of human society had been linear and not, as Gibbon had thought, cyclical.[57] Drawing on the new disciplines of archaeology and geology to some extent, it could be shown that cavemen who lived by hunting had given way to village farmers, who in turn yielded to townsmen living by trade. At each stage of this process, wealth, leisure and education, the qualifications for rational thought and indeed the holding of political views, had become more widespread. There was therefore demonstrable 'improvement'. Jeffrey, writing an article on Millar for the *Edinburgh*, thought that executive power itself would ultimately be conquered by the impact of 'this increase of industry and opulence upon the character and understanding of the people at large'.[58] For the Hollands, it raised the possibility of giving the Foxite creed a 'scientific' basis. For the Reviewers, it became their intellectual stock in trade.

56. D. Forbes, 'Scientific Whiggism: Adam Smith and John Millar', *Cambridge Journal*, vol. 7, no. 2, 1954.

57. For a full discussion of this theory, see W.C. Lehmann, *John Millar of Glasgow 1735-1801* (Cambridge 1960). Millar's most influential works were *Observations Concerning the Distinction of Ranks in Society* (1771) and the *Historical View of the English Government* (1787).

58. *Edinburgh Review*, iii 175-6.

The Hollands established close links with Scotland at an early stage. 'The Scotch Foxites' had suffered badly in the 1790s and Holland accepted that they had 'a right to lean on me for such support as I can afford them'.[59] They made their first visit to Scotland in 1799.[60] Other Scots were encountered when Holland became a member of the King of Clubs Society in 1799, at whose monthly dinners in the Strand he first met James Mackintosh.[61] It was, however, John Allen's establishment at Holland House that confirmed the Scots connection. Himself a Reviewer, Allen became the main link between Edinburgh and the Hollands, providing news, searching out new talent and arranging introductions. When the Hollands again visited Scotland, in 1810, Allen was sent on in advance to arrange their ordered progress through the intellectual life of Edinburgh and Glasgow. Jeffrey, Horner and Brougham were already familiar figures at Holland House. Now they wanted to meet other reviewers like John Clarke who had chosen to remain in Scotland.[62] In 1814, 1819 and 1822, Allen was sent back alone to collect information on the latest developments, and, on the last occasion, he was commissioned to introduce Holland's eldest son to the leading Scots Reviewers. As he subsequently recorded: 'I never knew Allen give his opinions such vent as he does here, where he thinks they are heard with pleasure and certainly where he acquired them.'[63] In short, the Hollands pursued the Reviewers with the passion of trophy hunters.[64]

If Stewart, Millar and Black were the prophets of 'the movement', their pupils interpreted their words in the *Edinburgh* to the extent that it became the Testament of their ideas. Jeffrey, its first and greatest editor, was a complete convert to the faith they promulgated, Allen describing him as 'another Pangloss' who 'sees nothing but the progress of

59. Holland to Brougham, 31 Dec. 1831; *The Life and Times of Lord Brougham*, iii 449.
60. Add. MSS. 51735, f 47; Holland to Caroline Fox, c 9 July 1798.
61. *The Pope of Holland House*, pp. 333-40.
62. Add. MSS. 52172, f 17; Ailen to Lady Holland, 27 July 1810. See also Add. MSS. 52172, f 28; Lady Holland to Allen, 2 Aug. 1810.
63. *The Journal of Henry Edward Fox*, pp. 117 seq.
64. See also my article 'The Edinburgh Review and the Lake Poets' in *Essays presented to C.M. Bowra* (Oxford 1970).

liberty & liberal opinions and the certainty of a long and general peace'.[65] As the Hollands recognised, Jeffrey had created a powerful instrument of propaganda. Accordingly, when he was in London, he dined with them, and, when he was back in Edinburgh, he remained one of their most faithful correspondents.[66] Through him and his associates, the teaching of the Scots universities trickled into Holland House and into English Whiggery. It is inconceivable that the Hollands would not have been profoundly influenced by their protégés, even if they had shown any reluctance to accept new ideas. In fact, they welcomed the Scots with open arms. When the first volumes of the *Edinburgh* appeared, the Hollands were in Spain, but Caroline Fox sent out copies as soon as they were printed. Holland's verdict was unequivocal. Writing from Madrid in 1803, he announced that 'the Edinburgh Review is clearly the cleverest periodical criticism ever published', even if the Reviewers 'have full as much of the Executioner as of the judge in their composition'.[67] Their pursuit of this quarry stemmed directly from this assessment.

It is easy to demonstrate the close relationship which grew up between what Jeffrey described as the 'ever loved & honoured Holland House'[68] and the Edinburgh Reviewers. Few Holland House dinners were held without one of them being present. It is therefore reasonable to claim that contact of this kind over a period of nearly forty years must have represented one of the channels whereby the teaching of Edinburgh infiltrated Whig thinking. Nothing in the Scots' ideas demanded a modification of basic Foxite thinking. Rather it gave it a new dynamic. From being a static rehearsal of views aired in the 1790s, Foxite opinions could now be defended as being in line with 'the movement'. In the situation of 1832 for example, it might be more comfortable to argue for Parliamentary Reform as a simple aligning of political life with social and economic developments than as a fearful concession to a mob. The more contact politicians had with

65. Add. MSS. 52172, f63; Allen to Lady Holland, 14 June 1814.
66. Add. MSS. 51644, f155; Jeffrey to Holland, 29 June 1832.
67. Add. MSS. 51736, f276; Holland to Caroline Fox, Nov. 1803.
68. Add. MSS. 51644, ff 165-6; Jeffrey to Lady Holland, 14 Nov. 1844.

the *Edinburgh* and its ideas, the more likely they were to accept the changes of 1832 with equanimity. Setting Foxite values in a 'movement' over time, possibly as part of a notion of 'progress', was a benefit of a quite extraordinary kind. The Hollands seem to have encouraged this development and to have joyfully engaged in the intellectual challenges it presented. Much more difficult is the problem of evaluating the extent of Edinburgh influence on Holland House and of demonstrating its explicit operation. Certainly, there was no precise overlap of ideas. The Hollands were always impressed by the gloomy forebodings of Malthus, for example, which to an extent ran counter to the Scots' optimistic assessments of the future.[69] Similarly, as has been noted earlier, Holland House took no interest whatever in problems connected with political economy, which was the study perhaps most closely associated with ideas about progress and 'movement'. Whereas Adam Smith had become a god to the Reviewers, he was rarely mentioned at Holland House. Therefore, even if the Hollands shared the Scots enthusiasm for 'the movement', they were unwilling or incapable of going too deeply into the economic arguments which gave the general theory substance. It was predictably a dinner table acceptance of new ideas rather than something to be pursued in a study. Holland never spoke on economic issues, and seems to have been content to take his views on trust from John Allen for whom these matters were more vivid. This refusal to absorb the economic background for arguments about movement and progress must be taken as a clear limiting factor on Scots influence. At best, Holland would publicise these views without really understanding them.

Education could be cited as another area in which Holland House found itself out of step with Edinburgh. It was reasonable to expect that, once 'sociological evolutionism' had begun to operate, bringing in its wake a massive increase in wealth and leisure, the necessity for more educational opportunities would have been obvious. The Reviewers on the

69. Add. MSS. 51753, f 195; Holland to Henry Fox, 11 Nov. 1834. See also Add. MSS. 51741, f 9; Holland to Caroline Fox, 7 July 1817.

whole acknowledged this fact. The Hollands did not. Lady Holland was rather against the whole notion of extending education facilities. As she told her son, in 1822: 'Jack [Allen] would have scowled hearing me run off in my usual strain against public education to Staël, ignorant that he had timed his arrival so as to speak upon the general meeting for the advancement of knowledge all the world over.'[70] Her husband's views were less firm. In the Lords, he supported the idea of setting up parish schools in 1807,[71] and spoke in favour of a government-sponsored system of education in 1839,[72] but there was a marked lack of enthusiasm on both occasions.

Holland's real views on the question of education are perhaps represented by a pamphlet he published in 1813 on the proposal to set up a university in Malta. Ominously, it was entitled 'A Dream'. In it, Holland adopted the device of having the matter debated in heaven by a group of eighteenth-century worthies. At the conclusion of the discussion, Holland summed up as follows:

> They manifestly considered it as an incontrovertible axiom of policy, that the improvement of mankind, whether by the extension of knowledge, or the refinement of morals or taste was in itself a good which those intrusted with any portion of human power were, from motives of duty and glory, alike bound to promote. This lamentable simplicity must account for the wildness of their projects.[73]

Such a tepid response from Holland House to the educational potential implied in the Scots notion of improvement is significant in itself, and must again be conceded as a limiting factor on Scots influence in general.

It is clear therefore that, although the extract from the Greville diary quoted earlier in this chapter makes it clear that the Hollands fully subscribed to 'the movement', it was very much on their own terms. Their approach was exactly that of the proprietors of a salon. They accepted general principles

70. Lady Holland to Henry Fox, 20 May 1822; *Elizabeth, Lady Holland to her Son*, p.11.

71. *Parl. Deb.*, vol. XLV 1175; 11 Aug. 1807.

72. Add. MSS. 51757, ff 59-70; Holland to Henry Fox, 5 July 1839.

73. Holland, *A Dream* (London 1813), p.34.

but refused to follow detail. They took on the faith of progress without necessarily comprehending the articles on economics or education. They provided the forum for discussion and allowed others to formulate the terms of the debate. Above all, these ideas were not seen to require an extension of governmental activity which men like Peel, starting from quite different premises, believed essential. All these factors circumscribe their influence but in no way alter the fact of its existence. Holland House remained one of the principal meeting places for London Whigs and Scots Reviewers. The interchange between them was supervised and encouraged by the Hollands. The Foxite core of the party was thereby immeasurably enriched.

In one crucial area, however, the theories articulated by the Edinburgh Reviewers correlated exactly with those held at Holland House. It is likely that the Review was merely expressing prejudices already held in the Fox family, but by that very expression it gave definition to them. The area in question was that of literary criticism. At first sight, this might appear of relatively trivial concern when compared to the political role of the Hollands, but in fact literature and politics were closely related. The intellectual challenge of the French Revolution had been made over such a wide compass that literature too was brought within its scope. After 1789, to belong to a literary movement was a political act. To write prose or poetry was likewise to raise a political standard. It is not unfair to claim therefore that, because the Hollands closely followed the *Edinburgh*'s literary preferences, they were also likely to subscribe to its other prejudices, since literature could no longer be considered as something standing apart from other areas of enquiry. An exploration of this correlation in the pages of the *Edinburgh* is therefore well worth undertaking.

Above all, the *Edinburgh* loathed the poetry of the Lake School. Wordsworth, Coleridge and Southey were pursued through its articles with unyielding ferocity. However, its motives were complex. Jeffrey read the work of all these men with great pleasure in private, and yet encouraged its demolition in public articles. The explanation lies in the overlap between politics and literature referred to above. Judged simply as a literary production, Lake School poetry, as Jeffrey freely admitted, showed unmistakable talent. Its implications in politics, however, were damnable. As a result, it should be praised in private and condemned in public. The Hollands were even more severe. They saw no merit in it in either context. For them, Dryden, Swift and Pope remained unrivalled. Even so, they fully agreed with the three-pronged attack levelled by the Reviewers against the Lake poets. On each count, the offence was political in nature.

The first charge concerned subject matter and idiom. The Whig Reviewers could not allow that shepherds and cottagers were proper subjects for the poet, unless, as in the work of Burns, they were presented in their own idiom and context. By contrast, the Lake School endowed such people with the thoughts that properly pertained only to other social groups. The danger was obvious. Quite simply, in the post-1789 world, to endow a rustic with philosophic ideas undermined the arguments on which he was denied a vote. The preservation of the idioms peculiar to each order in society was of crucial political importance. In reviewing Southey's *Thalaba*, Jeffrey made the point well:

> Now the different classes of society have each of them a distinct character, as well as a separate idiom; and the names of the various passions to which they are subject respectively, have a signification that varies essentially, according to the condition of the persons to whom they are applied ... The question, therefore, comes simply to be – which of them is the most proper object for poetical imitation? It is needless for us to answer a question, which the practice of the world has long ago decided irrevocably. The poor and vulgar may interest us, in poetry, by their situation; but never ... by any sentiments that are peculiar to their condition, and still less by any language that is characteristic of it.[74]

This is an authentic Whig voice. 'Improvement' there would be as the laws of progress took hold, but, until that time, literature must not flatter the democracy.

Associated with this point was the preference that the Lake

74. *Edinburgh Review*, i 63.

Poets seemed to give to individual emotions. According to the Reviewers, literature was a function of that rational approach to society which alone guaranteed ordered advances. To give equal weight to instinct and emotion therefore was to attack one of 'the numberless restrictions important to the well-being of our species'.[75] In particular, to give importance to such feelings in unenfranchised people compounded the felony described above. Sydney Smith asserted that 'when a human being believes that his internal feelings are the monitions of God, and that these monitions must govern his conduct ... it is impossible to say to what a pitch of extravagance mankind may not be carried, under the influence of such dangerous doctrines'.[76] According to the Whigs, rational argument was only possible with the leisure and education that came with property-holding. It was the sole qualification for a voice in politics. To elevate instinct and emotion to the same level was therefore again fraught with danger.

Worst of all, the Lake Poets seemed to be profoundly unimpressed with the whole idea of 'movement' and progress. Instead of welcoming industrialisation and the possibilities it raised, they were intent on turning their backs on the whole process. It was a childish or immature refusal to accept and profit by change. The fact that, in politics, these men started as Radicals and ended as Tories came as no surprise to the Whigs. They were simply changing from one form of lunacy to another. By 'a close contact with the general mass of intelligence',[77] they would have avoided these errors. As Jeffrey observed:

> A splenetic and idle discontent with the existing institutions of society seems to be at the bottom of all their serious and peculiar sentiments. Instead of contemplating the wonders and the pleasures which civilization has created for mankind, they are perpetually brooding over the disorders by which its progress has been attended.[78]

There was a simple analogy to be made between Lake Poets

75. ibid., ii 172.
76. ibid., ii 356.
77. J. Greig, *Francis Jeffrey of the Edinburgh Review*, p.225.
78. *Edinburgh Review*, i 71.

5. Lord Holland by Sir Edwin Landseer

6. Samuel Rogers by Landseer

objecting to industrialisation and Tory peers refusing to face the political challenges that arose directly out of that process. As a result, the Reviewers were inclined to praise Wordsworth and Coleridge in private and to damn them in public.

In all these opinions, the Fox family followed the Reviewers closely. In Fox's long correspondence with his nephew, the masters of poetry, apart from Classical authors, are held to be Tasso, Ariosto, Dryden and Pope. When Wordsworth presented Fox with a copy of *Lyrical Ballads*, he was met with the rather chilling remark: 'I am very glad to see you, Mr Wordsworth, though I am not of your faction.'[79] Similarly Rousseau, whom Jeffrey identified as one of the major influences on Lake Poetry,[80] was always a very poor third, in Fox's mind, to Voltaire and Montesquieu. He admitted on one occasion that he had begun to read *Du Contrat Social*, but that he had had to give it up because he found it 'so extravagant'.[81] In semi-retirement, after his secession from Parliament, in 1797, he returned with obvious pleasure to the editing of the Greek poet Lycophron.

Consistent with their view that the nineteenth century represented only a decline in letters, the proprietors of Holland House were only too happy to fall in with their uncle's tuition in this area, as in so many others. John Allen encouraged Jeffrey 'to sharpen his weapons for Southey'.[82] Lady Holland, after giving dinner to Wordsworth in April 1831, found him unimpressive and dull. She felt it absurd that ink should be wasted on a 'man who wrote about caps and pinafores and that sort of thing'.[83] In this remark, she is simply making the same kind of criticism about the democratic subject matter of Wordsworth's work that Jeffrey developed at greater length in the pages of the Review itself. After reading Rousseau's *Confessions*, she felt only 'disgust': 'One abhors the man; not even the magic of the style covers the atrocity of his mind. Naturally suspicious & selfish, he

79. A. Dyce, *Reminiscences and Table Talk of Samuel Rogers* (Edinburgh 1903), p.55.
80. *Edinburgh Review*, i 63.
81. Lord J. Russell, *The Life and Times of Charles James Fox*, ii 360.
82. Add. MSS. 52172, f 26; Allen to Lady Holland, 1 Aug. 1810.
83. *The Chronicles of Holland House*, p.135.

confirmed the latter propensity by thinking & writing eternally of self, self.'[84] Again, such a comment, less well-turned than those that came from the pens of the Reviewers, exactly matches their views. The investigation of emotion had no place in literature, particularly when such an investigation took place within a 'democratic' milieu.

In his *Memoirs*, Holland himself devoted space to a retrospective assessment of the Lake Poets. He remained unimpressed. They were 'a knot of young enthusiasts', who 'were at their outset, scarcely less extravagant in their principles, and much more so in their projects, than the materialists of Godwin's school, though they had the good fortune to escape all legal persecution'. Their works 'all inculcating the wildest maxims of German metaphysics, and all combating the principles upon which the institutions of property as well as the distribution of political power, are founded in society', were distinguished by 'a sickly sentimentality and real immorality'.[85] It is not hard to align these words with the criticisms levelled by Jeffrey and his friends. Political considerations as well as personal preference made Holland House blind to the appeal of Wordsworth and his kind. In Holland's view, the Augustans had never been superseded. When Byron died, he believed that the greatest living poet was Crabbe.

To a critical mind, this insensitivity to Lake poetry could be associated with the other areas in which the Hollands resembled eighteenth-century whales stranded on nineteenth century beaches. Their Foxite politics rested on the events of the 1780s and 1790s. Just as their deism found the reformation of manners of the 1830s hard to understand, so they continued to praise the Augustans rather than the Romantics. There is some truth in this description. Particularly after 1832, the Hollands complained loudly that there was unfamiliarity about many aspects of life. The assumptions on which people acted had changed dramatically. Intelligent young men

84. Lady Holland to Henry Fox, 19 May 1823; *Elizabeth, Lady Holland to her Son*, p.23.

85. Holland, *Further Memoirs of the Whig Party*, pp. 383-4.

insisted on interesting themselves in subjects which, to a late eighteenth-century mind, were either irrelevant or boring or both. Stanley's Anglicanism was puzzling, Althorp's deep piety almost funny. No doubt therefore, their unswerving belief that literature was declining in quality in the nineteenth century owes something to the depths of the intellectual roots they had put down in the preceding century. The invocation of Fox's name conjured up a view of literature as well as of politics. The disapproval of a popular subject matter and idiom in literature could be accounted for in this way.

All the same, the Hollands would not have argued in these terms. As they saw it, their objections to Lake poetry were very contemporary. It was Wordsworth's insistence on the values of a non-industrial world that was really anachronistic. Whereas the Hollands subscribed to 'the movement', if in a salonard and undetailed way, the Lake poets seemed to regret its very existence. Their preference for the Augustans was not part of a generally backward-looking stance, but simply the expression of an aesthetic judgment. If the whole effort of Holland House was to keep abreast of everything new, the Lake poets were determined to ignore anything that reflected on contemporary trends. Their defence in literature of 'the movement', 'the progress of improvement' in Greville's definition, was vigorously undertaken for good reasons. As Scots ideas flowed into Holland House, it reinvigorated and, in a sense, made contemporary, much of what Fox had laid down as a proper view of politics. Everything seemed to lead to the same conclusions. The Hollands' involvement with the literary world therefore brought great profit. As guardians of the Foxite temple, they had been able to give the creed a new justification. Brougham, Jeffrey and the other Scots dined well at Holland House, but they also added a new dimension to the politics of their host and hostess.

8

The Hollands and Europe, 1789-1830

Foreign travel and foreign company probably gave the Hollands more pleasure than any other form of activity. As linquists and travellers, they built up a foreign acquaintance which it would have been hard to equal in the England of the early nineteenth century. Much of the period 1791-1809 was spent abroad. After the extensive tour of France, Italy, Germany, Austria and Denmark between 1791 and 1796,[1] there was a further excursion to Germany in 1800.[2] Between 1802 and 1805 and again in 1808-9, the Hollands travelled in Spain and Portugal, and in the process developed such an intense interest in the politics of the Iberian peninsula that it became one of Holland House's special subjects. After 1810, illness circumscribed their travelling opportunities, but regular visits to Paris were undertaken almost up to the moment of Holland's death. The conclusion to be drawn from these facts is obvious. While the Foxite tradition rooted them firmly in English politics, it was developed by being placed in a European context. Holland found it almost impossible to discuss a point in English politics without relating it to a European parallel. To understand Holland House society is to put proper emphasis on the closeness of this relationship. At dinner, among English politicians and Scots Reviewers, would be the ambassador, the refugee, the traveller and the *gens du monde*.[3]

1. Holland, *Memoirs of the Whig Party during my Time*, pp. 3 and 46.
2. Add. MSS. 51735, f 174; Holland to Caroline Fox, 1 July 1800.
3. The apotheosis of this aspect of Holland House entertainment was perhaps

Although Fox never had the expertise which his nephew developed in European affairs, in this area, as in almost all others, he had established ground rules. In his view, the experience of the French Revolution created a struggle between light and darkness in Europe of a manichaean intensity. On one side were the French who, in spite of excess and mismanagement, represented what Fox chose to call 'liberty'. On the other, the Coalitions of monarchs attacking France represented the opponents of 'liberty'. There was no middle ground. A clear choice had to be made between these alternatives. By allowing England to join the first Coalition, Pitt involved all Englishmen in such a choice. Further, unlike earlier eighteenth-century wars, victory and defeat became absolutes. If the Coalition kings and emperors crushed France, authoritarian systems of government would be established from London to Moscow. If the French prevailed, some variation on the theme of 'liberty' might predominate over the same area. It was a stark reading of events. By it, the Fox family had to support France, bewailing more often than not the intemperance and violence of Frenchmen.[4]

The major conclusion to be derived from this teaching was that all authoritarianism was bad and all constitutionalism was good. Princes under no restraints but God and their own conscience inevitably became ogres. Almost all of them developed, for example 'a love of military glory which is a fine word for a love of cutting people's throats'.[5] Assassination in these circumstances became almost a civic duty. Reflecting on the murder of Paul I of Russia, Holland wrote: 'There is no mitigation of the excesses of despotism; violence alone can remove them. Those, therefore, who are in contact with such disorders must, both in principle and practice, be more familiarised with forcible remedies, and more pardonable in supplying them, than persons who never have to deal with

---

reached in July 1837, when the Hollands gave dinner to the ambassadors of Russia, Prussia, Austria, France, Sardinia and Portugal at the same table. See *The Chronicles of Holland House*, p.238.

4. This view marks a major revision of Whig attitudes to France. Before 1789, the France of Louis XIV and his successors had been held up as the major threat to England and her liberties.

5. Add. MSS. 51757, f 227; Holland to Henry Fox, 30 June 1840.

symptoms so dangerous.'[6] The one enduring consequence of the French Revolution was, as Holland told his sister, that no people need ever again tolerate the burden of despotism against their wishes:

> The Prussians say, that it is a good produced by the horrors of the French revolution that people now know to what revolutions may lead – be it so, & this is a good produced by this horrible & abominable war, that people now know that if they have a mind to change their governments, it is not foreign force & combined Monarchs that can prevent them.[7]

The Hollands' experience of the behaviour of English kings naturally complemented this view.

A loathing of kings was so inbred in Holland's personality that it frequently led to naive or unbalanced judgments. His *Foreign Reminiscences*, which were published in 1851, were greeted with a unanimous chorus of abuse. All its critics made the same point. The whole book was vitiated by what the *Quarterly Review* called 'a greedy appetite for all the profligate stories that private malice could invent, and Jacobin rage propagate, against every class of royalty. All Kings and Princes are knaves or idiots – all Queens and Princesses shameless prostitutes – one sex fit only for Bedlam or Newgate, the other for Bridewell or the Magdalen.'[8] Lord Aberdeen, with more resignation, simply noted that 'a senseless hostility to all legitimate Kings and Queens, and a ludicrous exaltation of "that great prince" Bonaparte might have been expected.'[9] Even the *Edinburgh Review* had to admit that the criticism was in large measure just.[10] *The Times* dismissed the book as 'a farrago of idle gossip and misstatement which Henry Edward Lord Holland has not thought it unbecoming the son of his father to publish'.[11]

In mitigation, it might be suggested that Holland's basic

6. Holland, *Foreign Reminiscences*, p.181.
7. Add. MSS. 51735, f 187; Holland to Caroline Fox, 6 Aug. 1800.
8. *The Quarterly Review*, vol. 88, p.492. See also *Blackwood's Magazine*, vol. 69.
9. Aberdeen to Croker, 21 Feb. 1851; *The Correspondence and Diaries of J.W. Croker*, iii 225.
10. *Edinburgh Review*, vol. 93, pp. 137 seq.
11. *The Times*, 27 Jan. 1851.

fault was less on unreasoning vindictiveness than undue credulity for stories retailed by his friends. There is no doubt, for example, that Talleyrand's friendship with Holland was a powerful influence on the book. The story of Axel Fersen being surprised in Marie Antoinette's bedroom when Versailles was attacked in October 1789 came directly from him, for example. Further, Holland's comments on Charles IV and Marie Luisa of Spain, both of whom he had met, were derived from his numerous Spanish connections. Even so, the general criticism stands. The Fox family was blinkered in its appreciation of kings and Holland was no exception to the rule. The *Foreign Reminiscences* had a didactic purpose in illustrating the dangers of authoritarianism. As such, they formed a natural corollary to the two volumes of memoirs on English politics. The issues at stake in England and on the Continent were the same.

It followed from all this that every regime could be safely placed on one side or the other in the battle between despotic darkness and constitutional light. In addition, further points of discrimination could be made. Among the ranks of the evil, some were more evil than others, and equally, among the virtuous, some were better than others. In fact, there was a quite clear spectrum in Holland's mind on which all countries and all governments could be given a place. The object of policy therefore became to decide which power represented the greatest good in any situation, and then to support it to the hilt. Even if a dispute largely concerned two criminal powers, it was important in Holland's view to support the least felonious. Very reasonably, Holland was frequently accused of subordinating the narrow self-interest of England to larger ideological ends. Holland's reply would have been that, since England was unavoidably a part of Europe after 1789, the triumph of constitutionalism over the whole Continent was itself a point of self-interest. As part of that process, Holland found the concept of a spectrum of powers between the very good and the diabolical to be invaluable.

Leaving aside France and Spain,[12] about which the Hollands entertained such intimate and complex views that

---

12. See below, Chapters Nine and Ten.

they deserve detailed attention, the country which most consistently exemplified the virtues of constitutionalism was the United States. The Whig party colours of buff and blue had been taken from Washington's uniform in the War of Independence, and the Fox family admired without reservation the republican freshness of the New World. When Congress, in 1825, paid tribute to the work of his old friend Lafayette in cementing Franco-American relations, Holland noted with evident pleasure that 'they prove, as indeed what does not? the superior taste eloquence & grandeur of popular institutions when compared with the pomp and ceremony & senseless adulation of Absolute Monarchies. What miserable coxcombs & pedants are Lewis 18 or Lewis 14 in comparison to Mr Clay! The whole scene was worthy of Greece or Rome & had made a great sensation.'[13] The Americans were seen as the most successful of the Whigs' protégés who were to be treated with friendly condescension. Holland reflected with family pride on 'the predilection it is so gratifying to think the Americans have for our name', and hoped that the passing of time would 'make them better Foxites than ever'.[14] Lady Holland was prepared to overlook the fact that the wife of the American ambassador spoke English so oddly that 'she is often herself unintelligible'.[15]

The crucial point about America was that it was the one country where constitutional practices seemed absolutely secure. The same could not be maintained, in Holland's view, about any European country including England. The more the growing power of 'the enlightened government of the United States'[16] had influence in Europe therefore, the more likely it was that liberalism would survive. America in fact was an obvious counterweight to the autocratic empires of eastern Europe. As England and America tried to re-establish links after the trauma of the War of Independence, no one was more anxious than the Hollands to promote reconciliation. The major point of contention after 1793 was the extent to which

13. Add. MSS. 51749, f 72; Holland to Henry Fox, c 14 Feb. 1825.
14. Holland to H.S. Fox, 28 Feb. 1838; Bodleian MSS. Eng. Lett. c 234, f 104.
15. Lady Holland to Henry Fox, 27 Dec. 1836; *Elizabeth, Lady Holland to her Son*, p.164.

England could stop and search America's neutral shipping as part of its war effort against France. Holland consistently took the view, stated as early as 1795,[17] that to enrage American opinion on this issue was to put tactics before strategy, for if England and America were estranged, the liberal cause in Europe was thereby diminished. Only close cooperation between constitutional powers could defeat autocracy in Europe.

In 1807, Holland was delighted to find himself appointed one of the Commissioners to settle with Monroe and Pinckney the question of neutral shipping rights. His colleague, Lord Auckland, paid tribute to his earnestness: 'We are honorably disposed to remove all real causes of complaint & to promote every practical measure of National friendship & Conciliation. You have indeed persuaded Messieurs Monroe & Pinckney to see the Matter in this just point of view; & nothing more can be desired.'[18] When the negotiations foundered, due largely in Holland's view to Canning's duplicity, he regarded it ever after as one of the greatest disappointments of his political life.[19] The War of 1812 between England and America might well have been avoided. Its occurrence jeopardised Wellington's efforts in Spain, and served to demonstrate how a breach with America prejudiced the success of liberal movements in Europe generally.[20] Too much could be built on Anglo-American understanding to risk its disruption in the pursuit of narrow objectives.

Still excluding France and Spain from consideration, the only other country which suggested a hopeful outcome of the war between autocratic darkness and constitutional light was Portugal. For most of their political career, the Hollands saw Portuguese affairs as a corollary of events in Spain, and they were kept well-informed by Portuguese liberals like Palmella, the future ambassador and prime minister. In the long civil war between the liberal Queen Maria and her autocratic

16. *Parl. Deb.*, 14 July 1807; vol. XLV 806-7.
17. Add. MSS. 51733, f 30; Holland to Caroline Fox, 18 July 1795.
18. Add. MSS. 51532, f 31; Auckland to Holland, 7 Sept. (1806).
19. ibid., f 80; ibid., 3 April 1807.
20. *Parl Deb.*, 28 Feb. 1812; vol. LVII 1057-1066.

uncle, Don Miguel, Holland actively supported his friends.[21]
In 1826, he went as far as to urge British intervention in
Portugal on the liberal side, even if this action involved
fighting the Spain of Ferdinand VII and the France of Charles
X. His speech on that occasion illustrates the important point
that, in discussing any particular country, Holland never lost
sight of the war in Europe as a whole between liberalism and
autocracy. The Portuguese battle was a specific example of a
general theme: 'If we did enter into a war with Spain, it would
not be with a wretched, feeble and faithless monarch, but with
a fanatic and tyranical faction, not only militant in Spain but
dominant elsewhere – powerful, not merely from its
uncontrolled sway in that country, but from its extensive
influence all over the continent of Europe.[22] In supporting
Portuguese liberals, Holland was fighting a European-wide
system, which he termed 'the Ultra Metternich & Apostolick
faction'.[23]

It is already clear from such remarks that Holland House
associated liberal promise with those states which bordered
the Atlantic. England, Portugal, North and South America,
and, with luck, Spain and France together represented an
alternative to the autocratic empires of the east. The Rhine
became a veritable Styx, on the far side of which shadowy
figures moved about in an unrelieved gloom. Italy might be
disputed ground, but nothing could be done for Poland. From
an early date, the emphasis in Holland's thinking was put on
the building up of an association of liberal states which in
many ways prefigured Palmerston's Quadruple Alliance of
1834.[24] Within such a context, sea power might assist liberal
efforts, and the wealth generated by trade between the
Americas and Europe might guarantee the prosperity of
liberal states. Such a view fitted neatly the cultural preferences
of the Hollands themselves. These countries covered the area
they knew well from personal experience, and from which they
drew most of their foreign friends.

21. Add. MSS. 51717, f 85-6; Comte de Flahault to Holland, 16 May 1823.
22. *Parl. Deb.*, 12 Dec. 1826; vol. XLIII 343-7.
23. Add. MSS. 51750, f 135; Holland to Henry Fox, 31 July 1827.
24. Involving France, Britain, Spain and Portugal.

In a spiritual sense therefore, enemy territory for the Hollands began on the Franco-German border. Germany was in fact 'that detested country'.[25] The Hollands were wholly unsympathetic to the culture and language of the German states and they found their governing groups unsophisticated and unenlightened.[26] Germans, and particularly Humboldt, appeared at Holland House functions from time to time, but never seem to have enjoyed the favour reserved for Frenchmen, Spaniards and Italians. Within this blanket disapproval of all things German, however, some distinctions could be drawn. Prussia, for example, was thought to be marginally preferable to the other principalities because her people had shown some response to French ideas after 1789,[27] and because her policies were too often dictated by the bullying pressures exerted by Russia and Austria.[28] On this line of defence, certain of the Rhineland states could also make pleas for sympathetic attention. Even so, these arguments only mitigated criminal attitudes. The attitudes themselves remained intact as far as Holland House could see. Prussia's continued membership of the repressive Holy Alliance was ultimately inexcusable.

In this bleak German world, Austria stood out as the source of all evil. Holland had visited the Hapsburg Empire only once, in the spring of 1796, and what he saw made him disinclined to return. Metternich dined at Holland House in 1814, but his host described him as 'a lively clever man, with a most false expression of Countenance'.[29] About the Emperor Francis II, Holland was even more uncomplimentary. As the man who imprisoned Lafayette after his flight from France, Francis was unlikely to endear himself to the Hollands, and, when they met him on a visit to London, their worst fears were confirmed. They dismissed him with the remark that 'his manners ... seemed such as might have been expected from a

25. Lady Holland to Henry Fox, 8 Jan. 1839; *Elizabeth, Lady Holland to her Son*, p.171.

26. Add. MSS. 51682, f 5; Holland to Lansdowne, 1 Sept. 1793.

27. Holland, *Foreign Reminiscences*, p.47.

28. Fox to Holland, 7 Nov. 1805; *The Memorials and Correspondence of C.J. Fox*, iv 121.

29. Add. MSS. 52172, f 76; Holland to Allen, 24 June 1814.

German who had studied French vivacity in the fashionable novel of the day'.[30] In March 1824, the Austrian government paid Holland the indirect compliment of naming him among a group of European radicals who were never to be allowed into Hapsburg territory. With a nice sense of propriety, Princess Lieven thought that 'they might at least have done him the honour of naming him in a separate document'.[31] Such a point of courtesy would hardly have impressed the Hollands. The Austrian government's distrust of them was returned in full measure.

Austria's greatest crime rested in its domination of the Italian peninsula. The Hollands knew Italy well. Both had spent the years 1792-5 as residents in various Italian cities, and their culture and language were immediately acceptable. In 1814-15, they made one further visit to evaluate Napoleon's impact in the peninsula. As usual, however, the traffic was not all one way. The first liberal refugee, Serafino Buonaiuti, arrived in 1800, and was immediately incorporated into Holland House as tutor in Italian to the Holland children. Giuseppe Binda arrived soon after. In September, 1816, Ugo Foscolo, the Professor of Eloquence from Pavia and a firm Bonapartist, joined the list of exiled Italians who looked to Holland House for patronage and protection.[32] As tutors and lecturers,[33] the Italians became a continual reminder of the liberal opportunities that had been lost from Sardinia to Naples. Holland's personal awareness of the Italian situation made it likely that he would be the English politician most anxious to keep Austrian misdemeanours in the public eye.

The views of Holland House were forthright enough. The Napoleonic impact on Italy had been almost entirely beneficial. Writing from Florence in 1814, Holland reported that:

30. Holland, *Foreign Reminiscences*, p.163.
31. Princess Lieven to Grey, 3 Sept. 1824; *The Correspondence of Princess Lieven and Earl Grey*, i 2.
32. E.R. Vincent, *Ugo Foscolo*, p.31.
33. In 1823, Holland organised a highly successful series of lectures by Foscolo on Italian literature at a subscription rate of five guineas for the series.

It is difficult to imagine such power founded entirely on military superiority producing less evil than his did on the provinces subjected by his troops. In this country that is *Italy* not Tuscany, I believe his contribution has done more good than harm, & the late change is perhaps for the worse than the better. It is certainly unpopular with the active part of the Community, all of whom wish for independence & most of whom if they are to have a Master prefer Bonaparte to any other & France very much to Germany.[34]

Lady Holland's comments on Rome in the same year echo these sentiments. Careers which had been thrown open to talent and ability were now closed again by corruption. Torture had been reintroduced. The convents and monasteries were again being filled by 'the credulous'.[35] The simplicity of Napoleonic law codes had been overthrown in favour of cumbersome Church law. Only the Grand Duke of Tuscany, 'a great Napoleonist', had managed to salvage something of the French legacy, but even he had closed all the literary clubs in Florence.[36] All movement towards regular forms of government, even constitutionalism, had been rolled back with the withdrawal of the French in order to restore the old corruption and superstition.

Holland's concern for Italy led him to take one of the oddest steps of his career. In April 1815, he and Allen sketched out proposals for a new constitution for Naples, and un-invited, sent them to Joachim Murat, whom the Allies had left in charge of that kingdom. Binda, who was acting as the courier, was stopped by the Austrians in Lucca, only narrowly escaped with his life, and saw the Holland proposals being redirected to Vienna.[37] Such an attempt to meddle in an area of agreed Austrian influence seriously embarrassed relations between London and Vienna at a very sensitive time. Even some of Holland's political allies were scandalised by this

34. Add. MSS. 51740, f 24; Holland to Caroline Fox, 10 Nov. 1814.
35. Lady Holland to J. Wishaw, 17 Dec. 1814; *The Pope of Holland House*, pp. 75-80. See also Add. MSS. 51740, f 29; Holland to Caroline Fox, 21 Nov. 1814.
36. Add. MSS. 51745, f 228; Lady Holland to Caroline Fox, 3 Nov. 1814.
37. Lord Burghersh to Lord W. Bentinck, 20 April 1815; *The Correspondence of Lord Burghersh*, pp. 152-3.

'scrawling out [of] Italian constitutions'.[38] Holland was simply too prominent an English politician for his actions not to reflect on his country's policies as a whole. The whole venture was misguided, and it gave Holland's critics the first evidence for the view that Holland House was too prepared to run a foreign policy independent of that pursued by the elected British government. Palmerston's later difficulties with Holland House are here clearly foreshadowed.

This 'Sketch of a Constitution for the Kingdom of Naples', apart from the repercussions it started, is also worthy of a more detailed study in itself. It gives a clear indication of the type of system that Holland would have liked to see developing all over Europe, and therefore some idea of what he took to be the proper constitutional expression of 'liberty'. He begins with a discussion of the advantages of limited monarchy over any arbitrary system, and insists that constitutional development must come slowly because such a thing is the product of 'the growth of time, not the invention of ingenuity'. He goes on to explain the necessity of two-chamber government, a franchise based on the holding of property and freedom of speech. The principle of no taxation without representation must be a firm assumption in government. As in his suggestions for a Spanish constitution written a few years earlier, there are also helpful hints on how to conduct debates and preserve parliamentary forms. If many of these points suggest an encomium of English practices, that would not be accidental. Holland consistently saw the English system as something that all Europeans should adopt as the starting point for their constitutional thinking. Even the depredations of George III had not impaired its essential usefulness. In the *Sketch*, the evolutionary nature of the English system is favourably compared to the erratic experimentation of the French.[39]

Predictably, the liberal risings of 1821 in Naples, Milan and other Italian cities excited Holland's keenest sympathy. In the

38. T. Grenville to Lord Grenville, 3 July 1815; Hist. MSS. Comm. 30 *Fortescue* X, p.404.

39. Holland, *Sketch of a Constitution for the Kingdom of Naples suggested in 1815 to the Duca di Gallo by the late Lord Holland* (London 1848).

Lords, he demanded that the English government should at
least dissociate itself from the actions of 'the armed despots of
Troppau',[40] and express its firm disapproval 'of any war with
any nation founded on the principles of such interference in its
internal concerns'.[40] He went on to air the hope that 'the
power of tyrany, however formidable at the outset, cannot
long resist the united attacks of liberty and knowledge'.[41]
When the revolts were suppressed by Austrian armies,
Holland's language became more intemperate: 'We are all
very very anxious about Naples & if the Emperors go on as
they do I shall not only call them murderers but express my
sincere hopes of seeing them murdered.'[42] The 'anti-liberty
conspiracy' in Italy was 'quite sufficient to drive one to
Jacobinism'.[43] The events of 1821 effectively extinguished the
possibility that the Napoleonic experience might have drawn
Italy towards the liberal west. Under Austrian supervision,
the peninsula was returned to darkness. The discomfort of
Holland and his Italian friends was the proof of Austrian
power.

Beyond the German world, in an even lower circle of Hell,
was Russia. Voltaire's nickname of 'la Oursie' for that country
was one that the Hollands appropriated for their own use.[44]
The expansion of Russia in their lifetime was synonymous
with the spread of bearlike insensitivity and barbarism. As
Russian armies moved westwards into Europe after the failure
of Napoleon's 1812 adventure, the Hollands followed their
progress with mixed feelings. However complex were their
views about Bonaparte, they could not welcome his defeat if,
by that event, the controlling power in Europe became Russia.
The partitioning of Poland had appalled the Fox family,[45] and
it seemed to them that Russia's backing for the principles of
the Holy Alliance confirmed their fears for the future of

40. *Parl. Deb.*, 23 Jan. 1821; vol. LXXXI 17-23.

41. ibid., 19 Feb. 1821; ibid., 771-85.

42. Add. MSS. 51748, f 135; Holland to Henry Fox, 27 Feb. 1821.

43. ibid., f 137; Henry Fox to Holland, 1821.

44. Lady Holland to Henry Fox, 21 Nov. 1821; *Elizabeth, Lady Holland to her Son*,
p.7.

45. Add. MSS. 51731, f 46-7; Holland to Caroline Fox, 18 July 1791. See also Add.
MSS. 51731, f 125; ibid., 17 June 1793.

central and eastern Europe. Neither of them would have been surprised by the Russian intervention in Hungary in 1849. While most of their contemporaries were therefore obsessed with the ambitions of the traditional enemy, France, the Hollands were more concerned by the growth of Russia. In their lifetime, the Czars had swallowed up Poland, the Caucasus and the Crimea. The allied victories over Napoleon after 1812 could not be welcomed as each one brought the Russians further west.[46]

Under the ultimate patronage of Russia, the Holy Alliance could only have one purpose:

> It was, forsooth, an alliance of the conservation of the monarchical principle. And what was the monarchical principle? The right of one man to govern millions. It was legitimacy, not in the true sense of that word, but the establishment of military power in every country where hereditary princes were established, for their support; even after, by their misgovernment they should have forfeited their hereditary right, or the circumstances of the time should have required a change of dynasty.[47]

The historian's attempt to differentiate between liberal and illiberal elements in the policies of Catherine the Great, Paul I and Alexander I would have appeared ridiculous to the Hollands. In their view, all the rulers of Russia demonstrated the vices of unrestrained authority in full measure. The Emperor Paul was only to be distinguished by the fact that he was mad as well as vicious. Russia had led coalitions against Bonaparte, and, after 1815, seemed to have arrogated to itself the right to intervene in European affairs. The Hollands made no assessment of Alexander's or Catharine's attempts at

46. Lady Holland, who understandably had not been invited to join the Ladies Committee which commissioned Westmacott's statue of Achilles by way of celebrating the Allies victory over Bonaparte, took pleasure in retailing the following anecdote (Lady Holland to Henry Fox, 26 Jan. 1822; *Lady Holland to her Son*, p.8): 'A difficulty had arisen; & the artist had submitted to the female subscribers whether this immense colossal figure should preserve its antique nudity or be garnished with a fig leaf. It was carried for the leaf by a majority ... the names of the *minority* have not transpired.'

47. *Parl. Deb.*, 3 Feb. 1824; vol. LXXXVII 39.

reform. Rather, their black-and-white vision of European affairs precluded such discrimination.

Just as Holland's intemperance could embarrass Anglo-Austrian relations over the Binda affair, so he was quite capable of damaging Anglo-Russian arrangements single-handed. In February 1821, Holland was so swept away by his denunciation of Russian and Austrian policies that he openly declared that Alexander I had connived at the murder of his father.[48] The outcry produced by this remark was long and vigorous. Princess Lieven, the wife of the Russian ambassador in London, was not seen again at Holland House for eight years. In public, Holland was forced to issue a formal apology. In private, he was completely unrepentant. When a career diplomat protested at Holland's behaviour,[49] a sharp answer was returned:

> I can give you no explanation of my speech about Alexander ... Whether Alexander knew of Paul's murder or not, I think he has done much worse things lately and I can say nothing about him that will please Madame de Lieven ... who is a sensible woman and *not* a Russian, [and] knows very well that the Czar and his subjects where they mix with Europeans ne faut que jouer la comédie and that even the anger of being accused of murder is as much an affectation of sentiment, to which they are utterly strangers, as the religious horror or devotion of Talma in Oedipe or Hyppolytus. The historical fact is that Alexander *did* know of the intention of breaking in to his father's bedroom, and I can hardly suppose him so ignorant of the country he governs as not to have known the necessary consequences.[50]

In Holland's view, Alexander's best defence lay in the claim that he was simply abiding by the social habits of a barbarous country. His death was initially greeted with joy at Holland House, in that it allowed his brother Constantine's liberal reputation to be put to the test.[51]

Such opinions gave substance to the Hollands' view that a

48. Creevey to Miss Ord, 24 Feb. 1821; *The Creevey Letters*, ii 15.

49. Lord W. Russell to Holland, 1821; *The Chronicles of Holland House*, p.11.

50. Holland to Lord W. Russell, July 1821; *Lord William Russell and his Wife*, pp. 51-4.

51. Add. MSS. 51741, f 237; Holland to Caroline Fox, 22 Dec. 1825.

Holy Alliance of Austria, Prussia and Russia could be nothing but an unholy assault on the constitutional gains that Europe had made since 1789. Charles Fox had initiated the idea that the war between France and the Coalitions had presented all Europe with clear options. The war had come to an end officially in 1815, but Holland refused to believe that anything had really changed. The Alliance was more military than pious in character, and repeatedly showed its willingness to resort to arms. As for the liberal movement it had simply gone underground. The endless 'liberal' uprisings of the 1820s and 1830s gave evidence of its tunnelling operations under nineteenth-century society. For the Fox family, the war that began in 1793 had not ended in 1815. It had simply taken a different form. Similarly, just as Pitt had deliberately taken England into an ideological war, so Castlereagh's association with the Holy Alliance continued the theme. Though less dramatic than comparable battles in Europe, the Whig campaign for constitutionalism in England was believed to have European parallels. The only difference between the situation facing Holland and that which confronted his uncle was that Castlereagh's 'barbarisms have now found their way into solemn leagues as well as tedious harangues'.[52]

In this situation, the scope for the Opposition to modify or reverse Pittite commitments in Europe was limited. The national mood was too much engaged on the other side. All that Holland could do was to hope that even a Pittite government would ultimately dissociate itself from the policies of autocratic emperors: 'Surely, surely we do not mean to adopt the spirit of that mad declaration from Vienna? Can we answer the excellent papers printed in France? & will neither the publick debt persuade John Bull, nor his daughter & grandchild the Emperor of Austria to listen for once to the dictates of common sense & the feelings of humanity.'[53] He was forced to oppose the terms of the peace treaties of 1816 because they reimposed the Bourbon dynasty on France, and because 'they sanctioned the principle of guaranteeing

52. Add. MSS. 51748, f 53; Holland to Henry Fox, 26 Nov. 1818.
53. Add. MSS. 51740, f 112; Holland to Caroline Fox, 28 April 1815.

hereditary monarchies against the people, for whom and from whom they should alone derive their authority'.[54] For some years after 1815, Holland's appearances in the House of Lords were almost always connected with this probing of the extent to which English foreign policies were still associated with those of the Allies of 1815. On this point, Holland pursued Castlereagh and Liverpool with terrier-like persistence.[55]

On a more personal level, Holland House tried hard to help any individuals whom they saw as victims of autocratic persecution. In 1816, they launched an unsuccessful campaign in favour of Sieyès being allowed into England.[56] A year later, on a visit to Brussels, the Hollands were appalled by the pressure being brought to bear on the Dutch government to expel French refugees from Bourbon revenge: 'Nothing can be meaner or more cruel than the vexatious persecution of the French exiles by the Allied powers & I fear England & Wellington in particular ... It is curious that we who owe our Revolution & dynasty to the firmness of the Dutch in maintaining an asylum for the Whiggs in spite of Lewis 14 & Ch. & James 2 should now be forward in forcing them to desert them.'[57] The Aliens Bill of 1818 was looked on by Holland as clear proof that Liverpool had agreed to join the witch-hunt against anti-Bourbon Frenchmen.[58] Even more alarming was the suggestion that British subjects like Sir Robert Wilson could be put at risk in their own country at the behest of the French government. The case led the Duke of Sussex to conclude that 'even in this Country, *once* of Liberty, the House of Lords & Commons may shut up Shop when Castlereagh can ... inforce his Anti-liberal notions imported in a bad Phraseology from the Continent'.[59] The Hollands had never believed that English affairs could be divorced from European events, and, for them, the Holy Alliance menaced English liberties as clearly as it did those of Naples or Poland.

54. Holland, *Further Memoirs of the Whig Party*, pp. 216-17.
55. *Parl. Deb.*, 5 Oct. 1820; vol. LXXX 255-7.
56. Lady Holland to Grey, 2 Feb. 1816; Grey MSS. Box 33.
57. Holland to Grey, 11 July 1817; Grey MSS. Box 34.
58. *Parl. Deb.*, 14 May 1818; vol. LXXIV 652.
59. Add. MSS. 51524, f 106; Sussex to Holland, n.d.

Unfortunate as all this was from a Whig point of view, neither Russia nor the Holy Alliance were candidates for the position of the Anti-Christ. That title was unreservedly given to the Turkish Empire. In the same letters in which Holland castigates the crimes of Russian Czars, he is quite likely to develop these thoughts by wishing them good fortune in their expansion towards Constantinople. Balancing Russia against Turkey in a liberal scale left him with no other option:

> Alexander they say prefers legitimacy to conquest or religion. How far his armies and his people agree with him remains to be seen. In the meanwhile if we keep out of war we have no reason to complain as Englishmen, though both as such & as philosophers rather than Xtians we should I think rejoice, at least, I am sure I should, at any thing that led to the downfall of that cursed Turkish Empire – All the prevalent notions of the danger resulting from Russian preponderance in the Levant Archipelago & Mediterranean I believe to be very erroneous, & relate to a state of things much too remote to give any direction to our present policy.[60]

Missing from this analysis of course was any consideration of trading or strategic interests, but then Holland rarely brought such points into play. The relative, ideological purity of the two powers in conflict occupied his whole attention. The Russians were a terrible people, but the Turks were 'an anti-social race'.[61]

The application of such simple criteria to problems in the eastern Mediterranean once again brought an element of eccentricity to Holland House opinions. Many politicians would have agreed with Holland in his desire to see the Turks driven out of Greece, because it was a 'country from which we have derived no small portion of all those virtues which exult and dignify our nature, and to which we owe all that gives life and animation to our debates'.[62] Philhellenism touched the imagination. It was quite another matter, however, to countenance the disintegration of the Turkish Empire itself. For most Whigs and all Tories, the area involved strategic and commercial considerations of the first importance, not least

60. Add. MSS. 51546, f 144; Holland to Grey, 18 Nov. 1821.
61. *Parl. Deb.*, 29 Jan. 1828; vol. XCV 11-24.
62. ibid., 23.

those which guaranteed the overland route to India. To many of them Holland's complacency at the prospect of a Russian presence in Constantinople was simply incredible. Holland, in turn, attempted to justify his position by narrowing the debate to a discussion of the relative liberalism of the powers involved. For many of his contemporaries, this was a ludicrous simplification of the problem. Holland remained unrepentant, however: 'I hope our poverty will prevent our meddling to save the Turks – let 'em go & be d— say I & that is being a good Xtian.'[63]

Long before the Whigs took office in 1830 therefore, the Holland House stance on the Eastern Question had already acquired a reputation for eccentricity. Holland's unqualified delight at the news of the Turkish defeat at Navarino, in 1827, puzzled close friends as much as it irritated Tory opponents: 'Surely it must lead to the liberation of Greece & more remotely to the humiliation & dismemberment of the Ottoman Power in Europe. I suppose I am a bigot, a pedant or an enthusiast but I cannot but consider such a result as glorious to Christendom, favourable to learning & the arts & beneficial to the liberties & happiness of mankind – if so it must be advantageous & cannot be injurious to England.'[64] Grey was not impressed. To him and many other people, Holland's refusal to see that British interests would be jeopardised by a Russian occupation of Constantinople was childish in its simplicity. Further, Holland's views on the subject were expressed with such 'a degree of violence'[65] that any suggestion that he should become Foreign Minister in a Canning or Goderich government had, according to Grey, to be put firmly on one side. As Grey observed, 'the proceeding appears to me to have been most injudicious, and its result, I have no doubt, will be very unfavourable to him in the public opinion'.[66] When Grey's Whig Cabinet came to be formed,

63. Add. MSS. 51749, f 176; Holland to Henry Fox, 11 Feb. 1826.

64. Add. MSS. 51750, f 172; Holland to Henry Fox, 6 Dec. 1827. See also Add. MSS. 51547, f 133; Holland to Grey, 26 Dec. 1827.

65. Grey to Creevey, 15 Dec. 1827; *The Creevey Letters*, ii 141.

66. Grey to Princess Lieven, 19 July 1828; *The Correspondence of Princess Lieven and Earl Grey*, i 112.

Holland was only offered the Chancellorship of the Duchy of Lancaster. Palmerston, with a narrower and more pragmatic view of British interests, became Foreign Secretary.

It is hard not to sympathise with Grey's impatience at Holland's maverick behaviour. By 1828, the latter's preference for Russia over Turkey was absolute. Whereas Alexander I of Russia had been vilified in 1821 as a parricide, his more conservative brother Nicholas was now held up as the man who was to bring light into the Ottoman Empire. This fact, together with his discounting of Britain's major strategic and economic interests, made Holland's whole policy appear nonsensical. Even Princess Lieven, who now resumed relations with Holland House, found her host's enthusiasm for Russia to be so exuberant as to be positively embarrassing:

> I repeat, then, that all persons of intelligence are on our side, and among them Lord Holland deserves special mention. He is making ample amends for his former errors; he will not listen to argument on the subject of Turkey, but wishes her outside of Europe. He would be glad to see the Emperor arrive at Constantinople, that he might do as he liked with it, that we might have a port in the Mediterranean – in a word the only difficulty is to restrain him. He admires the Emperor beyond everything, and his wisdom above all other qualities. He is ashamed of the miserable policy of England.[67]

It was seriously believed in some quarters that attempts to secure Holland a place in the Cabinet in 1827 and 1828 were stagemanaged by this remarkable Russian ambassadress.[68] Not surprisingly, this episode did nothing to resolve doubts about Holland's overall judgment.

Being isolated in an opinion had never deterred the Hollands from pursuing the matter in the past, however, and indeed Holland himself rather relished the notoriety of holding 'opinions that other people do not hold'.[69] In spite of widespread criticism, he was determined to press his pro-

---

67. Princess Lieven to Alexander Benckendorff, 16 March 1828; *The Letters of Dorothea, Princess Lieven*, p.126.

68. *The Journal of Mrs Arbuthnot*, ii 149; Dec. 1827.

69. Lord John Russell to Lord William Russell, 27 Nov. 1829; *Lord William Russell and his Wife*, p.203.

Russian views. In 1829, the only aspect of the peace treaties worked out between Russia and Turkey that he seriously welcomed was the provision that Greece should become independent. Otherwise, the treaties were 'damned foolish'. The European powers, by their diplomatic intervention, had been far too hard on Russia and not nearly hard enough on the Turks. He told Grey: 'You see Peace is all but made & Constantinople has once more (I trust for the last time) escaped its inevitable fate – I rejoice at the first & am sorry for the last event. However Greece must be free, tho' I fear with small thanks to us.'[70] The vigorous preference for Russian influence over Turkish in the eastern Mediterranean was the most bizarre example of the application of a spectrum between good powers and evil powers, on which the Slav came out marginally ahead of the Turk. At no time did Holland allow the simplicity of the ideological yardstick to be modified by strategic or economic considerations. The consequences of such an approach to foreign policy formed the basis of the recurrent hostilities between Palmerston and Holland House which were to bedevil the Grey and Melbourne governments.[71]

Long before 1830 therefore, Holland House was held to be singular in its approach to foreign affairs. Its numerous contacts in Europe made it a centre of informed opinion and mischief-making. The Binda affair was not the first occasion that a Holland House initiative embarrassed government policy and it was certainly not to be the last. Further, the Hollands were utterly unimpressed by the criticisms which such activities excited, in that they continued to operate an eighteenth-century view of such things. Before 1789, governments exercised options in foreign policy, but they in no way bound individuals to follow the same options. It was, for example, perfectly easy to travel freely in an enemy country as a private individual in war time. It was considered just as legitimate to visit and correspond with friends in countries with which the British government was in conflict.

70. Add. MSS. 51547, f 179; Holland to Grey, 22 Sept. 1829.
71. See below, Chapter Eleven.

Governments fought wars, and private citizens were not directly involved. Many of these conventions were lost in the ferocity of the French Revolutionary Wars, but Holland's preference for them never changed. It continued to appear perfectly legitimate to put loyalty to foreign friends above loyalty to a Tory British government. Equally in Holland's view, there could be no objection to pursuing policies abroad which ran counter to those pursued by the government of the country of which he happened to be a citizen. By 1830, however, such a standpoint looked distinctly anachronistic. War was no longer a dispute between governments but rather a struggle between whole peoples.

Confident in the validity of his own assumptions therefore, Holland early developed the habit of giving Holland House its own foreign policy. The spectrum between good and bad powers provided him with a plausible, if blunt, intellectual system which could be applied in any context at any time. It had the advantage for Holland of having a decent Foxite parentage, and needed only to be expanded and developed. It also neatly fitted the assumption that the Armageddon between truth and untruth which Charles James Fox had described in Europe in the 1790s was still being fought in the 1820s and 1830s. Waterloo had produced a truce, not a final settlement. Over and over again, Holland House saw only ideological problems in foreign questions. There was no sympathy for Canning and Palmerston in their trumpeting of the primacy of commercial or strategic considerations. Even if these led them in liberal directions, Holland was inclined to insist that they had arrived at proper goals for the wrong reasons. Conversely, Canningite foreign ministers found Holland's meddling naive and blinkered. They could not deny his knowledge and experience. Ambassadors and refugees were too often in Holland House for that, but they deplored his influence. Holland House was one of the last private circles to attempt to develop its own foreign policies. As a result, in the early nineteenth century, its position was often highly equivocal.

9

Spain

Nowhere was the struggle between constitutionalism and autocracy more poignant than in Spain. The Spanish resistance to Bonaparte and the decades of civil war which followed the defeat of the French had epic qualities. For the Hollands, Spanish affairs involved an emotional commitment beyond that invested in any English issue. In letters, Holland frequently described himself as 'Esplanado', and Jovellanos, the leading Spanish liberal, described the Fox clan as 'la mejor, la mas amada de España, familia de Inglaterra'.[1] Both Lord and Lady Holland had fluent Spanish, and, after their travels in that country, they could honestly claim to have a personal knowledge of Spain that was unequalled among leading politicians. Indeed, in his *Foreign Reminiscences*, Holland thought it was the country he knew best.[2] He had many Spanish friends and some Spanish enemies. For Holland House, Spain was the test case of how far constitutionalism would be allowed to take root in Western Europe. Both the Hollands followed the fortunes of that country with the same intensity of feeling that would be aroused by a later Spanish civil war.

The Hollands established themselves as authorities on Spain by undertaking two celebrated and highly controversial journeys to that country, the first between 1802 and 1805 and the second between 1808 and 1809. In Madrid, in 1803, Lady Holland rented a house and began to give a series of dinner

1. Jovellanos, *Cartas*, ii 380.
2. Holland, *Foreign Reminiscences*, p.69.

parties at which the famous and infamous in Spanish society were systematically scrutinised.[3] In June of the same year, they were presented at Court. In the course of these visits, most of the major Spanish cities were inspected, and there was so much interest in the detail of Spanish life at all levels that Lady Holland's *Spanish Journal* has become a valuable piece of evidence for historians of Spain on the eve of Bonaparte's invasion. Nothing was thought so insignificant as to be unworthy of comment. To emphasise the educational nature of these excursions, the Hollands took two sons with them in 1802 and Lord John Russell in 1808. Spanish society was dissected with even more energy and thoroughness than they had expended on France.

Predictably, the Hollands returned home with very firm prejudices. In short, they had become the prisoners of Spain. They had found the people lively, imaginative, and, above all, responsive pupils. To read Lady Holland's *Journal* is to form a picture of a country which was determined on constitutionalism and the full, liberal prescription. The Hollands had no doubt that the only policy for England to follow was to assist them in realising that ambition. There was no aspect of Spanish life that could not be explained away. The limited role of women in society and politics was unfortunate, for example, but this fact could be put down to the baleful effects of clerical influence. Even though bull-fighting appalled her, Lady Holland, in justice to the Spaniards, concluded a passage on this subject by deploring 'the whining sensibility which has crept into the modern systems of education, when as much fine feeling is bestowed upon the sufferings of an earth worm as upon those of a fellow creature'.[4] As potential liberals and constitutionalists, the Spanish had to be given the benefit of all possible doubt.

The greatest obstacle to liberal values in Spain was the Catholic Church, and, if the notorious anticlericalism of

---

3. Ilchester, *The Spanish Journal of Elizabeth, Lady Holland*, pp. 100 seq. It should also be noted that Holland himself had first visited Spain between April and December 1793. It was in these months that he was first introduced to Jovellanos, who was to become the most important Spanish correspondent of Holland House.

4. *The Spanish Journal of Elizabeth, Lady Holland*, p.67.

Holland House smacks of Europe rather than England, this fact is hardly accidental. In Holland's view, the French Revolution 'furnished the priests with an opportunity of declaiming against all liberty, of confounding temperate toleration with determined irreligion and of persuading the people that freedom was only a softer name for Anarchy & Anarchism ... they are fallen at least fifty years back in prejudice'.[5] Similarly, Lady Holland's agnosticism was reinforced by her Spanish experiences. After being invited to smell the bones of St. Rosa de Lima, she merely noted: 'True it was that the bone had a strong odour, but to sceptical noses the musk was offensive.'[6] With the exception of the Jesuits for whose intelligence the Hollands entertained a certain respect, the clerical domination of education was believed to have been calamitous. Free thought was almost impossible, and liberal ideas were buried in obscurantist prejudice.

Alongside clericalism stood absolute monarchy. A knowledge of Spain allowed Holland to develop his family's preoccupation with the dangers of powerful executives in a quite new area. In his view, the Bourbon dynasty in Madrid demonstrated to the point of caricature 'the effects of an absolute government'.[7] Charles IV was half-witted. His wife, Maria Luisa, kept up a level of immoral behaviour that made her private life 'a topic of conversation with the muleteers'.[8] Their son, the future Ferdinand VII, was vain and cowardly in equal proportions, and was to prove himself willing to sell his people to the French. The details of his treachery were being freely distributed by his parents in Rome in 1814, and the Hollands checked the truth of this story by asking Murat when they arrived in Naples.[9] Only Godoy, Maria Luisa's lover and Charles IV's chief minister, evoked any sympathy from the Hollands, in that his venality and greed could not hide a basic intelligence. With the title of the Prince of the Peace, he had allowed Spain for many years to escape the

5. Add. MSS. 51733, f 121; Holland to Caroline Fox, 13 May 1793.

6. *The Spanish Journal of Elizabeth, Lady Holland*, p.170.

7. Add. MSS. 48226, f 116; Holland to Boringdon, 2 July 1793.

8. *The Spanish Journal of Elizabeth, Lady Holland*, p.28.

9. Holland, *Foreign Reminiscences*, pp. 111-33.

experience of war. In 1809, Holland asked Liverpool to allow him to enter England as a refugee.[10] On their last visit to Paris, in 1838, the Hollands made a point of visiting Godoy in the dingy hotel where he spent his last years.[11]

Even if the Hollands had ever been tempted to consider the possibility of Spain being regenerated through the efforts of her kings, their personal knowledge of the Bourbons would have quickly disillusioned them. In fact, conditions at the Spanish Court merely confirmed Foxite prejudices. If George III was an example of a dutiful king, Charles IV represented incompetence incarnate. Both personified the abuse of power that was inherent in an unbridled executive. The constitutional cause in Spain was therefore an extension of Whig battles in England. Not surprisingly, Holland looked with hope not to the Spanish monarchy as the agency of change but to liberal members of the Spanish aristocracy like Jovellanos and Infantado. It was these men who were counted the friends of Holland House. They were regarded as a species of Spanish Whig holding the same ambitions in politics as the Hollands themselves.

On his return to England, Holland published his biography of Lope de Vega, thereby confirming his reputation as an expert on Spain and its culture. The book was dedicated to the patriot poet Manuel Quintana, and was openly didactic in intention. Praise for de Vega's literary ability is mixed with criticism of his religious bigotry and his servile adulation of kings.[12] The intermixing of politics and literature is undertaken with great sensitivity and demonstrates Holland's mastery of Spain and its idioms. Between 1805 and 1808, Holland kept up a brisk correspondence with Spain, and counted among his informants Cevallos,[13] Saavedra, Jovellanos and Infantado.[14] As he relayed information to

10. Holland, *Foreign Reminiscences*, pp. 137-9.

11. ibid., pp. 332-9.

12. Holland, *Some Account of the Life and Writings of Lope Felix de Vega Carpio* (London 1806), pp. 92-4.

13. Add. MSS. 51624, ff 17-39; Cevallos to Holland.

14. Add. MSS. 51544, f 125; Holland to Grey, 12 Sept. 1808. All of these men were to take leading parts in the patriotic resistance to the French occupation.

Grey, it was obviously a matter of some pride that the leaders of Spanish liberalism should see him as the proper channel for conveying their views into England. As he himself put the point: 'I have so many & such *grand* correspondents in Spain.'[14] The boast was quite justified. By the time the Hollands left England for their second visit to Spain, in 1808, they were already distinguished by their expertise in that country's affairs. Their writing, travels and friendships gave them a distinctive character in early nineteenth-century society.

In March 1808, Charles IV was forced to abdicate in favour of his son Ferdinand. A month later, Ferdinand in turn abdicated in favour of Napoleon's brother Joseph. In the summer of the same year, the Spanish launched a guerilla war against the occupying French troops that was to last for four years. Predictably, the Hollands took the keenest possible interest in these developments. Their second visit to Spain was an attempt to share the excitement. Holland was not surprised that Charles IV and Ferdinand VII should have allowed themselves to become pensioners of the French. Monarchical incompetence had dragged Spain down to a position of dependence and was now incapable of regeneration. That task fell to the aristocratic juntas or councils which were leading the fight against France. For at least two years before 1808, Holland had been presenting his Spanish friends with a stark choice. Spain must either reassert herself by joining the war against Bonaparte, or face the consequences of being a client of the French, in the form of an English attack on her Latin American colonies:

> If Spain submits to be a secondary power in Europe, she must expect to be none at all across the Atlantic but we will forego our conquests & guarantee her Colonies if she will reassert her importance not by treaties & language but by actions [and] by introducing men of rank talents & character.[15]

The fact that the reassertion of Spanish dignity against Bonaparte's armies had been undertaken without any

15. Add. MSS. 51544, ff 27-9; Holland to Grey, 5 Oct. 1806.

assistance from Bourbon kings was a warming confirmation of Foxite views.

Once, however, the Spanish people began to resist the French in guerilla warfare, Holland had no doubt that English policy should be narrowly directed towards assisting them. He knew Spain too well to believe that the French occupation would be anything but an 'incomplete work'.[16] In public and private statements, Holland endlessly pressed the point that Napoleon could be pinned down in Spain and slowly bled to death. The failure of Sir John Moore's campaign should not lead to British disengagement but simply to more effective military planning.[17] Intervention in Spain therefore came to have a dual purpose. In military terms, it offered the best chance of influencing the larger struggle against Napoleon to England's advantage. At the same time, it allowed English constitutionalists to influence the outcome of a people's war. Holland's ideas on intervention in Spain always involved 'the arrangement of a system for conciliating the minds of the Spanish people by a redress of their grievances'.[18] Such meddling in the internal affairs of another country was simply the passing on of valuable experience. Constitutional forms were, after all, to be handed over to Europeans as a Foxite gift.

Holland's defence of the Spanish after 1808 again made him very distinctive among opposition politicians. Both Grey and Grenville were much more sceptical about the value of Spanish good intentions, particularly when the war effort against Bonaparte was divided among a number of squabbling juntas or councils, which seemed incapable of organising themselves into concerted action.[19] On innumerable occasions, Holland had to persuade his colleagues that the Spanish really were dutiful pupils of Whig instruction, when more often than not they behaved more like provincial-minded bandits. Holland never faltered in this line

16. Add. MSS. 51532, f 93; Holland to Auckland, 18 Sept. 1809.

17. Holland to Sir C. Vaughan, 26 June & 14 Aug. 1809; Vaughan MSS. c 55/7.

18. *Parl. Deb.*, vol. LIII 502-3; 8 June 1810.

19. Richmond to Bathurst, 23 May 1812; Hist MSS. Comm. 76 *Bathurst*, p.174. See also T. Grenville to Lord Grenville, 3 Dec. 1811; Hist. MSS. Comm. 30. *Fortescue* X, p.184.

of argument, however, and, towards the end of the Napoleonic
War, tried hard to see that provision for a Spanish Cortes or
parliament was written into the peace terms.[20] It was not a
priority that even many members of his own party thought
feasible as practical politics.

Distinctive as these views were, they were based on broad
experience. The 1808 revolution in Spain, which had brought
their friends to power, gave the Hollands the keenest pleasure
and excited them to new activity:

> You may easily imagine how much pleasure I feel at the Revolution
> in Spain, not that it is likely at present to lead to any thing
> advantageous to this country, but it is certain to do good to Spain ...
> Our friend the Duque del Infantado whom I hear is made Prime
> Minister is a man of excellent understanding & full of information ...
> he is the first Grandee in it who has manifested the slightest wish of
> being useful to his country.[21]

A knowledge of agriculture and chemistry were just two of the
new prime minister's accomplishments. Between April and
November 1808, the Hollands appointed themselves the
unofficial ambassadors of the new provisional government in
Spain. The Juntas of Murcia and Leon applied for English
loans by using Holland as a broker.[22] When accredited
ambassadors arrived in England, in July, it was almost
inevitable that they would move within a social ambit
prescribed by Holland House.[23] In the Lords, Holland
demanded that the English government should declare itself
willing 'to guarantee the integrity of the Spanish empire, and
to negotiate with any form of government which the Spanish
people were disposed to adopt, or with any family which they
might choose to call to the throne, if they decided on a
monarchical form, whether limited or unlimited'.[24]

20. *Parl. Deb.*, vol. LXI 517-18; 2 April 1813.

21. Add. MSS. 51549, f 15; Lady Holland to Grey, 29 April 1808.

22. Add. MSS. 51598, f 47; Holland to Canning, 2 Sept. 1808. See also Add. MSS.
51520, f 30; Holland to Prince of Wales, 30 Sept. 1808.

23. Lady S. Lyttelton to Lady Spencer, 6 July 1808; *The Correspondence of Sarah, Lady Lyttelton*, p.21.

24. *Parl. Deb.*, vol. XLVII 1108-1110; 30 June 1808.

While it was no doubt flattering for Holland, as an opposition politician, to be asked by Infantado, Jovellanos and other Spanish friends to be the intermediary between the new government in Madrid and England, the position was fraught with obvious constitutional dangers. Holland chose to ignore them. Without consulting Canning or official Foreign Office policy, Holland established his own policies towards Spain. He assured Jovellanos that 'la causa de España es la de la justicia y de la humanidad', and that English opinion was firmly committed to the liberal side in Spain.[25] By way of giving more practical assistance, Holland plied his friends in Madrid with all manner of helpful material on the subject of parliamentary practice, including copies of the House of Commons Rule Book and Charles Fox's *History of the Reign of James II*. The tendency for Holland House to conduct a foreign policy independent of that pursued by the British government was particularly apparent in Spanish affairs. The constitutional objections to such a practice were clear, but the Hollands could riposte that, in this particular context, they were probably more informed than the government could ever hope to be.

Predictably, Canning and the British government reacted sharply to such behaviour. When the Hollands applied for a passport for their second journey to Spain, they were told by Canning that it would only be issued if Holland made it abundantly clear that his views on Spain were peculiar to himself and not necessarily coterminous with those of the British government. Canning also announced his intention of making this point explicit to the Spanish authorities. Holland could not believe 'such an admonition to be in any way useful, becoming or necessary', but complied with Canning's terms.[26] When the Hollands landed at Corunna in November 1808, therefore, to begin their second progress around the Iberian peninsula, they were already highly controversial figures in the Spanish world. As they spent the next nine months

25. Holland to Jovellanos, Sept. 1808; *Cartas*, i 84-5 ('Spain's cause is that of justice and humanity').

26. Add. MSS. 51598, ff 57-60; Holland to Canning, 13 Oct. 1808. See also Holland to Morpeth, 20 Oct. 1808; Castle Howard MSS.

7.   Sydney Smith by Landseer

8. John Allen by Landseer

dodging French armies in Spain and Portugal, nothing was done to lessen their notoriety.[27]

To plunge into the middle of a war zone was in itself self-advertising to a degree, and Lord Auckland could only attribute this behaviour to 'a sort of Spanish fever, which still holds possession of him ... disgraceful to our political and military character'.[28] When the Hollands then proceeded to send reports to England criticising Sir John Moore and other English commanders for timidity, the outcry against them became vociferous. As they were ceremoniously fêted by the provincial juntas, it seemed that their judgment of events had been overborne by their pro-Spanish sympathies. Sir John Cradock, reporting from Spain to the War Office, observed:

> I saw a letter today from those shocking people Lord & Lady Holland (I always put them together) at Seville. His Lordship says the French never had so large a force in Spain as was represented in England, and, what is worse they [the French] made our army believe it. Was not his Lordship content with the loss we sustained? I believe he would give the lives of ten English to save one Spaniard.[29]

As the first Spanish resistance to Bonaparte crumbled, the quarrelling juntas were exonerated from all blame by the Hollands, who preferred to credit British armies with the full responsibility. Early in 1809, even Sydney Smith was moved to ask: 'Why my dear Lady Holland, do you not come home? It is all over, it has been all over this month; except in the Holland family, there has not been a man of sense for some weeks who has thought otherwise.'[30]

Much of the criticism was well-founded. There is little echo in the Hollands' writings on Spain of the divisions and antipathies which fissured the resistance movement. The tendency of the Fox family to see foreign affairs in crude blacks and whites was never more marked than in their diagnosis of Spanish events. Unfortunately, this imbalance too

---

27. *The Spanish Journal of Elizabeth, Lady Holland*, pp. 200 seq.
28. Auckland to Grenville, 29 Nov. 1808; Hist. MSS. Comm. *Fortescue* IX, 245-6.
29. Sir J. Cradock to E. Cooke, 26 Feb. 1809; *The Spanish Journal of Elizabeth, Lady Holland*, p.250.
30. S. Smith to Lady Holland, c. Jan. 1809; *The Letters of Sydney Smith*, p.150.

often neutered the impact of the real information they had to convey. The reason for this blinkering effect is not hard to find. The Spanish resistance to Bonaparte was the supreme example of a popular movement, undirected by kings or bishops, acting in the furtherance of a demand for a more constitutional system. To a Foxite, it presented an irresistible attraction. Equally, it was hard to admit that its initial impetus would founder on the deficiencies within the popular movement itself.

On the other hand, the 1808-9 visit dramatically reaffirmed Holland's standing among the Spanish. Romana, the principal resistance leader in the north, concluded a blow-by-blow account of Sir John Moore's retreat with the hope that 'je ne désire rien tant dans ce monde que de voir mon pays débarrasé de French dogs pour aller lui presenter mes respectueux hommages et couler deux ou trois jours heureux à Lord Holland's House'.[31] Among British Residents in Spain, the Hollands counted as friends Thomas Reynell in Gibraltar, Thomas Graham in Granada and George Jackson in Seville. Among the Spanish, there was Saavedra and Jovellanos.[31] The latter in particular was thought to have principles worked out 'by those of true philosophy & of the most accredited patriotism, such as Cicero & Mr Fox'.[32] Jovellanos was the best hope for seeing a Cortes established in Spain, and could even be used for more humble tasks like securing a passport for Jeremy Bentham. Both during their Spanish visit and after their return to England, the Hollands were kept informed in protracted correspondences of the course of events in the peninsula. The information was often partial, but it allowed the Hollands to claim an extraordinary expertise in Spanish affairs.

Above all, the second visit to Spain reinforced the Hollands' view that the French could never hold the country for long. In spite of moments of real doubt occasioned by the Spanish preference for 'reforms by bayonet' or 'generals as

31. Add. MSS. 51625, f 220; Romana to Holland, 4 July 1810. This volume contains the letters which the Hollands received from Spain between 1808 and 1810.

32. Holland to Jovellanos, 5 May 1809; *Cartas*, i 156. See also Add. MSS. 51738, f 149; Holland to Caroline Fox, 9 Feb. 1809.

legislators',[33] Holland House continued to see the Spanish war
as the crucial battlefield in the European struggle against
Bonaparte. As he told the English diplomat Sir Charles
Vaughan, 'in spite of all difficulties I do not think the French
can ever conquer Spain'.[34] The geography of Spain and the
temper of its people made such a prospect impossible. In
Holland's view, only failed English soldiers described the
situation as hopeless, and poured calumnies on the heads of
the Spanish as an excuse for their own military incapacity. In
fact, the situation was quite otherwise. The enduring
resistance of the Spanish was proof of it. In a long letter
written from Cadiz in May 1809, Holland tried to explain to
Grey that his criticisms of Moore and the other generals was
by way of defending the Spanish from unjustifiable abuse:

> If the reports given by our Generals & officers of the apathy of the
> people, the ignorance of the Government, the treachery of individuals
> etc etc were true, how could the whole coast of Spain from Barcelona
> to Corunna & from Ferrol to St Ander be in the possession of the
> Spaniards four or five months after so hopeless a state of things.[35]

Admitting that these views were 'Spaniolated',[36] Holland
nevertheless saw them as squaring with what he himself saw
and heard. Perspectives from London were obviously
different.

After 1809, Spain's symbolism became a dominant element
in Holland's thinking. In military terms, the war against
Napoleon was to be won in Spain. At the least, thousands of
French troops could be tied down in guerilla warfare. At best,
the English and Spanish together might be able to bring off a
major victory. For this to be possible, Moore's failure had to
be discounted. Rather, the military commitment to both
Spain and Portugal had to be reaffirmed. In addition, Austria
must be persuaded to open up a second front; 'to save Spain
there must be, first, an Austrian war; secondly, a British force

33. Holland to Jovellanos, 17 May 1809; *Cartas*, i 177.
34. Holland to Sir Charles Vaughan, 6 Nov. 1808; Vaughan MSS. c 55/4.
35. Add. MSS. 51544, ff 131-47; Holland to Grey, 20 May 1809.
36. Holland to Caroline Fox, 5 April 1809; *Sovereign Lady*, p.167. See also Add.
MSS. 51795, ff 105-7; Holland to Upper Ossory, 9 May 1809.

in Portugal, either determined to act offensively or at least
disposed to make demonstrations in favour of Spain.'[37] It was
maddening to find even such close political associates as Grey
and Bedford sceptical on this point.[38] In recognising the
military possibilities in Spain, Holland tentatively approached
Wellingtonian views.

The more important aspect of Spain's symbolism, however,
lay in its politics. Quite simply, Holland saw the Spanish war
as the test case for evaluating the liberal potential in Europe.
In 1808, there was an unparalleled opportunity for
introducing full constitutionalism. The old style of monarchy
had lamentably failed to provide any kind of national
leadership. The Catholic Church had been associated in its
disgrace. At the same time, the political consciousness of the
Spanish had been so awakened in reaction to the French
invasion that a return to the old ways was impossible.
Constitutionalism might be worked out within a monarchical
arrangement, but only if future kings recognised their
indebtedness to a Cortes. As Holland reported to his sister
from Seville:

> With respect to their liberty – all classes think something should be
> done & I am in hope the Cortes will please – what is certain is that
> with much loyalty to Ferdinand there is no notion even among the
> common people, that it is an encroachment on his rights to limit to a
> certain degree the authority of the Crown for not a grain of respect for
> the name of Charles 4th or Maria Luisa is left in the Country &
> Ferdinand is more beloved as an enemy of Godoy & a victim of
> French policy than as a King or a Prince.[39]

The old assumptions in Spanish politics had been destroyed
by the French invasion. As Holland himself stated the matter,
'in that country there must be either a French Army or a
Cortez'.[40]

This was a prospect too exciting for forego. Between 1808

---

37. Holland to Grey, 27 April 1809; Hist. MSS. Comm. *Fortescue* IX, 309-311.
38. Add. MSS. 51738, f 226; Holland to Caroline Fox, 17 June 1809.
39. Add. MSS. 51738, f 201; Holland to Caroline Fox, 27 April 1809.
40. Charles Arbuthnot to Liverpool, 29 Dec. 1824; *The Correspondence of Charles Arbuthnot*, p.71.

and 1812, Holland House followed the attempts at constitution-making in Spain with the closest possible interest, and actively tried to influence the course of events. With the exception of a short period in the summer of 1810, when differences among the Spanish liberals seemed to have reached impossible proportions,[41] Holland never doubted that some sort of parliamentary system would finally emerge. The old forces blocking constitutional progress in Spain were discredited. Something new had to be tried. The popular resistance movement against the French had created the conditions in which radical departures could be discussed. For Foxites, Spain represented, in almost scientific terms, an experiment for testing the assumptions on which they recommended constitutionalism to Europe. In more personal terms, they could hope to win in Spain a battle which they had almost lost in England. As Spain started afresh, there was some chance of realising a Utopia. A commitment to the Spanish cause was therefore emotional as well as political. Light and darkness played over the surface of Spain as an endless dilemma.

While in Spain, Holland tried hard to convince Jovellanos, Infantado and the several provincial juntas that the only possible answer to the problems they faced lay in the calling of a Cortes in Madrid to which they would all defer. In long tutorial-like letters, Holland set out the case for and described the forms of constitutional government. Most importantly, he insisted that the national cause and all future government must be given a popular basis. Even though he is no doubt giving a Whig value to the word 'people' in these letters, the explicit linking of popular involvement with final success is striking:

> I can only hope that those who are more afraid either of the enemy or of public disquiet will be more disposed than before to give the people its legitimate share in the management of affairs which, it should never be forgotten, are theirs. The more I see, the more I have

41. Holland to B. White, 6 Aug. 1810; Blanco White MSS. II i/229 iii; see also Lady Holland to Sir Charles Vaughan, 10 Oct. 1810; Vaughan MSS. c 61/1.

thought of this matter, the more I am persuaded that it is not only
badly judged, but also an injustice, not to popularize the cause of
Spain.[42]

In this long correspondence with Jovellanos, Holland again
and again returns to the same theme: 'I am sorry to emphasize
these points but truely we can't terminate this great fight
without giving in some way or other, real influence to the
people.'[43] The Cortes would quarantee the national struggle
and the long-term predominance of constitutionalism.
Without it, there might be a return to 'Oriental notions of
Government'.[44]

Holland House not only insisted on a Cortes, but showered
their Spanish friends with all manner of helpful advice on the
form that assembly might take. Sometimes the assistance was
given by way of an answer to a specific problem. When
Jovellanos asked whether Holland would prefer a bicameral or
unicameral system,[45] the latter came down strongly in favour
of an upper house to maintain a link between property and
representation and to stop the grandees going over to the
French. More often, the advice was tendered without any
prior warning. In May 1809, John Allen, drew up a proposal
for a new Spanish constitution 'sobre las formas de la Camera
de los Communes'.[46] It was sent to Spain together with the
Red Book which contained the forms and procedures of the
English Parliament. Although Allen prefaced his remarks
with an historical account of how the Castilian Cortes used to
work, the assumption behind the Holland House proposals
was clearly that the Spanish could do worse than adopt
English procedures wholesale. The forms as well as the theory
of constitutionalism were very much for export.[47]

42. Holland to Jovellanos, 12 April 1809; *Cartas*, i 137.

43. Holland to Jovellanos, 9 April 1809; *Cartas*, i 127.

44. Add. MSS. 51738, f 214; Holland to Caroline Fox, 20 May 1809.

45. Jovellanos to Holland, 11 June 1809; *Cartas*, i 259. 'Ah mi Mr Allen, y Vre mi
querido Lord! socorro! alumbrenme, les pido, en esta perplegidad.' (Oh, Mr Allen
and my most excellent dear Lord! Help! Enlighten me, I beg you, in this perplexity).

46. Holland to Jovellanos, 31 May 1809; *Cartas*, i 218-19.

47. The detail of his tuition may be found in Jovellanos *Cartas*, i 208 seq. See also J.
Allen to Sir Charles Vaughan, 13 Dec. 1808, Vaughan MSS c 8/1, and Add. MSS.
51653 f 32; Holland to Sir J. Mackintosh, 4 Nov. 1809.

Patronage verging on a cultural imperialism was by no means resented in Spain. The anglophilia of the Spanish liberals went deep. Jovellanos himself claimed to be working from a copy of Blackstone, and he and his friends had somewhat incongruously taken to celebrating George III's birthday all over the country.[48] When Allen's draft proposals arrived, Jovellanos declared himself delighted with 'los apuntamentos de nuestro Mr Allen; manjar no menos dulce y agradable que sano y provechoso. No solo lo comere sino que le rumiere para digerirle mejor.'[49] In fact, Holland's approaches to the Spanish liberals were a little less wooden than the evidence has so far suggested. It was less important that the Spanish should adopt English constitutional forms than they should adopt some forms. Such a view had an authentic Foxite pedigree:

> In talking to Spaniards on the Cortes and publick assemblies recommend them to study *the forms of our proceedings*, not because they are ours but because they are *forms* – I remember that My Uncle used to say that when a law could be made in *half an hour* there could be no liberty as it was his opinion that a want of respect for forms was one of the chief reasons of the violences & extravagances which the French assemblies & convention committed. Indeed the French have an inaptitude to forms & the Spanish have on the contrary a liking to them. This last feature in their character is fortunate & it is well they should know what advantage they can derive from it in the present circumstances.[50]

Everything was possible once constitutionalism took a practical form.

On their return to England, the Hollands continued to meddle in Spanish affairs by sponsoring a new journal, the *Espagnol*, which, under the editorship of Joseph Blanco White,[51] appeared in at least eight issues between April 1810

48. Jovellanos to Holland, 3 June 1809; *Cartas*, i 229.

49. ibid., 5 June 1809; ibid., i 232-3. ('The points raised by Mr Allen are a delicacy no less sweet and agreeable than healthy and useful. Not only will I eat it, but I will chew it over well to digest it better'.)

50. Holland to Sir Charles Vaughan, c. Aug. 1808; Vaughan MSS. c 55/1.

51. Joseph Blanco White, the grandson of an Irish Catholic, had been brought up in Spain. On reaching England, in 1810, he was introduced to Holland House and immediately found employment. For further details, see *Sovereign Lady*, p.220.

and June 1814. The aim of this new venture was avowedly didactic. It aimed both to influence English opinion in favour of the Spanish liberals and to offer advice and encouragement to the Spanish themselves. One of its principle customers was the government, which was anxious to keep Holland House foreign policy under surveillance. The history of the journal is marked by difficult relations with authority, and Holland, on more than one occasion had to advise caution to its editor: 'I hope that you will take care in any communication you have with L. Wellesley to convey to him strong assurances of your willingness & anxiety to attend to the wishes of the Government & to promote the chief & original object of your publication viz a Union of Sentiments & a mutual confidence between all that remains of the Spanish Empire & Great Britain.'[52] Even so, the *Espagnol* was widely assumed to be a new avenue by which Holland House hoped to conduct a foreign policy independent of that preferred by the English government.

There is no doubt that the journal could not have survived without Holland House support. Holland himself dictated editorial policy, and, by allowing his Spanish correspondence to be published, allowed White to claim that his journal gave the fullest information on Spanish affairs.[53] Not surprisingly its ideas strongly echoed those which Holland had already advanced in Spain itself. It saw the Cortes as the only possible solution to Spain's problems and repeatedly urged the provincial juntas to surrender their powers to a national body in Madrid. Holland congratulated White on taking such a line and read him a familiar lecture:

> I have read your Espagnol with great pleasure & am convinced that your information about our Parliament will be of great advantage to your country if the Cortes is really called together ... You have now shewn the Cortes the forms by which they should proceed, you should [in your] next number shew them the substance of their deliberations.[54]

52. Holland to White, 26 Sept. [1810]; Blanco White MSS. II i/229 vi.
53. Holland to White, [Sept. 1810]; Blanco White MSS. II i/229 v & xiv.
54. ibid., 4 Oct. [1810]; ibid., II i/229 viii.

By way of suggestions for what that 'substance' might be, Holland asked White to publish his views on army reforms, judicial and taxation systems, and imperial questions.[55] There was no doubt in Holland's mind that, with regard to the latter, 'the distinction between Mother Country & Colonies must be done away'.[56] In pleading for an all-powerful Cortes, he was hoping that it would draw representatives from Spanish America as well as from Spain itself.

It is almost impossible to evaluate the influence which Holland House exercised over the minds of Spanish liberals as they moved towards the calling of a Cortes in 1810. What can be demonstrated is that the *Espagnol* was read in Spain with great interest. Indeed, Holland received letters from some of his former friends protesting that, in accusing the juntas of provincialism, he was underestimating the difficulties inherent in Spanish politics. Holland was not inclined to make concessions. In July 1810, he told White:

Since you left Holland House I have received a letter from Quintana & I am sorry to say that the first number of the Espagnol seems to have made an impression at Cadiz somewhat different from that which I had before mentioned to you ... Quintana seems to think that it may have the effect of disgusting people here and elsewhere with the Spanish cause & that it is not only severe but unjustly severe on the late Government of the Central Junta.[57]

The letter goes on to make the point that Jovellanos had been ready to surrender his authority to a Cortes at the first meeting of the Junta, and to ask White to recommend this course of action in the next issue of the journal. Whether in Spain or in England, Holland never accepted any excuse for delay in summoning a Cortes. The meeting of such a body was a duty which Spanish liberals had to fulfil.

When a Cortes finally assembled in Madrid, the Hollands were predictably delighted. Eye-witness accounts of its early sessions began to reach Holland House in September 1810,

55. ibid., 25 July [1810]; ibid., II i/229 ii.
56. ibid., 20 Sept. [1810]; ibid., II i/229 iv.
57. Holland to White, July [1810]; Blanco White MSS. II i/229 i.

including one from Lord John Russell who found that the Spanish had shown 'a free & bold spirit'.[58] Puckishly, Lady Holland communicated these details to those Whigs like Grey who had doubted that such a body would ever meet: 'Tho' you are a most untrustworthy Spaniard, I cannot resist sending you the enclosed ... account of the first meeting of the Cortes. L.H. has received many other letters upon the same occasion which if he thought you would like should be sent to you.'[59] There was more than a little proprietary pride for the Hollands in seeing constitutionalism becoming such a force in Spanish life.

Nevertheless, the counselling of the Spanish through the pages of the *Espagnol* went on. After congratulating the Cortes on its decree giving full rights to the citizens of Spanish America,[60] Holland went on to ask Blanco White to turn their attention once more to the problems of establishing constitutional practice in Spain. Once again, English models are held up as precedents:

> Would it not be useful to state very shortly the books from which a knowledge of the English Constitution can best be derived, at the same time recommending an attention to the great principles of keeping the purse in the hands of the people, of preserving the freedom of the press, of securing the personal liberty of the subject, of administrating justice coram ora et in conspectu omnium, but disclaiming at the same time the notion of servilely copying the English laws & constitution & only urging the necessity of attending to the main principles & to the practical manner in which they are enforced.[61]

Schoolmasterly advice poured out of Holland House as the Cortes settled down to constitution-making.[62] No attempt to influence the affairs of another country was more determined or more blatant.

When the Spanish Constitution of 1812 finally appeared, Holland House was not entirely happy that its advice had

58. Add. MSS. 51677, f 19; Lord John Russell to Holland, 25 Sept. 1810.
59. Add. MSS. 51549, f 90; Lady Holland to Grey, 26 Oct. 1810.
60. Holland to White, c. Oct. 1810; Blanco White MSS. II i/229 xvi.
61. ibid., c. Nov. 1810; ibid., II i/229 xviii.
62. ibid., 20 Oct. 1810; ibid., II i/229 xii.

been properly digested. When Andres de la Vega, the President of the Cortes, sent a copy of the new Constitution to Holland as an act of courtesy, he was treated to a lecture by way of return on the deficiencies in the proposals. On too many points, according to Holland, English precedents had been ignored:

> As a plan or mould of Government, the want of a Second House of Commons and the want of any direct elections (by which alone the immediate connexion between the people and their representatives can be maintained) seem to me the most obvious omissions. The exaction of an oath, the institution of a permanent deputation of Cortes (a dangerous as well as silly contrivance) and the preposterous law against any alteration or revision for eight years appear to me the most striking defects, though the exclusion of all Members of the legislature from offices under the Executive Government, and of all members of the present Cortes from a seat in the next are yet more childish and inexcusable, and will perhaps be found, as they always have been where they have been tried, fatal to the Government of which they form a part. However, a popular assembly, the right of petitioning and the freedom of the press will it is to be hoped, give the people a taste for freedom, and enable them, whatever the canvass may be, to work out their salvation.[63]

In a twenty-page letter to Blanco White, Holland described the dangers inherent in the Spanish decision to divorce legislature from executive.[64] In this, as in so many other points, the Spanish had chosen to follow French rather than English models. Lady Holland accused them of having 'copied the Brissotine constitution'.[65] Lord John Russell, writing from Madrid, observed that 'a democracy will never do in the middle of Spain'.[66]

All in all, the Spanish Constitution of 1812 offered very little return for the political and emotional investment of Holland House in Spain. Again and again, the Spanish had chosen to adopt speculative French ideas when the Hollands had consistently pressed the claims of England's more practical

63. Add. MSS. 51626, ff 65-9; Holland to A. de la Vega, 12 Oct. 1812.
64. Holland to Blanco White, 9 April 1813; Blanco White MSS. II ii/230.
65. Lord Broughton, *Recollections of a Long Life*, i 143-4.
66. Add. MSS. 51677, ff 26-30; Lord John Russell to Holland, 16 July 1813.

arrangements. The Hollands were delighted that a constitution had emerged at all, but feared that it would prove unworkable. So little influence had been allowed the grandees, for example, that Holland feared that they might well be tempted to join Ferdinand VII in a reassertion of monarchical power. When this fear was realised in Ferdinand's decision to abrogate constitutional forms, Holland's irritation with his Spanish friends over their misguided behaviour in 1812 swiftly turned to pity. By 1816, they had been entirely forgiven. As Holland remarked to Sir Charles Vaughan: 'On Spanish politics I have neither time nor temper to speak. The impracticality & absurdity of those I knew are quite obliterated by their misfortunes & one only recollects their zeal their integrity & their patriotism & the infamous treatment they have received from a government which owes its existence to their exertions.'[67] Much of the year was spent in helping Brougham to organise financial relief for refugees from Ferdinand's new tyranny.[68]

Throughout the years 1808 to 1815, Holland rigidly applied the rule of testing régimes with ideological criteria. The options before the Spanish were monarchy in the old style, a Bonapartist system or some régime based on a constitution. The last option was a possibility because the resistance to the French had been on a popular basis. Holland had no doubt about his own preferences. Whereas Bonaparte in so many other parts of Europe was to be applauded as a destroyer of the ancien régime, in Spain he was to be opposed as the block to popular rights. He remained preferable to Charles IV or Ferdinand VII, but had to take second place to Infantado or Jovellanos. Napoleon was thought to be a benefactor in Italy and Germany because so much of what he did awakened national feeling. All the same, the Hollands thought him a monster in Spain because he set himself in opposition to a mature, popular movement. The spectrum between light and darkness which the Hollands used to evaluate whole régimes could be just as useful in allowing them to discriminate

67. Holland to Sir Charles Vaughan, 2 Jan. 1816; Vaughan MSS. c 57/5.
68. Holland to Grey, 10 Feb. 1816; Grey MSS. Box 34.

between the domestic options of a particular country. The rule was simple but made for clear lines of action.

So close was Holland's involvement with events in Spain between 1808 and 1812 that it was inconceivable that he would ever again take a disinterested view. After 1815, the Hollands encouraged friends with business interests in Spain like William Marsh Greening and professional travellers like Sir John Bowring to make Holland House a sounding board for their impressions.[69] If Ferdinand's resumption of absolutist attitudes was depressing, the liberal revival of 1820 was exhilarating.[70] The Spanish, adopted as protégés by Holland House, were setting an example to Europe which even English Tories could not ignore:

> The Spanish business provokes government & D of Wellington in particular. I shall compliment them on not interfering & draw a good omen from that circumstance in favor of any other people on the Continent who may make an effort to recover their liberties, as a proof that the Confederate Sovereigns are not engaged to meddle with them & The Holy Alliance is a mere rhapsody of foolish words.[71]

The struggle between constitutionalism and autocracy may have been halted in military terms in 1815, but, as the Spanish demonstrated, was by no means resolved. When this new outburst of Spanish liberalism was crushed by a French army in 1823, Holland was disappointed but not depressed. Reaction could never survive in Spain for long because 'all the property of the Country save three or four Grandees & the Priests are Constitutional or at least anti Ferdinand & anti Gallican'.[72] If property demanded constitutional representation, no Whig could believe that it could fail. Spain would continue to be a symbol of resistance to the temporary victory of reaction in 1815.

Holland's enthusiasm for Spain had often led him into doubtful constitutional behaviour. It did so again between

69. Add. MSS. 51627, f 10 seq.

70. For a detailed discussion of these events, see R. Carr, *Spain 1808-1939*, Ch. 4.

71. Add. MSS. 51546, ff 114-15; Holland to Grey, 20 April 1820.

72. ibid., f 264; ibid., 14 Oct. 1823. See also Add. MSS. 51741, f 201; Holland to Caroline Fox, 4 Jan. 1823.

1820 and 1823. To Tories, it was outrageous that rebels should receive active encouragement from England. For good or bad, Ferdinand's régime was recognised as the official government of Spain by England and Holland had no right to deal with its opponents.[73] The refusal of Holland House to accept its situation as part of Great Britain where foreign policy was concerned was intolerable. Equally, Holland's insistence from 1822 onwards that, if the French invaded Spain, a British force should be sent to the peninsula, reinforced the opinion in cautious minds that his judgment left much to be desired:

> Our neutrality in such a war as is about to ensue between Spain & France would you say be disgraceful. I think so too unless ... I think our real policy is to countenance her independence by sending an Embassador to Madrid & an envoy to Portugal directly ... This with some naval armament would be sufficient to show the despots with which party we should ultimately side & would either Cramp their exertions, as to make their war unsuccessful, or so alarm them with the consequences as to deter them from making it.[74]

As in 1808, the liberals in Spain could count on Holland's unstinted support at whatever cost to his career or reputation.

The success of the French intervention in Spain in 1823 meant that Holland House was once again flooded with Spanish liberal refugees. For men such as General Mina and Don Agostia Arguelles, Holland and Sir Francis Burdett became patrons and protectors.[75] For other liberals trapped in Spain, Holland could only attempt to mitigate penalties and ensure that families were provided for.[76] To all intents and purposes, Holland House was as much at war with Ferdinand VII as any Spanish liberal. His disaffected subjects were sheltered. His empire in South America was to be encouraged in its move towards independence, because he no longer represented anything in Spain except the wishes of the French

73. The Journal of Mrs Arbuthnot, i 226; 12 April 1823.
74. Add. MSS. 51653, f 121; Holland to Mackintosh 6 Dec. 1822. See also *Parl. Deb.*, vol. LXXXV 1202-1215 & vol. LXXXVI 200-7.
75. Add. MSS. 51569, ff 29-30; Sir F. Burdett to Holland, 6 Dec. 1829.
76. Add. MSS. 51627, f 179; L. de Torrigos to Holland, 19 Dec. 1831.

king and his Holy Alliance allies.[77] Hope for the future lay in
the birth of Ferdinand's daughter, Isabella, in 1830, which
would at least have the effect of excluding the reactionary Don
Carlos from the throne. The struggle between these two
claimants was to provoke another Spanish civil war, and
Holland's entry in his journal for 30 July 1831 was to prove
prophetic:[78] 'Passed the morning with my Spanish visitors &
in conversation on old Spanish stories. The state of [the]
Royal family in that country likely, even exclusive of political
opinions, to lead to a civil war on death of the king.'[79]

It must be clear from this record of Holland House
involvement in Spanish affairs that that country was regarded
as the most promising of its protégés. With or without their
consent, the Spanish were adopted by Holland House. They
were lectured, harassed and encouraged into constitutionalism. In their defence there was no risk that Holland was not
prepared to run. Again and again they disappointed him by a
refusal to accept English models of behaviour and by their
limitless capacity to argue amongst themselves. None of this
changed his basic assumptions. The experience of their travels
in Spain convinced the Hollands that no system based on
reactionary beliefs could survive there. The acceptance by the
men of property of their responsibility both to expel foreign
invaders and to construct constitutional government was a
textbook example of Whiggish good behaviour. 1815 settled
nothing in Spain. The duel between autocracy and liberalism
would continue. In this context, Spain, in microcosm,
represented the essential battle which was being fought all over
Western Europe. Spain acted as the symbol of European events
long before 1936. For the Hollands, its political experiences
represented everything that a Foxite would wish to
demonstrate about European affairs.

77. Add. MSS. 51547, f 25; Holland to Grey, 12 March 1824.
78. See below, Chapter Eleven.
79. Add. MSS. 51867, f 62; Holland's Political Journal, 30 July 1831.

10

France and Frenchmen, 1789-1830

Holland House was fascinated and bewildered by France. In one sense, it was the country that Lord and Lady Holland knew best, and in another it was the country which endlessly surprised them. They understood its language and culture intimately. Visits to Paris were considered essential for the continuing education of civilised people, and the French were usually represented at Holland House parties. Yet the violence of French politics, emanating from the most polished civilisation in Europe, was hard to comprehend. The Fox family admired France for its cultural achievements and feared it for its turbulence and unpredictability. As the greatest military power in Europe, France could either represent an irresistible force for political good or the shock troops of political evil. The Hollands tried to apply the same criteria, by which they judged the soundness of other European régimes, to successive French governments between 1789 and 1840, but it was harder to derive simple solutions. Was Bonapartism a good or a malign influence in Europe? Which party in France had most claim to the title of 'French Whigs'? Only one point was clear to the Hollands. They believed firmly that the nature of the régime in Paris determined the politics of at least Western Europe, and that Anglo-French relations might decide whether the continent as a whole was to have a liberal or an autocratic future.

According to Holland's son, the relationship between France and England had been 'the great hobby' of Charles

James Fox and 'still more' that of his own father.[1] No one was better equipped to follow this pursuit. Holland had arrived in Paris in 1791 for the first time, shortly after the death of Mirabeau. Under the guardianship of Lafayette, he was introduced to a wide spectrum of French political opinion, and contracted friendships that were to last for the rest of his life.[2] He came to France to observe the Revolution, firm in his uncle's belief that the events of 1789 were motivated by good, Whiggish ideas which had close English parallels. However depressing subsequent developments might be, Holland never wavered from Fox's view that the Revolution, at its inception, was liberal, generous and tolerant. Even at the highest point of the Terror, Holland took comfort in reflecting that the Revolution had been founded upon 'a principle which however it may be misconstrued and misunderstood is the same upon which our revolution in '88 was founded & the same upon which the existence of all free governments depend'.[3] The basic link between an English Whig and the French Revolution was a recognition that the events of 1688 and 1789 both involved a muzzling of despotism and autocratic power.

Predictably, both Holland and Fox followed the course of the Revolution with the keenest possible interest. Holland sent back regular reports and his uncle interpreted them and set them within a Whig context. Throughout this correspondence, the distaste for kings is paramount. Holland was in Paris during the flight to Varennes and heard Louis XVI's speech to the Legislative Assembly after his recapture. For him, it demonstrated the ineptitude and malevolence of Bourbon monarchy. Even Lafayette was taken to task for believing Louis XVI's protestations of good faith:

> The establishment of a Monarchy, with the view of ripening it into a
> Republick, was as mischievous to the community as unjust to the

1. C.R. Fox to H. Fox, 31 Oct. 1831; *The Chronicles of Holland House*, p.146.
2. R. Adair to Mme Recamier, 6 May 1836; Bibliothèque Nationale, n.a.fr. 14073, f 471.
3. Add. MSS. 51732, f 27; Holland to Caroline Fox, 2 June 1794; see also L.G. Mitchell, *Charles James Fox and the Disintegration of the Whig Party*, Ch. 5.

Monarch; and the notion that Lewis XVI could become a constitutional King, disposed to weaken rather than strengthen his own authority, after his intended flight, and with the Queen for his consort and adviser, was chimerical and puerile in the extreme.[4]

The acrimony and bitterness directed against Marie Antoinette in Holland's *Foreign Reminiscences* was culled from his experiences in Paris in 1791. The fall of the French monarchy and the September Massacres were provoked by the malevolence and incompetence of kings.[5]

The Fox family vendetta is unremitting. The trials and executions of Louis XVI and Marie Antoinette were unfortunate, but for Holland, the contemporary partitioning of Poland by kings was a crime of equal barbarism.[6] No Whig could shed tears over the destruction of autocratic governments, even though some of the attendant consequences were unpleasant and disturbing. As Holland told his sister: 'I fancy Hampden, Sidney or Somers would not be a little surprized were they to see their descendents spending their blood & treasure in order to restore an absolute monarchy to a neighbouring kingdom.'[7] Whatever qualms were felt about the deaths of the French king and queen were finally effaced by the publication of Dumouriez's *Memoires* in 1795, a highly coloured description of the Revolution which Holland accepted completely:

> It is sufficiently clear that the King & Queen were both acting a treacherous part and all the ingenuity of Jacobin violence and barbarity was necessary to put them so much in the right as they undoubtedly were after the tenth of August – that that bloody day was in fact rendered indispensable by the treachery of the court & intrigues of the Feuillans.[8]

Holland fully shared his uncle's view that the liberal hopes of 1789 degenerated into violence not because democratic intemperance became too great but because monarchical

4. *Foreign Reminiscences*, p.10.
5. Add. MSS. 51731, f 84; Holland to Caroline Fox, 8 Oct. 1792; see also C.J. Fox to Holland, 3 Sept. 1792; *Memorials and Correspondence of C.J. Fox*, iii 368.
6. Fox to Holland, 22 Aug. 1793; ibid., iii 47.
7. Add. MSS. 51731, ff 149-51; Holland to Caroline Fox, 28 Aug. 1793.
8. Add. MSS. 51733, f 51; Holland to Caroline Fox, 11 Aug. 1795.

trickery led politics into extremes. It was a theme that would be carried over into the nineteenth century and contribute to the evaluation of other French kings.

It was easy to identify villains, but much harder to find friends. The Fox family were depressed by the apparent inability of the revolutionaries to find stable solutions. The Feuillants would have allowed Louis a veto on all legislation, and 'he, who defends this, cannot be a Whig'.[9] The Girondins were sympathetic and talented but 'if one considers their vanity and indolence I believe one must own that they were little better than the Emigrants, the Feuillants or the Terrorists'.[10] Danton was 'a great Man' but 'lost himself by his corruption'.[11] Robespierre was 'that bloody fanatick of democracy'[12] or that 'despicable miscreant'. In 1795, however, Holland was busily collecting material for a life of Robespierre which ultimately had to be abandoned for a lack of hard evidence. Its purpose was to have been avowedly didactic and was to have presented a summing up of the Revolution as a whole:

> [It] will perhaps serve to prove first, that the proflicacy of internal intrigue, the Horror of foreign arms, & the profusion of English bribery contributed as much as any other circumstance to the calamities of France & the total prevalence of that system of Terror which deluged the country in blood & converted many mistaken but Honest men from the love of freedom to the acquiescence in hereditary despotism – secondly it will prove that ... the greatest Monster Modern History has seen ... had no commanding vices, no improving qualities, no firmness of soul, no brilliancy of talents to elevate his wickedness, to make us forget the tyrant in the Hero & lose the hypocrite in the consummate Statesman and Politician.[13]

To the Whig mind, pouring scorn on Louis XVI and Robespierre was to vilify the equal horrors of autocracy and democracy, but it came no nearer to finding a group in France

9. Fox to Holland, 20 Oct. 1792; *Memorials and Correspondence of C.J. Fox*, iii·371.

10. Add. MSS. 51733, f 68; Holland to Caroline Fox, 8 Sept. 1795.

11. ibid., f 100-1; ibid., 31 Oct. 1795.

12. Holland, *Memoirs of the Whig Party*, ii 215; see also Add. MSS. 51732, ff 88-9; Holland to Caroline Fox, 27 Sept. 1794.

13. Add. MSS. 51733, ff 120-1; Holland to Caroline Fox, 24 Nov. 1795.

that could be positively supported. In reality, after Lafayette's flight from France, in the summer of 1792, the Fox family had no position on French politics. Uncle and nephew could only point out the inadequacies of each new arrangement and hope that the 'Whig' spirit of 1789 would eventually be re-established.

The terrible weakness of the Foxite Whigs in having no cause in France that they could support after 1792 was only rendered less debilitating by the onset of war. If France was attacked by a coalition led by the Empress of Russia, the Emperor of Austria and the King of Prussia, political options once again became clear. The embarrassment of there being no individual Frenchman for whom genuine sympathy could be felt was lost in a defence of the French Revolution as a whole, in the face of a murderous assault by despotism in arms. Any crime perpetrated in France could be matched by the autocrats. The awfulness of the September Massacres paled into insignificance beside the Duke of Brunswick's threat to raze Paris to the ground. Holland reproved his sister for 'uttering your philippicks against the Massacres which sully but never can change the cause of Freedom in France without ever mentioning with one word of disapprobation the unexampled & infamous conspiracy not against France but against Liberty in general'.[14] To Fox and his nephew, the autocrats of the First Coalition were the true 'Barbarians'.[15] Even the excesses of the Committee of Public Safety were to an extent mitigated by the fact that the French

> are fighting to prevent the interference of other governments with their own, they are contending for the independence of their nation, fighting to prevent the dismemberment of their country and subversion of their rights as a people – I am willing to think that it is this principle & not any affection for the bloody government they have that fills their navies and armies and warms their heart with an enthusiasm which we have long imagined our times to be incapable of.[16]

14. Add. MSS. 51731, f 88; Holland to Caroline Fox, 23 Oct. 1792; see also Add. MSS. 47570, f 11; Fox to Holland, 20 Aug. 1792.

15. Add. MSS. 51731, f 91; Holland to Caroline Fox, 30 Oct. 1792; see also Fox to Holland, 14 June 1793; *Memoirs of the Whig Party*, i 66-7.

16. Add. MSS. 51732, f 15-16; Holland to Caroline Fox, 30 May 1794.

Once war between France and the First Coalition of kings had broken out, some choice had to be made. The Fox family opted for the lesser of two evils in the hope that it would produce long term good.

Predictably, England's entry into the war, in 1793, was greeted by Holland with profound alarm. Convinced that the motive for war was not, as Pitt claimed, a pragmatic defence of the Low Countries against French aggression but rather an ideological crusade to restore absolute monarchy in Paris,[17] Holland could only deplore any English participation. As Fox and his nephew amused themselves by drawing parallels between decrees of the Committee of Public Safety and Pitt's emergency legislation abrogating civil liberties,[18] it seemed that George III had at last been given the opportunity and excuse to perpetrate gross violations of the constitution. 1762, 1766, and 1784 fused with war to substantiate the Whig view of the king's malignity. Neither Fox nor Holland believed that the French could be browbeaten into a return to monarchy, but that, if such a calamity befell them, it would mark the end of all hope of political stability in that country. In a profound sense, 1789 could not be undone. The fall of Robespierre had made little difference to the French will to resist and nor did the overt corruption of the Directory.[19] The war was fundamentally futile because the French were filled with an ambition of 'preventing one nation from interfering with the internal government of another, and above all, of preventing *Crowned* heads from making a common cause against the rest of Mankind'.[20]

When England entered the war as an ally of autocrats in coalition, the constitutional battle which Fox had fought in England since 1784 fused with the larger struggle in Europe. As Holland mused on the disappearance of Habeas Corpus and the right to free assembly, he traced its origins back to the dissolution of Parliament in 1784, 'the greatest revolution we have experienced, the origin of all our evils & the most severe

17. Add. MSS. 47571, f 78; Fox to Holland, 3 Nov. 1793; see also Add. MSS. 48226, f 125; Holland to Boringdon, 4 Jan. 1795.
18. Add. MSS. 47571, f 85; Fox to Holland, 7 Nov. 1793.
19. Add. MSS. 51732, f 65; Holland to Caroline Fox, 19 Aug. 1794.
20. Add. MSS. 51733, ff 35-6; Holland to Caroline Fox, 23 July 1795.

blow the constitution ever received'.[21] War naturally strengthened the power of executive government all over Europe. It had eliminated moderate men from politics in both England and France. Fox and his nephew, by 1795, found themselves in an eery limbo. The Whig party had ceased to exist as a credible power base. Their friends were no longer powerful in France. It seemed to Fox and Holland that they lived 'in times of violence and extremes, and all those who are for creating or even for retaining checks upon power are considered as enemies to order'.[22] Never had the Foxite obsession with muzzling executive power been more unpopular. Their political views were dictated by events. If war underpinned executive power in France and England, 'moderate' men must be for peace. If there was only the dismal choice between George III and the Directory in France, 'moderate' men must oppose the greater evil in the hope of better days.

If, according to Holland, the war with France was being fought to impose on the French a constitutional settlement which they would never accept in the long term, it followed that the Fox family should support the idea of a peace which recognised the events of 1789 and 1792. It was only realistic to recognise the demise of monarchy in France:

> We must acknowledge the French republick without qualification, we must acknowledge a revolutionary right inherent in the people of that Country, and consequently of all countries, by renouncing any intention of interfering with their internal affairs upon any plea or pretext whatsoever, we must either restore part of our spoils or leave the French in quiet possession of theirs in doing which we break through all our treaties like cobwebs and leave the tattered fragments as the monuments of our mischievous ingenuity.[23]

Throughout the 1790s, Holland supported all attempts to promote peace on the basis of a recognition that what had

---

21. Add. MSS. 51733, f 52; Holland to Caroline Fox, 2 Oct. 1795.
22. Fox to Holland, c 28 Dec. 1793; *Memorials and Correspondence of C.J. Fox*, iii 61.
23. Add. MSS. 51733, ff 161-2; Holland to Caroline Fox, 5 Jan. 1796.

happened in France was irreversible.[24] Some of his earliest speeches in the Lords were attempts to block subsidies for England's autocratic allies,[25] and only once in Holland's correspondence is there any suggestion that the French might be equally to blame for the continuing fact of war.[26] Rather, in Fox family mythology, peace was unobtainable because George III and Pitt saw too many advantages in war.[27]

When a brief peace was concluded at Amiens in 1802, the Fox family were predictably delighted. The recognition of Bonaparte was in some measure a recognition of the Revolution. They could, as Lord Morpeth pointed out, 'indulge [their] pacific dreams for some time longer'.[28] But, as he went on to demonstrate, the Fox family reaction to the French Revolution was eccentric and lopsided. They had consistently underestimated its dynamism and novelty. Their insistence on comparing 1789 with the carefully managed 'revolution' of 1688 was ultimately misleading. The aggressive and proselytising aspect of the Revolution was too long denied by Fox and his nephew, for whom the phenomenon of Bonaparte was a puzzle rather than a warning. Not until the peace negotiations of 1806, in which Fox himself was intimately involved, did the family as a whole come to appreciate the darker face of the new France. On the other hand, Fox and Holland always insisted, through the 1790s and beyond, that the French world had irrevocably changed. The hope that the French Revolution would finally settle down into a kind of political Englishness may have been naive, but their insistence that there could be no return to the Ancien Régime in France was profoundly helpful. It was not easy for Fox and Holland to identify a party in France that shared an unshakable Whig belief in constitutionalism, but at least they

24. Add. MSS. 48226, ff 127-8; and ff. 137-8; Holland to Boringdon, 8 April 1795 and 6 Oct. 1797; see also Add. MSS. 51577, ff 87-8; Morpeth to Holland, 19 Oct. 1797.
25. *Parl. Deb.*, 21 March 1798; vol. XXXIII 1327 and *Parl. Deb.*, 11 June 1799; vol. XXXIV 1063-5.
26. Add. MSS. 51734, ff 63-5; Holland to Caroline Fox, Oct. 1796.
27. Fox to Holland, 24 Feb. 1795; *Memorials and Correspondence of C.J. Fox*, iii 99.
28. Add. MSS. 51577, ff 97-8; Morpeth to Holland, 15 Dec. 1802.

recognised that French politics could not be stabilised by imposing a monarchical solution on an unwilling nation.

All these fears were realised by the restoration of the French monarchy in the person of Louis XVIII in 1814. The Hollands put no faith in him or in the written constitution which theoretically bound him to constitutional practice. The arrangement was forced on the French by the weight of arms[29] and its overthrow had, in Holland's view, to become an article of the Whig faith. He told Grey that 'as to foreign policy, I am I fear a little more unreasonable. In short, my dear Grey, unless relinquishment of the policy by which we maintain at the risk of war & at the expence of our National character & constitutional security, an odious Government in France, becomes an article in our political creed as a party, I really do not know how I can honestly profess myself to be within the pale of our Whig Church'.[30] A garden party at Chiswick House was ruined by a public quarrel between George Tierney and Lady Holland on the subject of the credibility of the new French constitution. To Tierney's plea that it should be given a fair trial, Lady Holland simply replied: 'All humbug, my dear Tierney.'[31] Everything in the Hollands' experience of France convinced them that Bourbons could not be constitutionalists when Hanoverians found it so hard to be. The 1815 settlement was therefore hypocrisy.

In the autumn of 1814, the Hollands hurried to Paris to test the water of French politics for themselves, and found that 'the old emigrants were more absurd than they were before the Revolution and very much discontented with the Government for not restoring their estates'.[32] It was therefore with some personal knowledge of the situation that he outlined his views to the House of Lords on his return:

> It was clear that we were not to have a peace establishment in the true sense of the word. For could that be called a peace establishment when we were to keep on foot as large a body of troops to preserve,

29. Holland to C.R. Fox, April 1814; *Sovereign Lady*, p.204.
30. Holland to Grey, 4 Dec. 1816; Grey MSS. Box 34.
31. The Journal of Lady Elizabeth Foster, 1815; *Dearest Bess*, pp. 202-4.
32. J. Wishaw to S. Smith, 18 Sept. 1814; *The Pope of Holland House*, pp. 60-1.

forsooth, the Bourbons on the throne of France, as we had ever done at a former period to oppose the ambition of this same family ... the restoration of that family in 1814 was a complete farce, and entirely owing to the presence of foreign bayonets.[33]

As he had witnessed the duplicity of Louis XVI towards constitutional obligations in the summer of 1791, so now Holland saw Louis XVIII behaving in exactly the same way. According to Fox family experience, any attempt to find a stable and liberal settlement for France had to be concentrated outside France's ruling house. Since the 1790s, Holland had argued that no Bourbon had wholeheartedly accepted the fact of the Revolution, and nothing that he saw in France in 1814 led him to change his mind.[34]

From the outset therefore, Holland predicted that the Restoration Monarchy would not last long. Visits to Paris in 1817, 1821 and 1825-6[35] confirmed the Hollands in the view that the government of Louis XVIII and Charles X suffered from two fatal weaknesses. First, it was as obvious to the bulk of the French people as it was to the Hollands that kings had been brought back by foreign armies, and that the strength of the régime lay in the good offices of a consortium of other rulers. The peace treaties had no permanence because the French believed that their interests had not been properly consulted. Prophetically, Holland identified the Belgian clauses of the treaty as particularly transitory.[36] He described the 1815 settlement as 'not a mere interference of a conqueror with the affairs of a conquered country but it is, disguise it as they will, a conspiracy of the Governments of Europe against the people, an agreement to render the Kings the sole judges of other King's titles & actions & to deprive the governed of that Right which nature & reason have given them, the choice

33. *Parl. Deb.*, 19 Feb. 1816; vol. LXVIII 664-5.

34. Holland to Grey, 6 Feb. 1816; *The Whigs in Opposition*, p.87.

35. Their already extensive knowledge of France was further extended by the fact that an old Christ Church contemporary of Holland's, Granville Leveson Gower, was ambassador in Paris between 1824 and 1828 and again between 1830 and 1841. See Castalia, Countess Granville, *The Letters of Lord Granville Leveson Gower* (London 1916), and F. Leveson Gower, *The Letters of Harriet, Countess Granville* (London 1894).

36. Add. MSS. 51740, ff 77-8; Holland to Caroline Fox, 11 Feb. 1815.

by whom they shall be governed'.[37] Régimes built on such foundations must, according to Holland, falter.

Secondly, Holland believed that the Restoration Monarchy laboured under the weakness of having a king who could not escape the obligation of being a party leader. For émigrés and Churchmen who had suffered so much since 1789, the re-establishment of monarchy meant only the possibility for revenge. Even without the complicating factor of their own personalities, Louis XVIII and Charles X were not kings of France but leaders of a section of Frenchmen. As early as 1814, Holland could identity the reasons for the Monarchy's eventual collapse. He told his sister to 'read the last sentence of my Uncle's[38] introduction (I quote from recollection only) speculating on the events which were probable at James's accession & substitute Church lands & confiscated property for Church establishment & religion & it will be as applicable to Lewis 18th's as to James 2nd's accession.'[39] Visiting Paris in 1825, Holland was not surprised to find that Charles X 'who is an honest and sincere man, very unlike Louis 18, is entirely governed by a small Junto of fanaticks'.[40] For those who had lost by the Revolution, Bourbon kings brought the hope of restitution. According to Holland therefore, the whole régime was grounded in a denial of 1789 and, as such, could not last long. For nearly forty years, Holland had observed the Bourbons and found nothing to his liking.

If Bourbon monarchy could not provide France with long-term stability, the Hollands were much less clear about the phenomenon of Bonapartism. After 1815, Holland House acquired a reputation for being fanatically and uncritically Bonapartist, and, to an extent, this reputation was justified.

37. Holland to Grey, 9 Jan. 1816; Grey MSS. Box 34.
38. Holland is here referring to C.J. Fox's unfinished *History of the Reign of James II*, (London 1808). The sentence in question reads as follows. 'From this observation we may draw a further inference that, in proportion to the rashness of the Crown, in avowing and pressing forward the cause of Popery, and to the moderation and steadiness of the Whigs, in adhering to the form of monarchy, would be the chance for the people of England, for changing an ignominious despotism, for glory, liberty, and happiness.'
39. Add. MSS. 51740, f 15; Holland to Caroline Fox, c 26 Aug. 1814.
40. Holland to Caroline Fox, 3 Oct. 1825; *The Chronicles of Holland House*, p.68.

Very early in his career, Bonaparte was thought 'the Most Extraordinary Man of the Age' by Caroline Fox, for which predilection she was teased by her brother.[41] Lady Holland's devotion to the Emperor was so warm and unqualified that it was taken to be further evidence of her political unbalance.[42] A bust of 'the hero' by Canova stood in the gardens of Holland House in the company of other Whig gods.[43] Yet the attitudes of both Charles James Fox and his nephew were more cautious. Napoleon certainly fascinated both of them. Nearly a third of Holland's *Foreign Reminiscences* is devoted to a discussion of the implications of the Bonapartist experience in Europe. At the same time, they could never give him unalloyed approval. From the moment that their interview with Bonaparte in 1802 was interrupted by a delegation from the Senate asking him to become Consul for life, the opinions of Holland and his uncle became a compound of admiration and deep suspicion.[44]

In short, Bonaparte presented the Foxite Whig with an almost insuperable problem. So much that Bonaparte was to accomplish both within France and in the rest of Europe was worthy of support. On the other hand, as the Fox family recognised, the agency for accomplishing change was executive power which grew inexorably stronger in France down to 1815. Was it possible for a Whig to applaud the outcome of Bonapartist activity if the means employed were so profoundly suspect? No consistent answer was ever worked out to this dilemma. Holland once again took refuge in the application of a spectrum between good and evil and placed Napoleon on it. In Holland's correspondence, Bonaparte is

41. Add. MSS. 51734, f 71; Holland to Caroline Fox, 30 Nov. 1796; see also Add. MSS. 51735, f 153; Holland to Caroline Fox, 19 Nov. 1799.

42. Bedford to Lady Holland, June 1814; *Sovereign Lady*, p.216.

43. At the base of the bust was the following inscription:

> He is not dead, he breathes the air
> In distant lands beyond the deep,
> Some distant sea-girt island where
> Harsh men the hero keep.

Sovereign Lady, p.210.

44. *Personal Recollections of the Life and Times of Lord Cloncurry*, pp. 183-4.

endlessly compared with the alternative of the moment. If he was found fighting a greater evil, he was to be supported. If he was discovered oppressing a greater good, he was to be condemned. There was some consistency in this policy, but it was not always easy for Holland's contemporaries to follow the twists and turns of its working out. It was easier for them to take Lady Holland's uncritical Bonapartism as typical of the Fox family as a whole. This was, however, to arrive at a half-truth only.

Holland's reaction to Napoleon's impact on France was therefore all ambivalence:

> Bonaparte like the grand Cardinal a fait trop de mal pour en dire du bien et a fait trop de bien pour en dire du mal. He seems to like dwelling on the horrors of the revolution in order to disgust people with the name of liberty – but while he does so one must also acknowledge that he does much to do away the effect of those horrors & that placed in the singular situation of being the creature of the republick without being a republican & the protector of royalists without being their king he redresses the grievances & adopts the doctrines of the latter in a mode if not less dangerous to freedom at least less likely to produce reaction confusion & bloodshed than any Bourbon King could do. Many of the advantages resulting from the revolution such as equalization of taxes, abolition of all embarrassments & obstacles on internal trade, & the encouragement of all talents civil & military from the road being open to all competitors are perfectly compatible with a strong not to say an arbitrary government, but would all be lost were that arbitrary government in the hands of a Bourbon.[45]

Holland disliked Mme de Staël's idea that Napoleon was 'point un homme mais un Système',[46] which had either to be wholly accepted or wholly rejected. He preferred a more eclectic approach. Napoleon had brought stability to a country on the brink of civil war.[47] He more than anyone else bound the French together in a common purpose.[48] Talent was recognised in the Empire, property-holding had become a

45. Add. MSS. 51736, f 62; Holland to Caroline Fox, 6 Aug. 1802.
46. Lady Holland to Sir C. Vaughan, 30 June 1813; Vaughan MSS. c 61/8.
47. Add. MSS. 51578, f 84; Holland to Carlisle, Oct. 1821.
48. Holland, *Foreign Reminiscences*, pp. 256-7.

possibility for thousands of new people, and the roads ran straight.[49] So much that English Whigs had found offensive in the old system had been rectified.

On the other hand, all these good results had been achieved by executive power, and, as Bonaparte moved from Consulate to Empire, all checks on the exercise of that power were gradually removed. No Whig could applaud such a development. Holland could blame Napoleon's marriage to the daughter of the Austrian Emperor for his giving in to a desire 'to assimilate his government more and more to other monarchies',[50] but such a ploy only explained vice without excusing it. Consistency demanded that the Fox family critique of executive power be applied to Bonaparte as well as to his enemies. By 1814, Holland's responses to the Emperor had almost been paralysed in ambivalence. He told his sister that 'it is difficult to know what to wish. I hate & detest Bonaparte more than ever & yet I am not sure if he were to fall that the *legitimate* sovereign would not be restored & that in my mind is the last of misfortunes – bad for France, for liberty & for Mankind & in a narrower view bad for England'.[51] If nothing else could be said on Bonaparte's behalf, he was at least a prophylactic against even greater evil. On the Holland scale between good and evil, Bonaparte stood nearer to the light than the Bourbons.

The problem of accounting for Bonaparte was even more acute in the area of foreign policy. Traditionally the Whigs had feared France. As the greatest military power in Europe, France endlessly threatened England's trade and England's security. While the Bourbons ruled France, absolutism could call on military might. The fact that the Fox family could find anything to say in favour of Bonapartist France led to the accusation that they were abandoning customary Whig views. Grenville lectured Holland on 'the necessity of a resistance [to] the preponderating power of France in Europe'.[52]

49. Holland to Grey, 14 Sept. 1815; Grey MSS. Box 34; see also J. Mallet to J. Wishaw, 28 Jan. 1815; *The Pope of Holland House*, pp. 307-9.
50. Holland, *Foreign Reminiscences*, p.187.
51. Add. MSS. 51939, f 222; Holland to Caroline Fox, *c.* April 1814.
52. Add. MSS. 51530, ff 19-20; Grenville to Holland, n.d.

Holland replied that the new factor in the situation was that, for the first time, the military power of France was in quasi-liberal hands. The trading and strategic threats might continue, but at least in ideological terms there might now be aspects of French policy that Whigs could support. There could, however, be no clear line. As with Bonaparte's domestic policies, it would be necessary to choose carefully what could and what could not be applauded.

Writing from Germany in July 1815, Holland eloquently described the beneficial effects of the Napoleonic experience

> For my part so far from believing that these events [Waterloo] lead to any permanent peace I expect to see interminable wars in every part of Europe spring up from the ashes of this ... I write however from a country which is manifestly so much improved by its late connection with France, so much attached to Napoleon & so much disgusted with all that has succeeded him that I may be drawing general conclusions from particular facts which do not warrant it. The left bank of the Rhine had gained wonderfully in agriculture, intelligence, education, administration of justice ... during its connection with France ... but who that had to chuse between German feudalities & French government would hesitate in deciding for the latter.[53]

The irresistible fascination of Bonaparte lay in the observable fact that he had almost literally moved mountains. The France, Germany and Italy that the Hollands visited in 1814-15 were profoundly different from what they had known in the 1790s. The Vienna treaties would prove impermanent because the imagination of whole peoples had been irreversibly stirred.

It followed that, whenever Napoleon confronted 'the northern barbarians' of Russia and Prussia, Whigs should support him. The Hollands followed the French retreat across Europe in 1812-14 with dismay.[54] Personal experiences gathered on their European journey convinced the Hollands that, wherever the Allies reestablished themselves, everything that promised a liberal and constitutional future was snuffed out. He told Thomas Grenville that he was 'more than usually

53. Add. MSS. 51740, ff 147-8; Holland to Caroline Fox, 4 July 1815.
54. Add. MSS. 51545, f 106; Holland to Grey, 4 Dec. 1813; Add. MSS. 51549, f 127; Lady Holland to Grey, 4 March 1814; Add. MSS. 51739, f 146; 21 Oct. 1813.

soured with the northern barbarians – for such, in spite of
their acknowledged courage, I must consider them – from
having witnessed their odious and vexatious conduct to their
subjects and their friends on the Rhine and in Flanders'.[55]
Setting patriotic considerations aside, a Foxite had no choice
but to support Bonaparte as the greater good. As a result, the
notoriety of Holland House as a place where farouche foreign
politics were peddled was in no way diminished. To deplore
the Allied successes after 1812 was distinctive to say the least.
In March 1814, 'Lady Holland was fool enough ... to say
before ten people that she hoped Bonaparte would let but few
of the Allies get back to Frankfurt. This is very disgusting even
in a woman of such an irregular mind, and does a mischief
and discredit beyond belief.'[56] For some, the vaunting of such
views made Holland House 'unapproachable'.[57] These
opinions were born of an appreciation of what was positive in
Bonaparte's contribution to Europe and an absolute refusal to
support systems that were visibly worse.

Once again, however, although Lady Holland lavished
unstinting praise on Bonaparte, Holland himself was never as
uncritical of the French Emperor as many of his
contemporaries thought. In other parts of Europe, where
Bonaparte fought against national feeling, Holland
unhesitatingly attacked him. Lady Bessborough found this
puzzling: 'We dined at Holland House yesterday; it was very
pleasant, except for every now and then that tone of
incredulity or indifference to our successes – not in Spain, for I
cannot make out the consistency of their views; they would
defeat Bonaparte in Spain, but let him defeat the allies in
Germany. This is beyond my Politicks, and makes me ...
cross.'[58] The problem was not deep. Applying the Holland
House spectrum between good and evil, Napoleon was to be
cheered for bringing elements of liberalism to areas of Europe
formally dominated by autocrats, and damned for opposing

55. Holland to T. Grenville, 15 Sept. 1815; E. Tangye Lean, *The Napoleonists*, p.166.
56. T. Grenville to Lord Grenville, 15 Feb. 1814; H.M.C. 30 *Forestcue* X, p.380.
57. ibid., March 1814; ibid., p.384.
58. Lady Bessborough to Lord G. Leveson Gower, 22 Oct. 1813; *The Letters of Lord
Granville Leveson Gower*, ii 485.

liberal nationalists in Spain and Portugal. The application of this principle would have the happy effect that in both Spain and Poland, Holland would be supporting his friends, the constitutionalists. As he told the House of Lords in December 1813, he was 'bred in a school of politics that deprecated every encroachment upon national independence and the just liberty of mankind'.[59]

If Napoleon was to be praised or criticised according to context, and if he was neither an unqualified force for good nor a committed agent of the devil, it was relatively easy to pursue the idea that peace with France was possible as long as the Allies ceased to insist on a restoration of the Bourbons.[60] In Holland's view, it was perfectly feasible to envisage a peace which left Bonaparte as ruler of France. In 1800, both Holland and his uncle accepted the French overtures for peace as genuine and insisted that Bonaparte 'had given every proof of his sincerity'.[61] In the view of the Fox family, the failure of this initiative and the breakdown of the Peace of Amiens was entirely due to the British government's mishandling of Bonaparte and their insistence on making the war an ideological struggle to reimpose the Bourbons on France.[62] When war was resumed, in 1803, Holland told his sister: 'As to the war, I am so mad at it that it seems to me that as Addington's father made the king sound, his son has made the people mad — Mad indeed they must be if they approve this war ... to break treaties for the sake of being ruined, what is it but to rob on the Highway not for the love of the money but of the gallows.'[63] On this view, the ideological commitments of successive British governments had driven Bonaparte into extreme courses of action which might otherwise have been avoided.

It was perhaps this persistent willingness to give Napoleon

59. *Parl. Deb.*, 20 Dec. 1813; vol. LXIII 289-99.

60. Fox to Holland, Jan. 1800; *Memorials and Correspondence of C.J. Fox*, iii 174-7.

61. *Parl. Deb.*, 28 Jan. 1800; vol. XXXIV 1233 seq. See also Add. MSS. 51735, f 165; Holland to Caroline Fox, 21 Jan. 1800 and Melbourne to Lady Melbourne, 8 Feb. 1800; *Lord Melbourne's Papers*, p.21.

62. Fox to Holland, 6 June 1803; *Memorials and Correspondence of C.J. Fox*, iii 220-4. Add. MSS. 51577, ff 99-100; Morpeth to Holland, 17 April 1803.

63. Add. MSS. 51736, f 188; Holland to Caroline Fox, 1 June 1803.

the benefit of the doubt which most contributed to contemporary descriptions of Holland House as hopelessly Bonapartist in sympathy. Holland saw a good possibility for peace after Tilsit in 1807.[64] He fully subscribed to Sydney Smith's satirical rejection of English attempts to blockade France: 'the French, driven to the borders of insanity by the want of coffee, will rise and establish a family more favourable to the original mode of breakfasting. I have ventured to express doubts, but am immediately silenced as an Edinburgh reviewer.'[65] Above all, Napoleon's disastrous invasion of Russia in 1812 opened up real possibilities of a fair and negotiated peace.[66] There was then no question of the French dominating Europe, and, if the war had been fought to muzzle France, that objective had now been achieved. If the English government refused to offer peace terms, it could only confirm the Fox family belief that, from its inception, the war had been inspired by ideology alone, 'the indulging [of] extravagant and impracticable notions of humiliating Bonaparte & gratifying vanity & resentment'.[67] At no point did Holland abandon the proposition that a long-term peace with Bonaparte was possible as long as proper objectives were set out, particularly with regard to the Iberian peninsula, and as long as all commitment to Bourbon politics was abandoned.[68]

There was a certain logic in the view that, once monarchical solutions for France were discarded, a general European peace became a possibility, but to many contemporaries the Holland House line was simply not credible. For the Grenville family and many others, the years 1799-1812 proved that Bonaparte could not be trusted and that his removal from power was a precondition of taming France and restoring a balance of power in Europe. Just as many people could not follow the serpentine line of thought that allowed the Hollands to support Bonaparte's behaviour in central and eastern

64. T. Grenville to Lord Grenville, 9 Dec. 1807; H.M.C. 30 *Fortescue* IX 159.

65. S. Smith to Lady Holland, 9 Dec. 1807; *The Letters of Sydney Smith*, i 129.

66. Add. MSS. 51653, f 42; Holland to Mackintosh, 24 Dec. 1812.

67. Add. MSS. 51545, ff 24-6; Holland to Grey, 11 Nov. 1812.

68. Holland to Whitbread, c 1812; Whitbread MSS. 4208; see also *Parl. Deb.*, 13 Dec. 1812, vol. LX 322-3 and 29 June 1813, LXII 957-8.

Europe but not in Spain or Portugal, so their insistence that, properly handled, the French Emperor could become a stable element in a new European order looked equally odd. Outside the charmed circle of Holland House, it was easier to ignore the distinctions that Holland tried to draw and simply daub the building with accusations of outright Bonapartist loyalties. The issue added yet another element to the Hollands' well-established reputation for political idiosyncrasy. To many the Hollands were simply 'Bonaparte mad'.[69]

With this ambivalent response to Bonaparte, the period between his escape from Elba and his final defeat at Waterloo was for the Hollands one characterised by an extraordinary mixture of alarm and pleasurable anticipation that never quite left them.[70] Once again, Holland was more circumspect in his response than his wife. Writing home to his sister from Italy, he described his feelings as follows:

> Here's a job. Bonaparte escaped from his goal! Where is he going? What are his chances of success? Whatever be the result I think it a misfortune. If he fails he must be sacrificed & who can contemplate the extinction of such genius & activity with thorough indifference? If he succeeds we must have twenty years more war ... We are preparing for an excursion to Paestum but the escape of the *hero* has set Ldy Holland's spirits in such a flurry & agitation that I suspect she will not be calm & sedate enough to enjoy the imposing gravity of Dorick Architecture.[71]

They were both under no illusions about the depths of real Bonapartist feeling in France, but had to admit that this very popularity would probably take military form.[72] Awed and fascinated, Holland was neither for nor against Bonaparte during the Hundred Days. He continued to employ his standard device of weighing the Emperor against alternatives.

69. H. Bunbury to H.S. Fox, 30 Aug. 1815; Bodleian MSS. Eng. Lett. c 234, f 48.
70. Add. MSS. 51748, f 73; Holland to Henry Fox, 14 Feb. 1820; see also *Samuel Rogers and his Contemporaries*, i 181.
71. Add. MSS. 51740, f 93; Holland to Caroline Fox, 8 March 1815.
72. Holland to Grey, 12 July 1815; Grey MSS. Box 34.

In spite of this, Napoleon allowed the Hollands to travel back to England on an official passport signed by himself.[73]

After Waterloo and the Emperor's abdication, there was no element in the situation which a Whig could positively support. Peace had come but it had brought the Bourbons into Paris again in its wake. The military threat from Bonaparte had been snuffed out, but so had all his admirable contributions to Europe. There seemed to be no option in European politics that had a liberal or constitutional face. The experiences of 1814 and 1815 brought Holland's views on France to the point of neutered immobility:

> We have heard of the *abdication* but cannot yet understand the nature of it. Peace is my wish, if it comes with the triumph of Kings & restoration of Bourbons it comes as much embittered to my palate as so sweet a thing can be – I am in opinion to the full as violent perhaps more so than in 1793 but I have not so much feeling or affection for persons directly or indirectly concerned & am thank God more indifferent than I then was.[74]

Encouraged by his wife, Holland continued to receive Bonapartists in London,[75] and indeed initiated a major campaign to try to save the life of Marshal Ney,[76] but his essential dilemma about Bonapartism remained. How was it possible to acknowledge the benefits that Napoleon had brought to France without deploring the executive power by which these reforms were effected. How was it possible to cheer Napoleon's fostering of Italian and Polish nationalism without deploring his behaviour in Spain. For a Foxite Whig there was no clear-cut answer to any of these problems. In what looked like a groping and hesitating manner, Holland could only measure Bonaparte against his adversaries and judge accordingly.

It is really in the period 1815-21 that Holland House earned

73. Lady Holland to Caroline Fox, 6 March 1815; *Sovereign Lady*, p.210.

74. Add. MSS. 51740, ff 140-1; Holland to Caroline Fox, 27 June 1815.

75. T. Grenville to Lord Grenville, 15 & 26 Dec. 1815; H.M.C. 30 *Fortescue* X 408-9.

76. Holland to Grey, 24 Nov. 1815; Grey MSS. Box 34.

its reputation for madcap Bonapartism. Lady Holland's devotion to 'the greatest man of our times'[77] was undiminished. In spite of official attempts at obstruction, Lady Holland succeeded in sending out chests of presents to St Helena, for which she was formally thanked by the Emperor himself. The gifts ranged from food to eau de Cologne, but, as Holland informed Napoleon's sister, 'l'idée qu'ils n'ont pas été inutiles et qu'ils ont pu adoucir quelques instans de ce cruel exil est bien la plus chère et la plus flatteuse pour Lady Holland'.[78] Further, now that the capacity of Bonaparte to threaten and oppress had been removed, Lord Holland himself could safely reflect on the man's achievements without fearing his abuse of executive power. On 8 April 1816, Holland entered a lone protest in the Lords' Journal against the exiling of Bonaparte to St Helena. As he put it, 'to consign to distant exile and imprisonment a foreign and captive chief, who, after the abdication of his authority, relying on British generosity, had surrendered himself to us in preference to his other enemies, is unworthy of the magnanimity of a great country'.[79] In his view, the St Helena exile was a form of judicial murder.[80]

The Greek tragedy being played out on St Helena became a matter of overwhelming interest to Holland House. Designated the 'digne héritier de l'immortel Fox'[81] by members of Bonaparte's family, Holland did everything in his power to mitigate his terms of imprisonment. The *Edinburgh Review* was used to publicise information about Bonaparte which was provided by his brothers and sisters via Holland House.[82] Holland himself kept up a vigorous, Parliamentary campaign about conditions on St Helena,[83] and, at one point,

77. Lady Holland to Bathurst, 16 Sept. 1820; H.M.C. 76 *Bathurst*, p.487.
78. Holland to Pauline Borghese, 11 Aug. 1821; *Sovereign Lady*, p.228; see also Lady Holland to Grey, 25 Sept. 1815.
79. *Parl. Deb.*, 8 April 1816; vol. LXIX 1020.
80. Add. MSS. 51748, ff 80-1; Holland to Henry Fox, 18 Feb. 1820.
81. Lucien Bonaparte to Holland, 25 April 1819; *The Chronicles of Holland House*, p.14.
82. Creevey to Miss Ord, 21 July 1822; *The Creevey Papers*, ii 39.
83. J. Wishaw to S. Smith, 11 March 1817; *The Pope of Holland House*, p.176; see also Holland to Ebrington, 11 Jan. 1817; Fortescue MSS. 1262 M/FC 75.

he and his wife took on Napoleon's gaoler, Sir Hudson Lowe, as a dinner guest, in a vain attempt to influence him in their new protégé's favour. The same charity and concern was extended to the Emperor's entourage.[84] No cause could have been more unpopular. Odium was heaped on Holland House, but with little effect. Anyone connected with St Helena would be squeezed dry of every last point of information about the Emperor, his thoughts and general way of life.[85] Holland House was never so Bonapartist as it was after 1815.

News of Napoleon's death reached Paris while the Hollands were paying one of their periodic visits to the French capital, and they were appalled by the Bourbons pretending grief:

> The Court here affect to speak of the great man they dreaded and persecuted, with tenderness and even admiration – LXVIII is no Caesar, but
>
> > 'Caesar would weep, the crocodile would weep,
> > To see his rival of the universe
> > Lie still and peaceful there.'[86]

In his will, Bonaparte left Lady Holland a snuff-box which had been a present from Pius VI. It was handed over by two of Napoleon's companions in exile, Bertrand and Montholon, at Holland House on 18 September 1821. To many, it became a token and symbol of the Hollands' longstanding and traitorous leanings towards Bonapartism. The Earl of Carlisle poetically advised its rejection:

> Lady, reject the gift! 'tis tinged with gore!
> Those crimson spots a dreadful tale relate.
> It has been grasp'd by an infernal Power
> And by that hand which seal'd young Enghien's[87] fate.[88]

84. Mme. de Montholon to Holland, 31 Jan. 1820; *Foreign Reminiscences*, pp. 333-5; Holland to Ebrington, 17 Nov. 1818; Fortescue MSS. 1262 M/FC 76. Lady Holland to Mrs Creevey, Sept. 1817; *The Creevey Papers*, i 226.

85. The manuscript of Lord Ebrington's conversations with Bonaparte are in the Holland House collection. Add. MSS. 51525.

86. Lord Holland to S. Rogers, July 1821; *Samuel Rogers & his Contemporaries*, i 309. (Dryden, *All for Love*, Act I, Scene I.)

87. On Napoleon's orders, the Duc d'Enghien was kidnapped and shot in March 1804.

88. R. Prothero, *The Works of Lord Byron*, VI 82.

Lord Holland swiftly replied in kind:

> For this her snuffbox to resign
> A pretty thought enough
> Alas, my Lord, for verse of thine,
> Who'd give a pinch of snuff.[89]

The snuff-box remained at Holland House. For Lady Holland, it was the gift of the hero of his age. For Lord Holland, it came from a man whose crimes and achievements were both of monumental proportions.

In fact, the Hollands determinedly kept up their connections with the surviving members of Bonaparte's family. Jérôme Bonaparte was a regular guest whenever he came to England.[90] Joseph, the ex-ruler of Spain came in 1833, and was found 'as handsome, plain, well-meaning an ex-king as one could wish to see on a summer's day'.[91] The Hollands' favourite, however, was Lucien Bonaparte, because on his regular visits to Holland House, he 'expresses a great love of rational liberty & attributes the evils of despotism, which he is not disposed to palliate, to the nature of despotism rather than the character of the individual despot'.[92] On a number of occasions, the Hollands tried to assist members of Bonaparte's family who had become associated in his disgrace.[93] Inevitably, such activity confirmed suspicions about the Hollands' true feelings. Lady Holland was as lavishly devoted to Napoleon as her critics liked to suggest. At no point was this true of her husband.

Reflecting on the whole Napoleonic adventure, Holland came to the firm conclusion that, like the Bourbons, the Bonaparte family too offered no long-term stability for France. He believed that such a régime would inevitably overflow into military adventures. He deplored any suggestion that the Bonapartes might be plotting a coup[94] and, although he was

89. *The Chronicles of Holland House*, p.16.
90. Lady Holland to Henry Fox, 18 Feb. 1840; *Elizabeth, Lady Holland to her Son*, p.182.
91. *The Chronicles of Holland House*, pp. 160-1.
92. Add. MSS. 51740, ff 49-50; Holland to Caroline Fox, Dec. 1814.
93. ibid., f 134; ibid., 16 June 1815.
94. Add. MSS. 51752, f 199; Holland to Henry Fox, 7 May 1833.

delighted to discover that his son had become the friend of Louis Napoleon, he was very severe on the latter's recklessness and lack of political sensitivity.[95] A Bonapartist restoration in France would inevitably lead to European war, either because the other great powers would never accept such an event, or because the new Bonaparte would only feel safe by imitating his uncle. Either way the family would only bring disturbance. Whereas Lady Holland worshipped the Napoleonic myth blindly, her husband measured its attractions against the alternatives. In French terms, it was to be preferred to the Bourbons, but rejected if other solutions became possible.

In fact, Holland never abandoned the view that a fully constitutional settlement was possible for France and that such an outcome rested with the Orléans family, Talleyrand and Lafayette. All of these men were known in Foxite circles before the Revolution, and Holland found it irritating that, although they all enjoyed the friendship of the English Whigs, they could so often dislike each other more than their opponents. In particular, the suspicion which existed between Lafayette and the house of Orléans fissured liberal hopes. These 'French Whigs', as Charles Fox had called them, represented a genuine constitutional alternative for France if they could only be brought to act in concert. Holland, in promoting their cause, was merely following family tradition once again.[96] The essential link between French and English 'Whigs' was what Lafayette described to Charles Fox as 'cette Sympathie de Liberté et de patriotisme qui Unira toujours, j'ose le dire, Certaines Ames'.[97] The Bourbons and the Bonapartes lived on disruption. The Orléanists, as supporters of a monarchical tradition which accepted the initial aspirations of the Revolution, offered most hope of reconciling the divisions within French society on a constitutional basis.

The Orléanist reputation for liberal politics had been started by Philippe, Duc d'Orléans, nicknamed Egalité, who, as Louis XVI's cousin, represented the cadet branch of the French royal house. Both he and his son, the future Louis

95. Add. MSS. 51756, f 230; ibid., 26 Sept. 1836.
96. For a discussion of the Fox family's French connections before 1789, see L.G. Mitchell, *Charles James Fox and the Disintegration of the Whig Party*, Ch. 5.
97. Lafayette to Fox, 6 Nivose 1800; ibid., p.154.

Philippe, were thought to foster a keen Anglophilism, one aspect of which was their support of the Revolution up to the fall of the monarchy in August 1792.[98] It followed that they had accepted the Constitution of 1791, which, with its limited franchise based on a property qualification, was found pleasing in Whig circles. Although Holland was forbidden by Lafayette to see Orléans during his visit to Paris in 1791, he had already met him in England two years earlier. As someone suffering the persecution of the French Court, and of Marie Antoinette in particular, Orléans was immediately given a warm reception in Foxite circles. Although Holland recognised that Orléans' career as a roué and libertine had left him so jaded as to be beyond the necessity of emotion, 'le besoin de s'émouvoir',[99] both he and his uncle found his political behaviour impeccable. During their visit to Spain, in 1802, the Hollands visited Egalité's widow as an act of piety.[100]

Contacts were kept up in the next generation. Louis Philippe dined at Holland House for the first time in May 1802, and himself played host to the Hollands on their visits to Paris in 1815, 1825 and 1829.[101] Lady Holland proudly reported that her husband 'was received quite dans l'intérieur en famille with the Duke of Orleans ... he was, as one must always be, pleased at the Duke's conversation'.[102] On these visits, the Hollands took care to become acquainted with the major figures in Orléanist politics, and, by 1830, they could count Casimir Périer, Guizot and the Duc de Broglie as friends.[103] All these experiences confirmed Holland in the family view that 'in France, a Bonaparte or an Orleans is much more reconcilable with safe and free government than a prince whose title is exactly derived from primogeniture and

98. Egalité himself followed the Revolution even further, voting for the death of his cousin in January 1793. He was himself guillotined in October of the same year.

99. Holland, *Foreign Reminiscences*, p.29.

100. *The Spanish Journal of Elizabeth, Lady Holland*, p.4.

101. Add. MSS. 51524, ff 184-96. Lady Holland to Grey, 25 Sept. 1815; Grey MSS. Box 33.

102. Add. MSS. 52172, ff 93-4; Lady Holland to J. Allen, Feb. 1826.

103. Add. MSS. 52175, f 88; J. Allen to Henry Fox, 25 Jan. 1822; Add. MSS. 52173, ff 101-4; Lady Holland to J. Allen, 1 March 1826; Sydney Smith to Mrs Smith, 21 April 1826; *The Letters of Sydney Smith*, i 434.

lineal descent'. The Fox family had always insisted that Egalité and his sons were country members of the Whig party. By the 1830s, comparisons were drawn between Louis Philippe and William of Orange. Holland saw the house of Orléans as 'affording a sort of compromise (not very dissimilar to that of William and the House of Hanover in our country) between the bigoted Royalists on one side and the lovers of liberty on the other'.[104] Orléanism guaranteed the advantages of the Revolution without involving the elevation of executive power in either Bourbon or Bonapartist hands. From the Hollands' point of view, the July Revolution of 1830 was to be wholeheartedly welcomed. It offered France stability. It made an old friend King of the French.

The same Revolution brought Talleyrand back to London as French ambassador at the age of seventy-six. Holland had met him for the first time in 1791, and made a point of re-establishing contact whenever he visited Paris.[105] In gratitude for the Hollands' assistance when he was a political refugee in the 1790s,[106] Talleyrand received all members of the Fox family in Paris with high solemnity. During the 1825 visit, he even lent Lady Holland his cook for a time.[107] After 1815, relations between Talleyrand and Holland House became increasingly close. Talleyrand's memoirs were read in manuscript there in 1823. There was the exchanging of birthday presents and some attempt at joint Anglo-French co-operation in the defence of European liberals persecuted by autocrats.[108] Talleyrand seemed to acknowledge the comparisons which Holland was anxious to make between the English Whigs and Orléanist politics, once his rôle in Bonapartist foreign policy had faded from memory. When the Hollands graciously offered the title of 'Foxite', Talleyrand graciously accepted it: 'Je vous remercie de m'avoir, dans une circonstance qui vous intéresse, compté comme un des votres. C'est un titre que Mr Fox m'a permis de porter depuis

---

104. Holland to ?, 1832; *Foreign Reminiscences*, pp 350-1.
105. Holland to ?, 1832; *Foreign Reminiscences*, p.34 seq.
106. Add. MSS. 51731, ff 208-9; Holland to Caroline Fox, March 1794.
107. *The Journal of Mrs Arbuthnot*, ii 20; see also Add. MSS. 51740, f 6; Holland to Caroline Fox, 13 Aug. 1814; *The Journal of Henry Edward Fox*, pp. 75-6.
108. Add. MSS. 51635, f 5; Talleyrand to Holland, n.d.

longues années.'[109] It could only be a good omen that a man who willingly addressed the Hollands as 'vous qui êtes nos maîtres'[110] should be sent to London as the representative of the July Monarchy.[111] Here was another old friend who had accepted the Revolution until it degenerated into violence in 1792.

The third man to be catapulted back into political prominence by the revolution of 1830 was Lafayette, the Fox family's closest friend in France and someone who had been known and respected since the late 1770s. Lafayette was Holland's host on his visits to France in 1791 and 1802,[112] and his respect for the part he played in the Revolution was such that it led to one of the few instances in which he felt self-confident to challenge his uncle Charles' views on a particular point.[113] When Lafayette became a prisoner of the Austrians in 1792, after his emigration from France, the Fox family tried hard to assist him. Charles Fox formally asked the British government to intervene much to the delight of his nephew:

> Poor Fayette's Misfortunes have made me such an enthusiast that ... I do really think I should have gone to Luxemburg to have seen him – Good God! that after the great and honorable part he has acted in either Hemisphere, he should be at the age of 35 the prisoner of a parcel of unenlightened German Hussars or the Lord knows what.[114]

Lafayette's letters from prison brought Holland to the verge of tears.[115] By 1800, the Fox family and Lafayette could share a knowledge of persecution and ostracism for principles which they believed they held in common.[116] The experiences of the 1790s substantiated a friendship that was to last for the rest of their lives.

109. ibid., f 18; ibid., n.d.
110. ibid., ff 111-13; ibid., 30 Janvier c 1835.
111. Holland to Carlisle, 8 Oct. 1830; Castle Howard MSS.
112. Add. MSS. 47590, f 9; *Commonplace Book of Samuel Rogers*. The Hollands were delighted to discover that Lafayette had voted against Napoleon's being first Consul for life. Add. MSS. 51736, f 49; Holland to Caroline Fox, 27 June 1802.
113. Add. MSS. 51731, f 88; Holland to Caroline Fox, 23 Oct. 1792.
114. ibid., f 74; ibid., 14 Sept. 1792.
115. ibid., f 125; ibid., 17 June 1793.
116. Add. MSS. 51635, f 156; Lafayette to Holland, 1 Nivôse 1801.

After 1814, the correspondence between Holland and Lafayette was quickly resumed. Although the latter, unlike Talleyrand, never formally called himself a Foxite, he nevertheless claimed to favour 'une liberté universelle – cette caractère distinctif de la politique de l'oncle dont la mémoire m'est si cher, et du neveu a qui je renouvelle de tout mon coeur l'expression de mon attachment'.[117] One maxim of Fox's in particular was fixed in his mind. He confided to Holland in a letter that Fox had once told him that 'si nos deux pais peuvent avoir dans le même tems une administration libérale, la cause du genre humain est gagnée'.[118] Both Lafayette and Holland accepted this idea totally. If a liberal government could be established in France, the principles of 1789 could be safeguarded without danger to England or the rest of Europe. If a liberal government could be established in England as well, then a union of the greatest naval power in Europe with the greatest military power became a possibility which could only make every autocrat tremble. Such conditions would only be met after 1830. In the meantime, Lafayette could only chronicle the inadequacies of the Restoration monarchy and share with Holland his lamentations about the bullying of Italians, Poles and Greeks.[119] Anglo-French cooperation, which becomes the stock-in-trade of both men after 1830, was a theme built on old friendships and one which was thought to have Foxite origins.[120]

In the Holland House response to France therefore, there was none of the clear-cut approbation or disapprobation that was to be readily heaped on other countries. The shifting nature of French politics and the frequent changes of regime muddied the waters too much for simple formulas to be applied. In his long and affectionate connection with France, however, Holland fixed on certain themes as threads by which he could find a way through the labyrinthine events taking

117. Add. MSS. 51635, f 162; ibid., 15 Janvier 1816; see also Lafayette to Holland, 24 Avril 1814; Dean MSS. and Holland to Lafayette, 17 Sept. 1814, *The Letters of F. Horner*, ii 194-5.

118. Lafayette to Holland, 15 Dec. 1815; Cornell Univ. Dean MSS.

119. Add. MSS. 51635, f 185; Lafayette to Holland, 26 février 1821.

120. See below, Chapter Eleven.

place across the Channel. First, it was clear as early as 1791 that the Bourbons had become an anachronism. Louis XVI had physically run away from the Revolution and his brothers emotionally ran away from its implications after 1815. Bonapartism guaranteed the major gains of the Revolution but at the cost of the sanctification of executive power. In Holland's view, the true Revolution ran from 1789 to 1792, and was concerned to found a constitution on a propertied franchise. In a sense, the more English the French system became the more it found favour with Fox and his heirs. At the outset, Fox had likened the events of 1789 to those of 1688 in England. An imitation of those events was taken to be the Revolution's true purpose. The whole enterprise degenerated after 1792 because autocrats would not allow its natural growth.

On this reading of French events, the anglophilia of Louis Philippe, Talleyrand and Lafayette was instantly attractive to the Whigs. The old men of 1830 had been the young men of 1789. Although their political careers had diverged widely and although they could hardly be described as friends, they had all accepted the basic premises on which 1789 was built. They and the English Whigs had expressed a mutual interest and sympathy in American politics in the 1770s, English politics in the 1780s and French politics in the 1790s. A revival of that mutual sympathy was essential after 1815, in Holland's view, because the formation of a Holy alliance of despots could only be countered by something comparable on the liberal side. While Lady Holland looked to Napoleon as the saviour of Europe, thereby earning for Holland House its reputation for baroque Bonapartism, her husband preferred to cling to a family tradition that even predated the Revolution. Orléanism and the liberal aristocratic tradition in France, represented by Talleyrand and Lafayette, were to be the preferred allies of the Whigs. Their political record was less dangerous than that of the Bourbons; less volatile than Bonaparte's. If they could rule France and the Whigs England, it would represent 'la sainte alliance des amis de la liberté, en général plus honnêtes que la coalition des Rois'.[121]

---

121. Add. MSS. 51635, f 168; Lafayette to Holland, 9 février 1817.

11

The Conduct of
Foreign Affairs, 1830-40

In the Whig Cabinets of the 1830s, Holland had no official voice in the formulation of foreign policy. He sat in the Cabinet as Chancellor of the Duchy of Lancaster only. In fact, for most of the decade, Holland House operated a foreign policy of its own, which sometimes ran counter to and sometimes parallel with the official line of the Grey and Melbourne governments. Palmerston, as Foreign Secretary, was endlessly forced to battle with a Holland House mafia both within the Cabinet and in Europe at large. Neither Holland nor his wife were much concerned with the fact that, with no status in this area of policy, their meddling in foreign affairs raised large constitutional questions, and added further to their reputation for erratic behaviour. In their view, what they lacked in status was more than compensated for by forty years of European experiences. Their friendships and unrivalled expertise was all the status they required. The relative lack of interest which they showed in domestic matters was a product of the fact that all their energy was channelled into foreign affairs.[1] It would have been simpler if Holland himself had become Foreign Secretary.[2] As it was, guerrilla warfare broke out between himself and Palmerston. With the Whigs in power, the temptation to give practical expression to

1. See above, Chapter Six.
2. It is hard to know whether savage attacks of gout or a reputation for erratic judgments was the greater disqualification for Holland undertaking this office.

long-thought-out ideas about European affairs was irresistible.

Holland approached the possibility of an official career in foreign affairs from a totally prejudiced position. All the opinions he was to utter between 1830 and 1840 had long been foreshadowed. In particular, two ideas, which had been in gestation since 1789, now came triumphantly to the fore. First, whenever two powers were in conflict, it was incumbent on Britain to support the more liberal. While Palmerston might hedge this idea about with talk of strategic or trading interests, thereby betraying his Canningite origins, Holland never compromised this principle. The Eastern Mediterranean was only one of the areas where this difference of approach would bring the two men into conflict. Secondly, in Holland's view, an Anglo-French understanding should be the fulcrum on which all else turned. 1830 had brought liberal-minded governments into power in both Paris and London. This fact produced the possibility of a union of naval and military power that could act as a counterweight to the autocratic powers of Eastern Europe.[3] As the Duke of Sussex put it: 'With William IV our King and Louis XIX in France the Liberties of Europe will I trust be not only secured but extended.'[4]

It followed from both these principles that Holland House was distinguished by a firm francophilism. Once Louis Philippe was safely installed as King of the French, the Hollands were reluctant ever to believe that French policy could be inimical to England. It was an opinion which would drive Palmerston to the point of distraction. Disraeli would call Holland 'that old Gallomaniac'.[5] None of this impressed Holland, who, seeing European affairs solely in ideological terms, found the prospect of an entente between a liberal France and a liberal England too alluring to resist. For him, 1830 had cracked the system of oppression established at Vienna. In Belgium, Spain and Italy, there was a real chance

3. See above, Chapter Ten.
4. Add. MSS. 51526, f 91; Duke of Sussex to Holland, July 1830.
5. B. Disraeli to S. Disraeli, 15 Oct. 1840; *The Life of Benjamin Disraeli*, ii 95.

of constitutional gains. Even Poland and Germany might come nearer to liberal influences. As Holland explained the point to his son, who, living in Brussels, was much more sceptical about French intentions: 'I do not see much danger in politicks as long as England & France have no point in dispute between them & have no disposition to take any unwarrantable part in those of other powers – & where they are disposed to do it conjointly & not separately.'[6] If Holland had been asked to defend such a view, he would have claimed that all his experiences of Europe since 1789 pointed to this conclusion.

Certainly, the Hollands were magnificently prepared for the July Revolution in Paris. All through the 1820s, Flahault,[7] de Broglie,[8] Talleyrand and many others associated with Orléanist politics had briefed Holland House on the deteriorating position of Charles X's government. Firm comparisons were drawn between the English and French situations. When Wellington was forced to act as 'un libéral malgré lui' over Catholic Emancipation, Lafayette expressed the hope that Polignac might soon be forced into the same position.[9] For people so well informed on French affairs, the 1830 Revolution came as no surprise. Only fifteen months before becoming King, Louis Philippe and his son the Duc de Chartres had eaten their last dinner at Holland House.[10] As Holland explained to his son:

We all foresaw that the Ordonnances would be the ruin of the Ministry & dynasty, & for more than 15 years many, & among them I, have foretold that French revolutions would end in their natural euthanasia, a constitutional King of the House of Orleans – but who could have imagined that all would have been effected & so heroically & happily ended in 3 short days ... It makes me young again ... the middling ranks soberly but steadfastly approve, & a large majority of the upper ranks sincerely applaud.[11]

6. Add. MSS. 51751, ff 192-3; Holland to Henry Fox, 21 Feb. 1832.
7. Lord Stuart de Rothesay to Mrs Arbuthnot, 10 April 1830; *The Correspondence of Charles Arbuthnot*, p.125.
8. Brougham to de Broglie, 16 Aug. 1830; *The Life and Times of Lord Brougham*, iii 59.
9. Add. MSS. 51635, ff 198-9; Lafayette to Holland, 14 Avril 1830.
10. *The Chronicles of Holland House*, p.108.
11. Add. MSS. 51751, f 32; Holland to Henry Fox, 24 Aug. 1830.

At last the French had had the sense to discover a way to their own 1688, a bloodless path to constitutional government uncovered by French Whigs.[12]

Even though the occurrence of the Revolution came as no surprise to the Hollands, it was still 'great and glorious'.[13] As eye-witness reports from France came in from Lord John Russell and the Duke of Sussex,[14] Holland's excitement about the possibilities of the new situation grew almost fierce. He seriously considered travelling to Paris immediately to congratulate Louis Philippe in person and would have performed such an errand, as he put it, 'con amore'.[15] He was very flattered to receive a copy of the new king's acceptance speech,[16] and even more so when Louis Philippe wrote in his own hand to thank the Hollands for their good wishes:

> I am very thankfull for Lady Holland's kind messages & for your very flattering expressions on the subject of the part I have acted in the new situation to which I have been called so suddenly. The task that has fallen to my lot is a laborious one, & it is difficult after so great a convulsion to subdue the irritation, & to reestablish public confidence. I am striving incessantly to maintain the peace within & the peace without. War, bad as it is at all times, would be in the present state of Nations, attended with miseries & misfortunes unparalleled in any former wars.[17]

The reappearance of so many old friends in positions of power was positively rejuvenating. Lafayette and Tallyrand had forgotten their suspicions of Orléans to work in a common cause. As a result, Holland had almost as many friends in the French government as in the English.

Holland refused to believe that a France regenerated by a popular Revolution could be dangerous to England. Only by denying reform in France, as only by denying reform in

12. ibid., f 40; ibid., 5 Oct. 1830.

13. Holland to Brougham, 2 Aug. 1830; Brougham MSS. 14955.

14. Add. MSS. 51524, ff 109-110; Sussex to Holland, July 1830; and Add. MSS. 51677, ff 75-8; Lord J. Russell to Holland, 13 Sept. 1830.

15. Add. MSS. 51547, ff 233-4; Holland to Grey, 2 Aug. 1830.

16. Add. MSS. 51524, ff 178-9; L. de Chabot to Holland, 6 Aug. 1830.

17. ibid., ff 205-6; Louis Philippe to Holland, 9 March 1831.

England, could the possibility of upheaval come. Otherwise all was euphoria at Holland House:

> The Parisians have covered themselves with glory, their courage in atchieving & their moderation in using victory are beyond all example – & my old friend Lafayette! What a career! ... To what is this owing? but to the superiority of principle over talent & virtue over fortune. The choice of Orleans is most judicious ... Many here half like it, & some in their hearts must curse the final extinction of their favourite system of divine right under the false name of legitimacy.[18]

In Holland's view events in France had to be welcomed not only because they were right in themselves, but also because English opinion, girding its loins for the Reform Bill crisis, would not stand for any other response. Holland was hopeful that, if this liberal tide was taken at the flood, it might be made to wash over much of Western Europe.[19]

Holland's implicit belief in the value of Anglo-French cooperation could be infuriating to his colleagues. In the disputes over Belgium, Spain and Turkey, Palmerston saw as much to fear in French policy as Holland found to praise. Clashes between the two men punctuated Cabinet meetings throughout the 1830s. To Palmerston as Foreign Secretary, it was constitutionally and personally intolerable that Holland should use the accidents of private acquaintance to influence Anglo-French relations. To Holland, his singular friendships helped him to defuse Palmerston's blusterings in the interests of European liberalism as a whole. If constitutional problems were raised by Holland House behaviour, its defence lay in the fact that leading Orléanists genuinely shared Holland's reading of the Anglo-French entente. Sébastiani for example, who succeeded Talleyrand as French ambassador in London in 1834, declared that 'l'alliance entre la France et l'Angleterre assure la pais du Monde, l'ébranler, l'affaiblir, c'est tout mettre en question: c'est ce que désirent les enemis des deux pays: c'est je l'espère ce qu'ils ne parviendront

18. Add. MSS. 51751, f 30; Holland to Henry Fox, 13 Aug. 1830.
19. Holland to Grey, 23 Dec. 1830; Grey MSS. Box 34.

jamais à réaliser.'[20] After the experiences of the French wars,
Palmerston's doubts about French good intentions are
comprehensible. Holland's wider knowledge of French
opinion, however, allowed him to take broader views. There
would be much bluster on both sides.

The credibility of an Anglo-French understanding was
tested almost immediately in the Low Countries. In 1815, the
area which was to become the kingdom of Belgium had been
made a part of the Dutch state, in an attempt to create a
barrier against French expansionism to the north. In 1830, a
nationalist revolt broke out in Belgium, and in due course
French troops entered the country ostensibly to help the
insurgents against the Dutch king. The dilemma presented by
these events was acute. From Palmerston's point of view,
Belgian ports had been ideal bases for mounting an invasion
force against England in the past, and they remained points of
extreme strategic importance. If the French intended to
occupy the country permanently therefore, war would not be
too high a price to pay for dislodging them. For Holland this
was to overact ridiculously. Ignoring strategic considerations
and dealing only in the ideological, he maintained that the
French had gone into Belgium solely to assist in the expulsion
of an unpopular king, and that all troops would be withdrawn
as soon as that purpose was completed. The Belgian question
contained nothing that should jeopardise relations between
Paris and London. After the problem had been effectively
settled, Holland was for 'depending more on French
connections & French alliances ... from a conviction or at
least a confident hope, that it is the true interest & honest
purpose of France to cooperate in such views'.[21]

So great was Holland's concern that Belgium should not
involve a rupture between himself and his French friends that
he was led into some unWhiggish remarks on the subject. The
insurrection itself was 'foolish & unreasonable',[22] and

20. Sébastiani to Mme. Adelaide, 3 Oct. 1837; B.N. n.a. fr.12219, f 176; see also
Sébastiani to Mme. Adelaide, 30 Juin 1834; B.N. n.a. fr.12219, f 27 and Louis
Philippe to Thiers, 28 Sept. 1840; B.N. n.a. fr.20601, f 247-8.
21. Add. MSS. 51751, ff 166-74; Holland to Henry Fox, 10 Jan. 1832.
22. ibid., ff 40-1; ibid., 5 Oct. 1830.

Holland's son was treated to the unusual spectacle of his father contrasting the statesmanship of the Dutch king with the hysteria of his revolting subjects.[23] Holland knew that the Belgian situation represented temptation for the French[24] but hoped that they would be 'sensible enough not to sacrifice to the false glory of a little rhodomontade in the assembly, the solid advantage of a neutral state on her frontiers & of a real concert with England'.[25] Since Belgium had none of the racial or linguistic homogeneity by which aspiring nations were usually recognised, Holland even entertained doubts about its claims to this title. It seemed obvious as early as 1815 that Belgium could only exist independently as a diplomatic convenience, and that it had no feeling for nationhood within itself.[26] If this were so, Holland could argue that it might be better to face hard fact and divide the area between France and Holland. Whatever happened, it was madness to antagonise France on behalf of a struggling nationalism that never really existed.[27] To Palmerston, all these views were weak-minded to the point of lunacy.

Throughout the Belgian crisis, Holland insisted that, if Anglo-French relations became strained, the only beneficiary would be the Holy Alliance. He was sure that Russian policy

is to place us in an attitude towards France which if not that of actual war bespeaks our determination in case of war of favouring the anti-revolutionary & not the revolutionary side – & all this for Belgium! – a country which must ultimately either belong to France or at the very best be divided in a way that will practically give to France the disposal of the revenues of Hainault & Brabant & Liège.[28]

Both he and Lady Holland were half-inclined to believe that the whole Belgian insurrection had been stirred up by English Tories and their European allies in order to bring England

23. ibid., f 71; ibid., 17 Aug. 1831.
24. Holland to Carlisle, 29 Jan. 1831; Castle Howard MSS. LB 139.
25. Add. MSS. 51751, f 71; Holland to Henry Fox, 17 Aug. 1831.
26. Holland to Grey, 14 Sept. 1815; Grey MSS., Box 34.
27. Holland to Brougham, 7 Sept. 1830; Brougham MSS. 14956.
28. Add. MSS. 51548, ff 33-5; Holland to Grey, c 9 Feb. 1831.

and France into conflict.[29] Holland was confident, however:
'Do not imagine that France and England, Whigs &
Orleanists are such Spooneys to be driven or cajoled into
hostility.'[30] The entente between the liberal capitals of
London and Paris would hold, and the Russians would have
no choice but to be 'as tame as mice & satisfy themselves like
that peaceable race with nibbling at such morsels as may have
escaped our notice'.[31]

While Palmerston worried about the Belgian question in
terms of an historical French threat to the Channel ports,
Holland preferred to put the whole matter in a European
context. If Belgium only achieved independence at the cost of
a rupturing of the Anglo-French entente, the real losers by
that event would be liberals in Italy, Germany and Poland.
For these reasons, Holland set out with the idea that French
intentions towards Belgium were entirely honourable, and
never moved from that point of view. As Talleyrand had
assured him, at the outset, France 'was ready to acquiesce in
any arrangement that is not obviously injurious to their
interests or their honour',[32] and Holland chose to believe it. In
spite of momentary hesitations about the exact nature and
timing of the withdrawal of French troops,[33] Holland steadily
pressed this view in Cabinet against Palmerston's wish for
more demonstrative action.[34] Even so, it was a relief to
Holland when events vindicated his belief in France's good
faith. The establishment of Belgium as a new, constitutional
state in Europe, was taken to be the first fruit of Anglo-French
understanding. It represented a major advance of the liberal
cause in Europe, and it could be referred to as a hopeful
precedent when French actions were called in question in
other parts of the world.[35]

29. Lady Holland to Henry Fox, 16 Aug. 1831; *Elizabeth, Lady Holland to her Son*,
p.112.

30. Add. MSS. 51751, ff 94-5; Holland to Henry Fox, 13 Sept. 1831.

31. Holland to Carlisle, 29 Oct. 1832; Castle Howard MSS. LB 139.

32. Add. MSS. 51548, ff 1-3; Holland to Grey, 6 Oct. 1830.

33. Holland to H.S. Fox, 6 July 1831; Bod.Eng.MSS.Lett. c 234, f 89; see also Add.
MSS. 51751, ff 92-3; Holland to Henry Fox, 7 Sept. 1831.

34. For a detailed account of Holland's reactions to the Belgian crisis, see A.D.
Kriegel, *The Holland House Diaries, 1831-1840*.

35. Add. MSS. 51751, ff 112-14; Holland to Henry Fox, 25 Oct. 1831.

If Holland's confidence in the French was built on anything more than wishful thinking, it was based on his old friendship for Talleyrand:

> I am diverted but at the same time delighted at Talleyrand coming ambassador here again. I say again for I remember him in 1792 ... This & Lafayette at the head of the National Guard make me suppose myself young again & I have just now neither colick nor gout or ague to remind me that I am not so.[36]

The old man was not just the best dinner-table company in Europe,[37] but he was also the Frenchman who most sincerely shared Holland's emphasis on the Anglo-French entente.[38] In the middle of a debate on Belgian affairs in the House of Lords, Holland was moved to make the following testimony:

> He felt that there could be no good taste in dwelling upon the virtue and merits of a man's own acquaintance, in an assembly like that of their Lordships' yet he trusted that he might be allowed to observe that forty years' acquaintance with the noble individual ... enabled him to bear testimony to the fact, that ... there had been no man's character more shamefully traduced, & no man's public character more mistaken and misrepresented, than the private and public character of Prince Talleyrand.[39]

Talleyrand became Holland's major ally in his guerrilla warfare against Palmerston's bellicose trumpetings over Belgium.

In some measure, peace held between England and France because Talleyrand and Holland worked hand in glove to ensure this outcome. Their methods were highly irregular, and Palmerston endlessly complained that for a Cabinet Minister to deal directly with the ambassador of a foreign country was at least disruptive of the conduct of foreign affairs and potentially treasonable. To some outsiders it appeared that the Hollands had been completely taken in by their old

36. Add. MSS. 51751, ff 37-8; Holland to Henry Fox, 9 Sept. 1830; Sébastiani, who succeeded Talleyrand as ambassador in 1834, had dined at Holland House for the first time in 1816, as a refugee from the Restoration Monarchy; *The Chronicles of Holland House*, p.257.

37. Diary of Lady Dover, 8 Nov. 1830; *Three Howard Sisters*, p.157.

38. Holland to Grey, c Sept. 1832; Grey MSS. Box 34.

39. *Parl. Deb.*, vol. CIX 811-13; 29 Sept. 1831.

friend and that Talleyrand went 'every evening to Holland House, late, when every one else is gone, and sucks Hollands brains for an hour or two before he goes to bed'.[40] In fact, the commerce was a two-way affair. Talleyrand dined at Holland House two or three times a week, and undoubtedly was given up-to-date accounts of Cabinet decisions. In return, the ambassador allowed Holland to see his correspondence with Louis Philippe, Casimir Périer and Sébastiani, and to communicate whatever he thought fit to the English government.[41] In a very real sense, Holland House for a moment became the Foreign Office.

In constitutional terms, Holland was moving over the thinnest of ice. On at least one occasion, he was forced to apologise to Palmerston for prematurely leaking English plans to Talleyrand, thereby setting up a cross-current in the flow of official policy-making.[42] In his defence, Holland would have argued that, if everything had been left to 'the rough language'[43] of Palmerston, the Belgian question would have ended in the most calamitous of wars. The mutual sympathy and cooperation between Talleyrand and Holland played some part in avoiding that outcome. It was of some comfort to both men to know that each of them was unpopular with his own colleagues. Just as it was not easy for Holland to argue that the French should be trusted, so it was not easy for Talleyrand to turn French opinion away from the possibility of actually annexing Belgium. Both men tried hard to soften public statements, mute suspicions and tame their wild men. Both seem to have placed a trust in the other that was not misplaced. It was an extraordinary culmination of a forty-year friendship.[44]

40. Bedford to Lord W. Russell, 27 July 1831, *Lord W. Russell and his Wife*, p.234.

41. Holland to Grey, 3 Jan. 1832; Grey MSS. Box 34; see also Add. MSS. 51867, f 107; Holland's Political Journal, 27 Aug. 1831.

42. Holland to Brougham, [26 Dec.] 1831; Brougham MSS. 14965; and Palmerston to Holland, *Sovereign Lady*, p.301.

43. Holland to Brougham, 26 Dec. 1831; *The Life and Times of Lord Brougham*, iii 447-9.

44. Add. MSS. 51867, ff 70, 90, 112; see also Sébastiani to Talleyrand, 19 Jan. 1831; Quai d'Orsay 632 *Angleterre*, f 60; and B.N. n.a. fr. 20601, ff 39-40; Duchesse de Dino to Thiers, 4 Oct. 1830.

The Belgian affair set a pattern for the 1830s as a whole. For Holland's enemies, the divine right of the Fox family to meddle in foreign affairs had reached intolerable heights. The battle which was joined between Palmerston and Holland would last throughout the decade. In government or out of it, the Hollands too easily turned their dinner guests into couriers, agents and sources of intelligence. At times, it was hard to know whether their first loyalty lay with the British government or with some larger commitment to European liberalism. For Holland himself, Belgium had proved many things. It had demonstrated that the French could be trusted. It had shown that Russia and her autocratic allies could not sustain the Vienna settlement indefinitely. Above all, it had shown that 'the only true Holy Alliance is England & France'.[45]

If the Belgian question had an immediate and pressing importance, problems arising out of the Iberian peninsula came a close second. Geography dictated that France would have an interest in the area, and, as recently as 1823, the armies of Louis XVIII had entered Spain at the behest of the Holy Alliance to restore autocratic government. Equally, Wellington's achievements in the peninsula had given England some influence in the area and, as has been outlined above, Holland House regarded Spain and Portugal as peculiarly its own concern. The troubles which beset both countries after 1830 therefore again carried the risk of embarrassing Anglo-French relations, and of further embroiling Holland with Palmerston and official policy. Once again, Holland's long acquaintance with the leaders of the constitutional party in both Spain and Portugal allowed him to approach the crises of the early 1830s from a prepared position based on experience and prejudice, and to make Holland House the centre of pressure group politics in the liberal cause.[46]

Dom Pedro, the eldest son of John VI of Portugal, arrived in England in June 1831, as a refugee from Brazil, demanding

45. Holland to Grey, 13 June 1831; Grey MSS. Box 34.
46. See above, Chapters Nine and Ten.

British recognition for the claims of his daughter Maria to the Portuguese throne, currently held by his younger brother Miguel. Historically, there was some reason to see Pedro and his daughter as representing a constitutional future for Portugal, with Miguel ranged on the side of autocracy. In 1830, Holland had described the latter as 'that bloody tyrant and usurper of a country which is of more importance to this nation than any other country in Europe'.[47] Not surprisingly, Pedro and his chief adviser Palmella, who was an old friend of the Hollands, selected Holland House as the channel by which their hopes for Portugal could be brought to the English Government.[48] Once again, therefore, Holland found himself representing to Palmerston, from first-hand knowledge, an important section of foreign opinion.[49] To one of the Hollands' 'adopted' sons, Lord William Russell, watching the flow of Portuguese politics in Lisbon, the Whigs moved too slowly and too late.[50] Whatever the truth of this criticism, Holland himself worked hard in the interests of the Portuguese liberals throughout the crisis.

Holland responded to the appeal of Dom Pedro and Maria with characteristic Foxite assumptions. Portugal was the latest battlefield in the European-wide war between constitutionalism and autocracy. There was a universal Toryism which had to be fought which 'could waft sighs and hopes alternately from the Tagus to the Thames, and from the Thames to the Tagus'.[51] The European comprehensiveness of the struggle was contained in his belief that 'there was no power on earth so hostile to the interests of Great Britain as that power in Portugal, and out of Portugal, which supported the pretensions of Don Miguel'.[52] It followed that, in Holland's view, England could not stand neuter. Rather, since

47. *Parl. Deb.*, 4 Feb. 1830; vol. XCIX 42-4; Holland to Ebrington, 14 April 1830; Fortescue MSS. 1262 M/FC 86.

48. Holland to H.S. Fox, 6 July 1831; Bod. MSS. Eng. Lett. c 234, f 87; see also Add. MSS. 51867, f 154; Holland's Political Journal, 20 Sept. 1831.

49. Add. MSS. 51867, ff 8-10; Holland's Political Journal, 15 July 1831.

50. Lord W. Russell to Holland, 21 July 1832; *Lord William Russell and his Wife*, p.254.

51. *Parl. Deb.*, 5 Aug. 1831; vol. CVII 814-5.

52. ibid., 19 Sept. 1831; vol. CIX 123.

France too was now governed by liberals, it would be sensible to make common cause with that country to demonstrate the far-reaching possibilities of Anglo-French understanding. With Talleyrand's invaluable assistance, Holland hoped to prove the point that 'Portugal could no longer rely upon our protection alone, but must rest upon France, too'.[53] If European Tories hoped to embroil Paris and London in Portuguese affairs, Holland hoped instead to confront them with an Anglo-French constitutional crusade.[54]

At the same time that Holland was urging his colleagues to trust the French in Belgium, he was also asking them to countenance an Anglo-French force landing in Portugal. In July and again in November 1831, Holland presented formal French proposals to this effect to his friends and asked that they be accepted. As he told Grey: 'I should not hesitate at once to sign a treaty with France acknowledging Dn Pedro – whether as Guardian of his daughter or as king matters little though I believe you are right in thinking the latter more likely to ensure success & facilitate arrangements on his accession.'[55] Holland had been deeply impressed by both Pedro's and Palmella's wish to act with 'England and to take no step but in concert with that court'.[56] Consequently, it was not only incumbent on a Foxite Whig to assist them in a moral sense, but to deny their request was to run the risk of throwing them into the arms of the French, the very thing that the opponents of intervention claimed to fear most.[57]

Holland's views on Portugal were steadily rejected by his colleagues. For some, the overwhelming pressure of Reform Bill politics made any question of foreign adventures impossible. For others, Holland's nostalgic francophilism had simply burst out of control. They feared that it might be easier

53. Lord Ellenborough's Diary, 5 Aug. 1831; *Three Early Nineteenth Century Diaries*, p.114.
54. Add. MSS. 51635, ff 15-16; Talleyrand to Holland, n.d., see also Add. MSS. 51548, ff 5-8; Holland to Grey, 10 Oct. 1830.
55. Holland to Grey, 2 Aug. 1831; Grey MSS. Box 34; see also Add. MSS. 51868, f 194; Holland's Political Journal, 1 Nov. 1831; and Holland to Grey, 2 Nov. 1831; Grey MSS. Box 34.
56. Add. MSS. 51867, ff 53-4; Holland's Political Journal, 31 July 1831.
57. Add. MSS. 51869, f 586; ibid., 20 May 1833.

to introduce a French army into Portugal than to secure its withdrawal. Holland found himself taunted in Cabinet for his 'predilection for foreigners & Portuguese in particular'.[58] Whenever Anglo-French cooperation was proposed, he found that most of the Cabinet 'were more disposed to start nice points ... than to seize the fair offer of concert'.[59] As a result, the Hollands were forced to observe the situation in Portugal as it degenerated into civil war. It was particularly galling when Maria herself turned her back on her early liberalism, in 1836, thereby provoking the comment from Holland that 'she has acted as persons of her Class almost always [do] ... Charles I and Lewis 16 over again to the end of the chapter'.[60] For nearly a decade, the Hollands followed Portuguese events, encouraging their friends in that country[61] and applauding any steps taken in a liberal direction.[62] They could do little more. All attempts to influence the Grey and Melbourne governments had come to nothing, and, in the view of Holland House, a unique opportunity for cementing an Anglo-French entente had been lost.

An exactly analogous situation developed in Spain, in 1833, with the death of Ferdinand VII. Liberals supported the claims of his infant daughter Isabella and conservatives those of his brother, Don Carlos. In view of the Hollands' long association with Spain, this situation was found even more exciting than that in neighbouring Portugal. Mendizabel, the leading Spanish liberal who had been resident in London since 1823, vied with Palmella for invitations to Holland House. It was not unreasonably assumed by everyone that Holland himself would be pressing for maximum British assistance to the cause of Spanish liberalism.[63] As soon as news of Ferdinand's death reached London, Holland asked Grey to recognise Isabella immediately. He was instrumental

58. Add. MSS. 51870, f 205; ibid., 14 Jan. 1834.

59. Add. MSS. 51867, ff 503-4; ibid., 31 July 1831.

60. Add. MSS. 51871, f 979; ibid., 20 Sept. 1836.

61. Lady Holland to Henry Fox, 16 July 1833; *Elizabeth, Lady Holland to her Son*, p.142.

62. Holland to H.S. Fox, 10 Oct. [1834]; Bod. Eng. Lett. MSS. c 234, ff 97-8.

63. Add. MSS. 51677, ff 117-18; Lord John Russell to Holland, 15 Oct. 1833.

in persuading the government to allow British volunteers to fight in Spain.[64] Many of the arguments he used on these occasions could be carried over from his speeches on Portugal, but his long, emotional involvement with Spain gave them new urgency and spirit.

In the Spanish case, however, to the general argument for assisting liberal movements anywhere in western Europe, Holland could add new points culled from his personal experiences and contacts. Spanish liberals wrote endlessly to reassure him that 'the vast majority of the nation is convinced, both of the dangers & the evils which *absolute power* occasions', and that 'the cause of the Queen which is that of civilization & improvement is sure finally to succeed'.[65] Holland chose to believe them. From his own knowledge of the country, he thought that the supporters of Don Carlos were 'a miserable party in point of numbers as of cause for ever. They do not bear one 4th of the proportion our Jacobites bore to the Hanoverians. But I wish the remaining 3/4ths or 5/6ths had a Sir Robert Walpole.'[66] The fact that the Spanish Church sided with the Carlists merely confirmed Holland's views about the unrepresentative nature of the movement.[67] It followed therefore, that, unless England acted to help Isabella, there could be little hope of influencing what would inevitably be the long-term government of Spain.[68] In Holland's view, even Palmerstonian self-interest should lead in this case to an expeditionary force being sent to the peninsula.

On a more familiar note, Holland again pressed for Anglo-French cooperation. He was convinced that, whereas French intervention in Portugal might or might not occur, it must be expected in Spain, thereby raising all the tensions and fears that the Belgian question had generated. When the British Ambassador in Paris reported that Louis Philippe had given guarantees that France would not act unilaterally in Spain, but would continue to work with her allies, Holland was

---

64. Add. MSS. 51871; Holland's Political Journal, 26 May 1835.
65. Add. MSS. 51628, f 5; Martinez de la Rosa to Holland, 28 Jan. 1834.
66. Add. MSS. 51755, f 151; Holland to Henry Fox, 26 Aug. 1836.
67. Add. MSS. 51548, ff 146-7; Holland to Grey, 15 Oct. 1835.
68. Add. MSS. 51754, ff 124-5; Holland to Henry Fox, 24 July 1835.

visibly relieved.[69] Once again, his confidence in the French had been vindicated.

> Palmerston thinks a civil war can hardly be averted but the good disposition of France & the accommodating language she holds gives reasonable hope that general war may be avoided & even the civil struggle soon extinguished in Spain & Portugal. In the first Ls Philip sacrifices ... all little personal whims about Salick law, to the interests of peace & close alliance with us ... In short all at home and abroad is couleur de rose.[70]

As long as neither England nor France were tempted to try to win an exclusive influence in Spain by sponsoring Don Carlos, his cause was ultimately doomed. Holland was only irritated that Whig governments were so reluctant to work with France militarily in order to decide the issue once and for all.[71]

Once again, Holland's francophilia outran that of most of his political associates. To most of them, French troops in Spain and Portugal would be as unwelcome a sight as they had been in Belgium. Paris was deterred from taking any such step not, as Holland insisted, out of a respect for the British alliance, but out of a fear of retaliation. They taunted Holland with the paradox of his advocacy of interventionist policies in the Iberian peninsula mingling with his condemnation of Russian behaviour in Poland. Holland could only reply that 'it is our duty & interest to make Portugal & Spain an exception to such rules',[72] and that action was allowed under the terms of the Quadruple Alliance to which all the countries concerned were signatories. Against Holland's wishes therefore, there was no large-scale, Anglo-French intervention in the Spanish and Portuguese wars, even though the decision of both London and Paris not to assist reaction greatly weighted the balance in the liberals' favour in both countries. As a result, the politics of Spain and Portugal remained

69. Holland to Grey, 8 Oct. 1833; Grey MSS. Box 34.
70. Holland to Ellice, 11 Oct. 1833; Ellice MSS. f 134.
71. Add. MSS. 51754, f 88; Holland to Henry Fox, 5 June 1835. For a detailed discussion of Spanish affairs, see Raymond Carr, *Spain 1808-1939*.
72. Add. MSS. 51754, f 103; Holland to Henry Fox, 2 July 1835; see also Add. MSS. 51628, f 21; Holland to Minto, 6 Aug. 1834.

disturbed down to and beyond Holland's death in 1840. In his view, a magnificent chance had been lost to add these two countries to the list of constitutional powers. Belgium had already proved what Anglo-French cooperation could achieve. The moment to act had been missed because too many members of the Grey and Melbourne governments were weighed down by the pressure of domestic politics, and because Palmerston's habitual suspicion of France allowed neither flexibility nor imaginative manoeuvre.

Throughout the Belgian, Spanish and Portuguese crises, Holland never lost sight of the wider battles of which they were just a part. His stock-in-trade theory since 1789 was that the whole of Europe was engaged in a struggle between darkness and light, and, although the revolutions of 1830 had shifted the balance of forces significantly, they had done nothing to resolve the underlying issue. Citing the suppression of liberal movements in Italy and Poland as evidence, Holland continued to believe that the autocrats of Austria, Russia and Prussia were interested only in the ideological reconquest of Europe:

> There is I fear much latent hope in the three military powers & their satellites that either by intrigue or by war the revolutions of 1830 may be undone – & they little think what is nevertheless true, that such a prospect is in substance an intention of conquering France, England & the West of Europe, throughout which all that constitutes strength is liberal, & would be made revolutionary by any attempt at unconscionable coercion. Their only chance of preserving what they have is by supporting Perrier in France & reform in England – & they are fools enough to fight against both – with the idle notion that England & France once separated, they may reconquer Europe & impose what Governments they like.[73]

Holland believed that this view was common ground between Ultra Tories in England and their European brethren.[74] A firm reply had to be made, 'otherwise if we effect nothing for the liberals in Belgium or Portugal, the silent progress of the Holy Alliance in Germany, Italy, Poland & Switzerland will

---

73. Add. MSS. 51752, ff 18-19; Holland to Henry Fox, 3 May 1832.
74. Add. MSS. 51753, ff 21 & 26-7; ibid., 5 & 9 July 1833.

seem to encompass us about & somewhat justify the mouvement party in sounding [the] alarm'.[75]

Just as he supported cooperation between England and France in individual situations, so Holland was fervently behind attempts to gather up these movements into a general, formal alliance. A firm counter-statement had to be made to the eastern autocrats, and only clear alliances might sufficiently impress them. Holland House accordingly followed the progress to what was to become the Quadruple Alliance of 1834 with the keenest possible interest.[76] The alliance might bring home to Vienna and Petersburg 'the truth & the truth is this – that if they involve themselves & others in any war with France & the liberal party in Europe no English Government be it Whig, Tory, Radical or what not can get a response from our people to *assist* them, though it is not equally impossible that many ... might be procured to *resist* them'.[77] When England's acceptance of the Alliance was prefigured in the King's speech at the opening of Parliament in January 1834, the relevant paragraphs had been first drafted at Holland House by Holland and Talleyrand together.[78] The signing of the treaty in the following April was a fitting conclusion to Talleyrand's ambassadorship.

The Quadruple Alliance marked the high point of Holland's francophile line of politics. He reported joyfully that its conclusion had 'made a grand sensation in Germany',[79] and that now it was obvious to all that 'if Northern & Eastern despots conspire, the constitutional States of the West will combine'.[79] Talleyrand reported home in the same sense:

L'état de la Péninsula est une question plus particulièrement du ressort de la politique Anglo-Française. En tout cas, je ne puis pas me persuader que l'alliance que nous venons de conclure, qui resserve notre intimité avec l'angleterre, et qui place dans notre dépendance l'Espagne et le Portugal, ne soit pas calculé à inspirer quelque respect aux Cabinets du nord.[80]

75. Holland to Grey, 10 Sept. 1832; Grey MSS. Box 34.
76. Add. MSS. 51869, f 541; Holland's Political Journal, 27 June 1832.
77. Holland to Grey, 30 July 1832; Grey MSS Box 34.
78. ibid., 18 Jan. 1834; ibid.
79. Add. MSS. 51753, f 109; Holland to Henry Fox, 24 June 1834.
80. Talleyrand to Sébastiani, 23 Avril 1834; B.N. n.a.fr. 6363, f 443. The state of

Holland hoped that henceforth 'the minor courts of Italy will do prudently to look to the Constitutional rather than the Despotick League for protection,'[81] and was sure that no Spanish or Portuguese autocrat could now achieve anything without first having to 'break a lance with the naval power of Great Britain & the military forces of France.'[82] The Quadruple Alliance was a talisman to be held up before the eyes of European liberals as a defence against political evil and as the promise of betterment. The distinctive francophilism of Holland House was for a moment vindicated.

It was for a moment only, however. In March 1834, the Duc de Broglie, an old habitué of Holland House, resigned from the French government, and Holland was aware of the significance of this event. If Anglophiles resigned in Paris, it could only be taken as a dark omen:

> Broglie's loss will be indeed irreparable. Can he not be prevailed upon to resume his portefeuille? – for tho' I agree with you in thinking that *under all changes* the real wish & interest of France will be to adhere to our alliance & cling to the connexion between us, yet confidence must depend on *Men* & is not easily transferable – at any rate it is the growth of time – & a twig however well disposed to shoot up cannot afford as much shelter as a tree.[83]

The de Broglie resignation was the most worrying in a series of worrying events. The Hollands, although thought to be in Palmerstonian circles 'foolish as usual'[84] about the Orléanist régime, had shown signs of nervousness. Louis Philippe's declaration of Martial Law in 1832 had been alarming[85] and the Press Laws of 1835 were decidedly unWhiggish.[86] By September 1835, Holland began to fear that 'our friend Louis

---

the Peninsula is a question which particularly concerns Anglo-French politics. In every respect, I cannot persuade myself that the alliance we have just concluded, which preserves our intimacy with England, and which makes Spain and Portugal dependent on us, is not calculated to inspire some respect in the cabinets of the north.

81. Add. MSS. 51753, f 83; Holland to Henry Fox, 9 May 1834.

82. ibid., f 154; ibid., 15 Aug. 1834.

83. Holland to Ellice, 4 April 1834; Ellice MSS. f 142; see also Add. MSS. 51753, f 76; Holland to Henry Fox, 4 April 1834.

84. Lady Cowper to Melbourne, 14 June 1832; *The Letters of Lady Palmerston*, p.195.

85. Holland to Grey, 4 July 1832; Grey MSS. Box 34.

86. Add. MSS. 51754, f 137; Holland to Henry Fox, 11 Aug. 1835.

Philippe has drunk deeper of the cup of kingship than becomes a Constitutional Monarch'.[87] Perhaps the temptations offered by the exercise of executive power had corrupted him, as the Fox family feared it corrupted all men. It is in the autumn of 1835 and spring of 1836 that the first serious doubts about France's good intentions creep into Holland's writings.[88]

It was comforting in a sense that Talleyrand should share Holland's concern about the changing face of French politics. When de Broglie wrote to him to give the reasons for his resignation, Talleyrand immediately showed the letter to Holland with obvious sadness.[89] Lady Holland noted that 'M de Talleyrand grows thin, & looks wretched since the news of Broglie's resignation'.[90] The Holland House circle all hoped that changes in French domestic policy would have no repercussions in foreign affairs, but no one could be sure. Talleyrand's departure from the London embassy in 1834 removed another guarantee of Anglo-French cooperation. On all fronts, Louis Philippe seemed to prefer 'hum drum men'[91] to ministers of real character and worth. In particular, the Hollands watched the prospering careers of Thiers and Molé with dismay. Instructed by Talleyrand, they believed that the first was too suspicious of England and the second quite definitely too fond of Russia. Although de Broglie briefly returned to office after 1834, Holland's closest French friends played a smaller and smaller part in the formulation of French policy as the decade wore on.[92]

Although uncertainties grew after 1835, Holland never forsook the French alliance. Intimacy may have been lost, but contacts were carefully fostered on both sides. When the Duc de Nemours, Louis Philippe's second son, visited London, he

87. ibid., f 176; ibid., 26 Sept. 1835.

88. Add. MSS. 51871, ff 928-9; Holland's Political Journal, 29 Nov. 1835; and Add. MSS. 51548, f 183; Holland to Grey, 22 Feb. 1836.

89. Talleyrand to de Broglie, 10 Avril 1834; B.N. n.a. fr. 6363, f 421.

90. Lady Holland to Henry Fox, 11 April 1834; *Elizabeth, Lady Holland to her Son*, p.146.

91. Add. MSS. 51753, f 197; Holland to Henry Fox, 14 Nov. 1834.

92. Holland to Grey, April 1834; Grey MSS. Box 34; and Holland to H.S. Fox, 28 Feb. 1838; Bod. Eng. Lett. c 234, f 106.

was exhibited at Holland House.[93] More impressive still, the French king occasionally wrote long, personal letters to Holland excusing his conduct and evoking old friendships. Clearly the French put great weight on retaining Holland's sympathy. A letter of May 1837 is worth quoting at length to demonstrate the depths to which Louis Philippe was prepared to stoop to conquer:

> One of the greatest difficulties I experienced, was not to convince the French Nation of the advantages of peace, but to make them understand the real way of securing peace, & to reconcile their national feelings to the line of policy which I considered as the only one to avoid war. These feelings had been sadly wounded, the irritation was great, & the public mind was but too well prepared for the insidious insinuations of the press, & even for their violent & calomnious attacks against those who upheld the pacific system, & of course against me. This was the form & extent of my offence. But, my dear Lord, when I tell you in a confidential letter like this, que j'écris en me faisant la douce illusion d'être encore à Holland House, causant avec vous dans votre belle Bibliothèque, c'est que, au moins dans nos pays continentaux, peace is the real guardian of freedom & real Liberty. The law must end where war begins ... Vous dites, my Lord, que je suis toujours dans le juste milieu, et j'en conviens volontiers ... Under the present circumstances of the world, France and England have but one & the same interest, the preservation of Peace, the maintenance of the present Status quo, without losses or conquests for everyone, & the Independence & security of every state.'[94]

Sébastiani, Talleyrand's successor as ambassador, reported that when Holland received this letter, 'il a été touché et pénétré'.[95]

Following the same line of policy, the French government turned the Hollands' last visit to Paris, in 1838, into a triumphal tour. The post horses bringing them from Calais were not to be allowed to travel at more than three miles an hour for fear of upsetting Lady Holland.[96] Once in Paris, the

93. Lady Holland to Henry Fox, 29 Sept. 1835; *Elizabeth, Lady Holland to her Son*, p.158.
94. Add. MSS. 51524, ff 210-2; Louis Philippe to Holland, 28 May 1837.
95. Sébastiani to Mme. Adelaide, 10 Juillet 1837; B.N. n.a. fr. 12219, f 169.
96. S. Smith to Lady Grey, 15 Nov. 1838; *The Letters of Sydney Smith*, ii 674.

Queen flattered Lady Holland with so much attention that the latter began to live up to her reputation as 'the only really undisputed monarchy in Europe'.[97] Holland himself was welcomed to the Tuileries by Louis Philippe for long conversations. Predictably, the Hollands were 'charmed with their stay in Paris'.[98] On meeting Molé again,[99] he was found to be less frighteningly pro-Russian than they had imagined, and all their old admiration for Louis Philippe was rekindled:

> What a clever fellow he is! It would be wrong in a Whig to laud a King for too much proficiency in the talent of government, but certainly one talks with no man in this country and few in any, whose conversation convinces one more that he is qualified to be the Minister of a great nation.[100]

To Palmerston and his friends, the Hollands' reception in Paris was simply the price that the French King paid to have a mouthpiece within the English Cabinet itself. It seemed that Holland's naivety or wilfulness prevented him from seeing the danger of becoming a French puppet. Close relations with the leading men of other countries can be of great diplomatic convenience, but they can all too easily be construed as stopping just short of the treasonable. The Hollands would have fiercely rebutted these charges. They were aware of and deplored the increasingly repressive nature of the Orléanist régime. Quite simply, however, the Anglo-French entente had been shown to be successful in Belgium and partially so in Spain and Portugal. Until France publicly demonstrated, by some overt action, that the old understanding was at an end, there could be no reason for precipitating that event. Even if Louis Philippe could no longer be held up as a model constitutionalist, all alternative allies were worse. Old friendships had to be balanced against Palmerstonian mistrust.

Long acquaintance was not the only factor to be thrown

---

97. Lady Granville to Lady Carlisle, Sept. 1838; *The Letters of Harriet, Lady Granville*, ii 270-1.

98. Princess Lieven to Grey, 27 Oct. 1838; *The Grey-Lieven Correspondence*, iii 279-80.

99. The Hollands had met Molé for the first time in England, in 1802.

100. *The Chronicles of Holland House*, p.246.

into the scales, however. Holland insisted on playing his old game of always setting one line of policy against the alternatives, and, on this count, the French alliance remained the best option because the Russians remained damnable. The Emperor Nicholas I, 'if not on the verge of Madness which is possible, has adopted from calculation a more entirely Muscovite policy than he has hitherto avowed'.[101] According to Lady Holland, the Russian Court was full of 'great hoydens full of practical jokes & gigglings',[102] and she could even feel sympathy with Princess Lieven when she was recalled home to Petersburg.[103] Poland remained, as Lafayette reminded Holland, 'la barrière de la civilization de l'Europe'.[104] The brutal suppression of the Polish national rising by the Russians in 1831 emphasised once again that no real alternative ally lay to the east of the Rhine. When Prince Adam Czartoryski, the Polish leader, arrived in London as a refugee, he was immediately taken up by Talleyrand and the Hollands. He was found to be 'interesting & melancoly'.[105] The Polish disaster convinced Holland that a liberal counter-statement by France and England in Western Europe was absolutely essential. No suspicion of France could overcome this priority.

Although geographical factors made Poland a very different proposition from Spain, Portugal or Belgium, Holland saw no reason why it should not provide another arena for Anglo-French intervention. According to Holland House and its French friends, 'il ne faudrait rien moins que l'accord et la fermeté des deux gouvernements pour empecher que la barrière polonaise ne soit anéanti par la despotisme et la vengeance des russes'.[106] In June 1831, Czartoryski formally applied to the French and British governments for assistance.

---

101. Add. MSS. 51754, f 211; Holland to Henry Fox, 26 Nov. 1835.

102. Lady Holland to Henry Fox, 1 June 1841; *Elizabeth, Lady Holland to her Son*, p.191.

103. ibid., 28 July 1835; ibid., p.157.

104. Add. MSS. 51635, f 213; Lafayette to Holland, 31 May 1832.

105. Add. MSS. 51868, f 272; Holland's Political Journal, 27 Dec. 1831; see also Lady Holland to Henry Fox, 20 Jan. 1832; *Elizabeth, Lady Holland to her Son*, p.127.

106. Add. MSS. 51635, f 202; Lafayette to Holland, 23 Jan. 1831; see also Add. MSS. 51717, f 117-18; Flahault to Holland, 11 May 1831.

A month later, the Cabinet discussed a proposal from Talleyrand that Anglo-French mediation should be offered, but only Holland and Carlisle supported the idea.[107] Palmerston and Melbourne were full of sympathy for the Poles, but were clear that any such intervention must lead to war with Russia, and this could not be contemplated in the fraught domestic circumstances of 1831. Such a view to Holland was 'idle squeamishness ... if not sheer pusillanimity & impudence'.[108] In August, Holland argued alone in Cabinet that Czartoryski should be officially recognised as the leader of a Polish provisional government, whatever the consequences might be, and that Russia would not dare to confront the military power of England and France in combination.[109] His colleagues were not convinced. In their view, Holland's isolation on the Polish question only added to the general idiosyncrasy of Holland House in foreign affairs.

It was even more strange to find the Hollands at one and the same time condemning Russian actions in Poland and supporting them in the near east, but, as Princess Lieven always remembered, even in her frostiest encounters with Holland House,[110] they had consigned Turkey to an even lower circle of Hell. The Sultan's government remained 'a vile & crumbling tyrrany'[111] to the Hollands, and in public speeches in February 1830, Holland announced that 'as a citizen of the world', he would welcome the arrival of the Russians in Constantinople.[112] His uncle could be quoted as holding the same view.[113] The recurrent crises surrounding the Turkish Empire in the 1830s allowed Holland to apply a set of priorities which had been worked out long in advance.[114] By applying the rule of always supporting the more civilised protagonist in any dispute, Russia was to be preferred to

107. Add. MSS. 51867, ff 20-2; Holland's Political Journal, 20 July 1831.
108. ibid., f 105; ibid., 26 Aug. 1831.
109. ibid., ibid.
110. Princess Lieven to A. Benckendorff, Nov. 1830; *The Letters of Dorothea, Princess Lieven*, p.276.
111. Add. MSS. 51754, f 129; Holland to Henry Fox, 31 July 1835.
112. *Parl. Deb.*, 4 Feb. 1830; vol. XCIX, 420-4.
113. ibid., 12 Feb. 1830; ibid., 424-7.
114. See above, Chapter Eight.

Turkey, and France to both of them. Above all, nothing in the diplomacy over the Eastern Question must be allowed to threaten the Anglo-French entente.

Unlike Palmerston therefore, Holland held to the view that Britain really had no interests at stake in the area covered by the Turkish Empire. The anti-Russian press was too full of 'vague phrases'.[115] He was impressed by the unanimity of expert opinion that Russian control of Constantinople must threaten the overland route to India and the resilience of British trade over a wide area of the Middle East, but confessed that he retained 'doubts about both these propositions'.[116] The Byzantine Empire was cited as evidence that control of the Dardanelles did not imply control of the Mediterannean generally, although it might even so be prudent to keep this stretch of water out of exclusively Russian control.[117] In his Journal, Holland maintained a lofty indifference to the fate of Turkey which Palmerston found infuriating: 'We must not allow our disgust, natural as it may be, at Russian insolence & oppression in Poland to involve us in a war for interests which are either not really English, or are quite unattainable.'[118] There was no way in which a Foxite Whig could be moved 'by an enthusiastik preference of Mussulmen over Muscovites',[119] or vice versa. It was simply a contest between the unspeakable and the indescribable.

In the crisis which followed the reappearance of Russian influence in Constantinople with the Treaty of Unkiar Skelessi in 1833 therefore,[120] Holland remained calm. He could not share Palmerston's concern that British interests were being undermined, and he positively disliked the idea of any Anglo-Austrian intervention.[121] Rather than act, Holland hoped that Russia would be led to 'softening her language & restraining

115. Add. MSS. 51753, f 147; Holland to Henry Fox, 29 July 1834.

116. Add. MSS. 51754, f 229; ibid., 11 Dec. 1835.

117. Add. MSS. 51755, ff 56-7; Holland to Henry Fox, 18 March 1836; see also Holland to Ellice, 3 Nov. 1835; Ellice MSS. f 152.

118. Add. MSS. 51871, f 931; Holland's Political Journal, 30 Nov. 1835.

119. Holland to H.S. Fox, 28 Feb. 1838; Bod. MSS. Eng. Lett. c 234, f 107.

120. For a detailed discussion of this crisis, see M.S. Anderson, *The Eastern Question*.

121. Add. MSS. 51523, ff 53-4; Sir H. Taylor to Holland, 12 June 1833.

her impetuosity'.[122] Holland House simply refused to become involved in the bickerings of two barbaric powers in the eastern Mediterranean in these years, when so much was at stake in the west. Holland's belief that 'there is more reason & ... less mischief in inculcating distrust of the Muscovite than of the French',[123] illustrates his obsession with the Anglo-French entente as the basis of policy. So concerned was he that Turkish affairs must not be allowed to disrupt that understanding, that, if France began to show an interest in that area, Holland was prepared to argue the rather odd line that 'next to Austria, France always has been, is, & must be the country most interested in preventing Russian encroachment in that quarter'.[124] Even the French early sponsorship of Mehemet Ali in Egypt was not sinister.

Such attitudes merely convinced Palmerston that Holland was indeed a French puppet. His blindness to the real British interests bound up in the fate of the Turkish Empire was maddening, and it is hard not to sympathise with Palmerston's irritation. Quite simply, the eastern Mediterranean held little interest for Holland House. It was an area of irredeemable darkness. Western Europe alone offered hope and opportunity to liberals. The Anglo-French entente guaranteed that hope, and therefore, if anything was to be done about Turkey, Holland House insisted that London and Paris should act together. In discussing the disruptive behaviour of Mehemet Ali in 1833, whose claims for autonomy threatened Turkish control over at least Egypt, Palestine and Syria, Holland concluded that

> the French will ultimately have him, if we do not ... but they have constantly uniformly & openly offered to share with us, share & share alike, all influence at Constantinople or Alexandria & even pressed us to take the lead, & we have constantly held back – If we refuse to act jointly we cannot in reason or justice complain of their acting separately.[125]

122. Add. MSS. 51753, ff 62-3; Holland to Henry Fox, 31 Jan. 1834.
123. Add. MSS. 51869, ff 613-14; Holland's Political Journal, 14 June 1833.
124. Add. MSS. 51753, ff 58-9; Holland to Henry Fox, 21 Jan. 1834.
125. Add. MSS. 51869, f 589; Holland's Political Journal, 22 May 1833.

The Eastern Question brought together so many strands of Holland House thinking, namely a preference for the ideological struggles in the west to the strategic and commercial squabbles in the east; a marginal preference for Russia over Turkey, for Austria over both of these; and for France over the whole world. Not surprisingly, the fate of the Turkish Empire was the issue on which Palmerston and Holland fought each other in Cabinet unrelentingly.[126]

In 1839, renewed Russian pressure on Constantinople coupled with new claims presented by France's protégé, Mehemet Ali, produced a new crisis in the eastern Mediterranean which was to dominate the politics of Holland's last years. His views on the subject had not changed:

> I am sadly afraid that it has produced a temporary estrangement between us & France – God send it may be well & speedily healed ... You who know how much I love a French, & how much I hate a Holy or rather unholy, alliance & how very little value I set on Syria & such remote concerns ... will easily imagine that the steps which have been taken in that matter & yet more the consequences which may ensue, have given & still give me no little uneasiness.[127]

Holland wished to believe that his old friend Louis Philippe 'likes & means peace',[128] and that even Thiers was basically trustworthy.[129] Throughout the crisis of 1839-40, Holland's central purpose remained to discover a 'facilité à vivre at Paris and in London'.[130] To Palmerston, England had no choice but to resist either a French or a Russian preponderance at Constantinople. Their acrimonious and violent disagreement exhumed the ghosts of their Foxite or Canningite origins.

Even in 1840, Holland would not admit that there was anything in the Turkish situation that materially affected England. Russia's 'ambition is not so black nor so restless as it is painted & ... in very many respects her interests are rather

126. Add. MSS. 51755, ff 22-4; Holland to Henry Fox, 2 Feb. 1836.
127. Add. MSS. 51757, f 238; Holland to Henry Fox, 18 July 1830.
128. ibid., f 167; ibid., 14 Jan. 1840.
129. Add. MSS. 51548, f 251; Holland to Grey, 12 Oct. 1840.
130. Holland to Ellice, 20 July 1840; Ellice MSS. f 193.

associated than opposed to ours'.[131] Her predominance at
Constantinople since 1833 had not put an intolerable strain on
British interests. The French and Mehemet Ali were even less
worrying;

> As to Mehemet Ali, I own I think any conclusion without blows will
> be acceptable – I cannot I own think the way to keep Russia out of
> Constantinople, (where for the last 50 years I have heard she must
> come) is by embroiling the different branches of the Ottoman Empire
> together. If Mehemet pays tribute & furnishes contingents to support
> Constantinople against Christians, the integrity of the Empire is
> preserved, & what signifies his being hereditary or nominated Pasha
> to us – or his having more or less territory in his Pashalicks.[132]

Much of the territory to which Mehemet Ali now laid claim
had been his de facto for a number of years without harming
England.[133] It was comforting to the Hollands that Sébastiani,
coming to the end of his term as ambassador, was just as
alarmed that, in order to prevent either a Russian or an
Egyptian take-over at Constantinople, the Anglo-French
entente might be abandoned.[134] For Holland House, such a
prospect was appalling:

> A Holy Alliance against Egyptian Jacobinism & Rebels, for the
> purpose of raising the Crescent, & the introduction of Infidel perhaps
> Muscovite troops into Turkish provinces to preserve the
> independence & *integrity* of the Ottoman Empire, would be an
> anomaly in Politicks almost amounting to a Contradiction in terms &
> a solecism in language – but if it lead to estrangement & war with
> France, God knows it is no laughing matter – ... It is enough to make
> a dog (Turkish or Christian) sick to think of it.[135]

When the Cabinet decided to explore the possibility of joint
action with the French, Holland simply noted 'liberavi
animam meam'.[136]

In Palmerstonian circles, the Hollands' views on foreign
affairs had always seemed bizarre. Now, their indifference to

131. Add. MSS. 51757, ff 1-6; Holland to Henry Fox, 1 Jan. 1839.
132. ibid., ff 213-14; ibid., 22 May 1840.
133. Add. MSS. 51872, ff 1161-2; Holland's Political Journal, Oct. 1839.
134. Sébastiani to Mme. Adelaide, 27 Jan. 1840; B.N. n.a. fr. 12220, f 203.
135. Holland to Ebrington, 3 Aug. 1840; Fortescue MSS. 1262 M/FC 96.
136. Holland to Melbourne, 27 Sept. 1840; *Lord Melbourne's Papers*, pp. 483-4.

what were seen as fundamental British interests, seemed positively threatening. Holland's seeming weakness for 'that aged afrancesado freebooter, Mehemet Ali',[137] was to bring Palmerston to the point of resignation.[138] The possibility of Russian warships having free access to the Mediterranean, the threat to English exports posed by the industrial development of Odessa and its hinterland, and even the security of the overland route to India if Palestine and Syria fell into pro-French hands were all topics which Holland House would not or could not take seriously. The longstanding francophilism of the Hollands appeared to have finally driven them mad. To those who had always suspected that the Hollands were nothing more than unpaid French agents, their behaviour in the crisis of 1839-40 proved guilt beyond all reasonable doubt.

The Hollands' defence rested, as it had done for the whole decade, on how far their resilient belief in French good intentions was in fact justified. On the evidence of the private papers of the French foreign office, the Hollands certainly had a case. When Guizot, yet another old habitué of Holland House, replaced Sébastiani as ambassador in London in February 1840, his Instructions were couched in Holland House language. He was told: 'Les dispositions du Gouvernement du Roi à l'égard de la Grande Bretagne soit aussi bienveillantes, aussi conciliantes qu'à aucune autre époque.' With regard to the crisis in Turkey, Guizot was told that

> Deux pensées ont constamment présidé aux propositions qu'elle a successivement adressées a ses alliés; faire sortir, s'il se pouvait, de cette crise ... un état de choses qui, en plaçant la Porte sous la protectorat collectif de l'Europe, mit fin, par le fait, à un protectorat exclusif, consacré en faveur de la Russe par le traité d'Unkiar Skelessi; établir entre le Sultan et son puissant vassal [Mehemet Ali] des rapports par que un sentiment d'irritation défiante ne les maintient pas, l'un à l'égard de l'autre, dans une attitude d'hostilité toujours manaçantè pour le tranquillité du monde.[139]

137. Palmerston to Clarendon, 13 March 1840; *The Life and Letters of the Earl of Clarendon*, i 185.

138. Palmerston to ?, 27 July 1840; *The Life and Correspondence of Viscount Palmerston*, i 375.

139. *Instructions données à M. Guizot*, 19 Fevrier 1840; Quai d'Orsay *Angleterre* 654, ff 173-4. Two thoughts have constantly guided the propositions which France has

Sébastiani's replacement by Guizot at such a delicate moment in Anglo-French relations had given concern to Holland House, but in fact the new ambassador's despatches dealt in sentiments that Holland entirely shared.[140] In writing to Thiers, Louis Philippe expressed surprise and dismay to see the violence of the London press in its comments on French policy.[141] When Guizot took Talleyrand's and Sébastiani's place at the Holland House dinner table therefore, he also took over their concern for the survival of the Anglo-French entente.

As ever therefore, Holland was fortified in his pro-French views by confidence and intimacies that were denied most of his colleagues. In the almost public quarrel between Palmerston and Holland on the Eastern Question, which began in July 1840 and ended only with the latter's death in October, Holland was once again singular in his ideas, apparently eccentric and very informed. For four months, with some support from Clarendon and Lord John Russell, he fought Palmerston's wish to take a strong line in the eastern Mediterranean. As Lady Palmerston's letters suggest, his behaviour could be exasperating:

> He (Palmerston) has had a hard battle to fight with some of his Colleagues, Holland really quite foolish and superannuated, but with a name, and following, and dinners, and activity of proselitism that was quite extraordinary, very good friends in the main with P. but thinking it quite fair to have all this cabal against him, and underhand work, and putting all springs in motion *not* to get him out, but to make him yield his opinions; in short friendly, but just as he would in opposition, and more vicious, and kicking and biting.[142]

---

successively addressed to her allies; to derive from this crisis, if possible, a state of affairs which, in placing the Porte under the collective protection of Europe, terminates, by that fact, the exclusive protectorate enjoyed by Russia in the treaty of Unkiar Skelissi; and to establish between the Sultan and his powerful vassal [Mehemet Ali] relations by which a feeling of defiant irritation does not keep them, one to another, in an attitude of hostility, which is always menacing for the peace of the world.

140. Guizot to Thiers, 5 March 1840; B.N. n.a. fr. 20610, f 1; see also Guizot to Thiers, 10 March 1840; B.N. n.a. fr. 20610, ff 25-6.

141. Louis Philippe to Thiers, 26 June 1840; B.N. n.a. fr. 20611, ff 151-2.

142. Lady Palmerston to Lord Beauvale, 12 Oct. 1840; *The Letters of Lady Palmerston*, p.235.

The Palmerstons certainly had some grounds for complaint. Holland, who had never been overpunctillious in his observation of constitutional formalities, now strained them to the limit in his determination to stop any disruption of relations between London and Paris. Holland was systematically obstructive in Cabinet and a veritable fountain of indiscreet leakages. On more than one occasion in the summer and autumn of 1840, Palmerston had formally to complain to Melbourne that 'the talking at Holland House is irremediable'.[143] Holland was purveying Cabinet secrets 'to all who come near',[144] and 'les Diplomates s'imaginent, à entendre ses badinages et ses causeries, qu'il y a de grandes différences d'opinion dans le Cabinet'.[145] From his privileged position as Holland's confidant, Guizot was rather smugly able to report to Thiers: 'Je connaissais bien les dissentiments intérieurs du cabinets, (et) les efforts de Lord Holland et de Lord Clarendon pour faire prévaloir une politique analogue à la nôtre.[146] In fact, Holland followed with Guizot the same tactics that had worked so well with Talleyrand. On both occasions, only absolute frankness could save the Anglo-French entente. It was Holland's only countermove against what he suspected was an attempt by Palmerston to instigate an anti-French policy with the help of the Tories.[147] The only way to assure the French that the whole Melbourne government was not in fact slipping into Tory attitudes was to resurrect the idea of a second outlet for Anglo-French communication based on Holland House. It was this goal that justified the bending of the niceties of Cabinet government. When Holland died, in October 1840, the controversial reputation of Holland House politics was wholly undiminished.

143. Palmerston to Melbourne, 19 Sept. 1840; *Lord Melbourne's Papers*, pp. 477-8.

144. ibid., 16 Sept. 1840; ibid., pp. 475-6.

145. Lady Palmerston to Princess Lieven, 18 Sept. 1840; *Lettres de François Guizot et de la Princesse de Lieven*, ii 213.

146. Guizot to Thiers, 3 Avril 1840; B.N. n.a. fr. 20610, f 42; see also Guizot to Thiers, 1 Juin 1840; Quai d'Orsay *Angleterre* 655, f 85.

147. The Diary of Lady Clarendon, 5 Oct. 1840; *The Life and Letters of the Earl of Clarendon*, i 211.

Nor did Holland's actual demise put an end to debate. In December 1840, Thiers delivered a speech in which he extravagantly praised Holland as being so much the friend of France as to be almost the enemy of his own country.[148] It allowed a number of newspapers, which were currently evaluating Holland's career, to question his overall integrity. Guizot was compelled to spend much time in smoothing over the consequences of his leader's action. With or without the Thiers speech, however, the same questions would have arisen. Holland's whole career had been peppered with personal initiatives, some in line with official policy and some running counter to it. The drama of 1840 merely accentuated a long-standing theme. In Holland's old-fashioned turn of thinking, cabinet responsibility was not the highest of political rules, and ministers who dissented from majority decisions should send the sovereign memoranda explaining their position.[149] Equally, on eighteenth-century principles, foreign affairs for Holland were international arrangements promoted by like-minded gentlemen and not the narrow pursuance of national interest. Guizot, like his predecessors, became 'a treasure',[150] and, as the Austrian Ambassador sourly put it, went every day to Holland House 'to get his tears dried'.[151] As in so much else, the Hollands' eighteenth-century ideas conflicted with nineteenth-century practice.

With Holland there died that internationalist system of politics, based on polished and well-tended friendships that had become a Fox family trait. No one in the early nineteenth century could match the depth and breadth of his foreign experiences. They excited both respect and envy. 'Francophile' and 'Esplanado' were used both descriptively and as terms of abuse. Many believed that the thin line between being cosmopolitan and becoming un-English had been overstepped. None of this criticism alarmed the

148. Palmerston to Princess Lieven, 10 Dec. 1840; *The Lieven-Palmerston Correspondence*, p.201; see also Guizot to Lady Holland, 3 Jan. 1841; *Greville*, iv 382 n.2.
149. Cabinet Minute of Dissent, 8 July 1840; *The Life and Letters of the Earl of Clarendon*, i 196-7.
150. Add. MSS. 51757, f 189-90; Holland to Henry Fox, 31 March 1840.
151. Sir C. Webster, *The Foreign Policy of Lord Palmerston*, p.710.

Hollands, however. Proudly adopting his uncle's title of 'citizen of the world', Holland also took over his views on Europe. From 1789 onwards, every country in Europe was involved in the battle between constitutional and autocratic values. A Foxite Whig therefore found foreign liberals more likely allies than English Tories. Holland House was a staging post for a liberal mafia tunnelling beneath European governments. It offered the English and European refugee the sympathy and entertainment that warmed old loyalties back to life.

The influence of Holland House on policy was rarely directly applied. For most of his career, Holland was out of office and often out of England. Only between 1830 and 1840 was Holland explicitly able to steer the Anglo-French entente through Palmerstonian squalls. It is perhaps important that no evaluation of the consequences of Holland's death appears in Guizot's despatches. Rather Holland House operated the less tangible system of influence based on the salon, less easily documented and defined. It was the only English equivalent of a style of politics that Europeans knew well. People met, dined and talked. Ideas were exchanged and new contacts made. Values were found to be held in common and that was comforting. It was not a world of career diplomats or bureaucrats, but rather that of an international aristocracy, which despised frontiers and passports, safe in the belief that its kind could be found anywhere in Europe. The impact of Holland House was assessed correctly by Guizot in a letter to Princess Lieven: 'Politiquement, je regrette beaucoup Lord Holland. Il n'avait autant d'influence que j'aurais voulu, mais il en avait plus qu'on n'en convenait. La désapprobation de Holland House gênait beaucoup, même quand elle n'empêchait pas.'[152]

152. Guizot to Princess Lieven, 6 Oct. 1840; *Lettres de F. Guizot et de la Princesse de Lieven*, ii 271.

Conclusion

In July 1841, the *Edinburgh Review* tried to sum up the importance of Holland House, and the result was one of the most famous passages in Whig historiography. The *Review* noted that anyone who had known the House in its greatest days

> will recollect how many men who have guided the politics of Europe – who have moved great assemblies by reason and eloquence – who have put life into bronze or canvass, or who have left for posterity things so written as it shall not willingly let them die – were there mixed with all that was loveliest and gayest in the society of the most splendid of capitals. They will remember the singular character which belonged to that circle, in which every talent and accomplishment, every art and science, had its place. They will remember how the last debate was discussed in one corner, and the last comedy of Scribe in another; while Wilkie gazed with modest admiration on Reynolds' Baretti; while Mackintosh turned over Thomas Aquinas to verify a quotation; while Talleyrand related his conversations with Barras at the Luxembourg or his ride with Lannes over the field of Austerlitz.[1]

It was precisely in this diversity of topic and personality that the *salon* as a species of social life took root and flourished. Holland House society represented a self-conscious attempt to bring the powerful and the best together for their mutual edification and enjoyment. It was meritocratic, inegalitarian and held mediocrity in abhorrence.

1. *Edinburgh Review*, July 1841; vol. LXXIII, p.560.

There was no reason for a *salon* to be a comfortable place. Some kinds of talent had to be cosseted, but most responded to provocation. No one loved Lady Holland except her husband, but no one ignored her. Lord Holland was kinder, but was equally dismissive of the commonplace. Their children were the principal victims of these attitudes, but many of their guests were racked as well. In most of the memoirs recalling Holland House, what is regretted is the unique society found there rather than its owners in particular.[2] The Hollands would have probably accepted this judgment. Confident in the affection that they had for each other, they saw their function as intellectual impressarios, coaxing and taunting talent, dominating and guiding careers. The Christian virtues had everything to recommend them except that they made for very dull evenings. Even in death, Lady Holland could not resist the temptation to score points. According to Samuel Rogers, she left 'to Lady Palmerston her collection of fans which though it was a very valuable and curious one, seems to me a little like making fun of that super fine, fine lady'.[3]

Holland House accordingly betrayed many of the characteristics of the self-conscious élite. There was a group loyalty which Lady Holland guarded and defined. Some like John Allen and Samuel Rogers were able to cope with this imperiousness. Others like Byron and Brougham felt compelled to break away, because the terms of membership were too high. For the aspiring poet or politician, Holland House, in true *salon* style, was the entrée to a career. In the early stages of such a progress, however, it would have required a close attendance and a deferential manner. George Canning and others could never bow quite low enough. It was no place for the squeamish or those whose personalities were too vulnerable to be dissected. The history of Holland House is peppered with quarrels and reconciliations, with the latter being quite often as pleasurable and dramatic as the former.

The whole pattern of dining and quarrelling was imitative

2. *The Chronicles of Holland House*, p.355.
3. *Samuel Rogers and his Contemporaries*, ii 272-3.

of the great European *salons*. The Hollands followed Paris in
trying to make their House a channel of patronage, an arena
for political discussion and an echo-chamber for gossip and
intrigue all at the same time. There was an incurably foreign
air about Holland House. In addition to the French doctors,
Spanish servants and Italian tutors, which formed a constant
element in Lady Holland's entourage, and the endless flow of
refugees and ambassadors, the whole project of entertaining
great men together was continental rather than English. The
London Season of course saw entertainment and the mingling
of men, but Holland House pre-eminently set out to entertain
in order to influence. The distinguishing feature of the *salon*
was that it set out to make a positive impact on those that
attended it. The Hollands had such an intention.

The moulding of opinion always took place within a specific
intellectual context. *Salons* traditionally had individual
characters and atmospheres, radical, pious, freethinking or
conservative. In the case of Holland House, the *table d'hôte* of
ideas was unvarying. For English politics, there was the Foxite
obsession with the dominance of executive power, which had
been again and again intruded into the careers of Holland and
his uncle. Slaves, Catholics, Dissenters and Whigs had all
been its victims. The Hollands met many kings and almost all
of them were found wanting. The onrush of centralised power
had to be contained in constitutional channels or it would
surge uncontrollably. This is the theme which links the
tribulations of Charles James Fox in 1784 with the relief of his
nephew in 1832. As Holland endlessly intoned the praises of
the Whigs of the 1790s, like a battlefield roll of honour, for the
benefit of the young politicians of the 1820s and 1830s, he kept
alive and handed on a core of belief. Disraeli, a rather sour
observer of Whig society, thought Holland's death important,
because 'it breaks up an old clique of pure Whiggery'.[4]

For European politics, Holland House simply generalised
the English theme. As Foxites fought autocratic tendencies in
England, so liberal nationalists fought autocratic emperors in
Europe. The struggle was essentially the same, as Fox had

4. B. Disraeli to S. Disraeli, 22 Oct. 1840; *The Life of Benjamin Disraeli*, ii 95.

always said it was. Foscolo and Czartoryski, Palmella and Mendizabel came to Holland House with sad tales of persecution. In response, the Hollands could offer sympathy and instruction to 'all Europe', since it was 'desirous of enjoying a representative Govt.'.[5] They also saw English and European problems as different engagements in the same war, and felt happiest when drawing comparisons and discussing the politics of one in terms of the other. The Hollands' journeyings, friendships and linguistic skills made them uniquely qualified to do so. The obvious danger that too great a concern with Europe might lead to accusations of indifference to British interests was completely unheeded. The francophilism of the Hollands was one aspect of the belief that the nature of the régimes in London and Paris could blight or guarantee liberal prospects over a wide area of Europe. At all times, the overriding motivation in assessing points of foreign policy was ideological. In their view, a lofty aloofness towards the Continent was not possible. The events of 1789 had made England firmly into a European state.

Over both domestic and foreign politics, the shadow of Charles James Fox was everywhere. So great was his authority that it guaranteed his nephew a place in politics in the next generation. While Holland filled the Journals of the House of Lords with lone protests, while his wife relayed Cabinet decisions over dessert, and while both of them saw no harm in conducting a family foreign policy alongside that of the elected government, the notoriety of these activities never endangered them. In the Cabinet-making of 1806 and 1830, Holland was unavoidable because he was Fox's heir. The name was a shield against penalties. For three generations, the Fox family had never shown themselves to be either rigorous in their moral attitudes or punctilious in their dealings with others, but equally, the name that Holland carried gave the Whig party of the early nineteenth century a core of belief and a reading of the immediate past which Macaulay and Mackintosh turned into history. The long friendship between

5. Lady Holland to Henry Fox, 19 March 1821; *Elizabeth, Lady Holland to her Son*, p.3.

Holland and Grey stood at the centre of that 'pure Whiggery' of which Disraeli spoke. Holland was his uncle's creature, expounded his views and, cocooned in his mantle, was invulnerable to the comments and criticisms thrown against him.

The weight of family tradition contributed to the very odd intermingling of old myths and new ideas that constituted Holland House conversation. Their involvement with the *Edinburgh Review* and the enduring presence of John Allen guaranteed a lively interest in the concept of progress and movement in society. Indeed, the Hollands preened themselves that they, unlike most Tories, were not unaware of or uninformed about the development of an industrial society from an agricultural community. Although bored by fiscal policy and the detail of government, they yet claimed to appreciate the pace of change. At the same time, the politics of Holland House was anchored in the events of 1784 and 1789. It peddled an eighteenth-century deism and its literary preferences were for the Augustans. All of this must have appeared somewhat old-fashioned in the Romantic or Evangelical world after 1815. There was no hope that a Wilberforce could inspire the Hollands with 'a call to seriousness'. Even the cosmopolitan nature of Holland House society more strongly resembled the eighteenth than the nineteenth century, when fierce nationalisms made contact across frontiers less easy. Greville, the diarist, called it the 'house of old Europe'.[6] Interested and concerned as they were with the problems of the nineteenth century, many of the Hollands' judgments had been determined before that century was born. To find Macaulay and Talleyrand at the same dinner table points the contrast.

Lord Holland died on 22 October 1840. His wife noted: 'This wretched day closes all happiness, refinement and hospitality within the walls of Holland House.'[7] The letters of condolence which she and John Allen received fill a whole volume of the Holland House manuscripts.[8] The *salon* closed

6. *Sovereign Lady*, p.298.
7. *Elizabeth, Lady Holland to her Son*, p.189.
8. Add. MSS. 52174.

abruptly. For the remaining five years of her life, Lady Holland moved into London, and only revisited Holland House on very rare occasions. Her taste for social success was not entirely extinguished, one of her last actions being the introducing of Palmerston to Thiers, but, with so many of her old friends disappearing, there was little incentive to maintain the tradition. John Allen's death in 1843 was a particularly severe blow. The last years were spent in increasing isolation and nostalgic remembrance of the past. Until her own death in 1845, Lady Holland was as conscious as many of her contemporaries that the closing up of Holland House represented the end of a particular style of life.

Much of Holland House was destroyed by enemy action during the Second World War. What remains has been turned into a youth hostel. The orangery now houses a series of improvised teashops and the lawns provide opportunities for sunbathing, impromptu cricket matches and the exercising of dogs. As visible signs of the democracy that they so deeply suspected, it is not hard to imagine what the Hollands might have said about such developments. In the Whig world, intelligence and civilised values were by definition restricted to a few, who might in due course hope to influence others, but who for the moment must act alone. Holland House society was clever and smug, intellectually concerned with everything, if too often oblivious of the detail in any problem. People went there to show their paces and to be brilliantly entertained. One might be affronted, but one would never be bored. Charles Greville, often a severe critic of Holland House, described it as follows, in 1832:

> Such is the social despotism of this strange house, which presents an odd mixture of luxury and constraint, of enjoyment physical and intellectual with an alloy of désagréments ... Though everyone who goes there finds something to abuse or to ridicule in the mistress of the house ... all continue to go; all like it more or less; and whenever, by the death of either it shall come to an end, a vacuum will be made in society which nothing will supply ... the world will suffer by the loss.[9]

9. *Sovereign Lady*, p.298.

Holland House had a unique position in early nineteenth-century society. Full of crankiness, history and good sense, it was one of the most exciting places in London.

Bibliography

This study was based on the Holland House manuscripts held in the British Library. They represent an exhaustive coverage of Lord and Lady Holland's correspondence and journals. In some cases, the references given are taken from a catalogue which is still provisional.

(a) *MANUSCRIPT SOURCES*

British Library

(i) Holland House MSS. (Add. MSS. 51520-52254) The Letters and Journals of Henry Richard Vassall Fox and his wife, Elizabeth, 3rd Lord and Lady Holland.

In particular, the following volumes have proved most useful:

Add. MSS.

51520-5 Letters to and from George IV, William IV, Queen Caroline, Duke and Duchess of York, and Louis Philippe.

51530-2 Letters to and from Lord Auckland, Lord Grenville and Lord Robert Spencer.

51544-7 Letters to and from Lord and Lady Grey.

51569 Letters to and from Sir F. Burdett and Sir J. Hobhouse.

51577-8 Letters to and from the 6th Earl and Countess of Carlisle.

51584 Letters to and from George Tierney.

51598 Letters to and from George Canning.

51623-8 Papers relating to Spanish affairs.

51635 Letters to and from Talleyrand and Lafayette.

51644 Letters to and from F. Horner, Jeffrey and John Murray.

51653 Letters to and from Sir J. Mackintosh.

51656-7 'An Account of Holland House' by Sir J. Mackintosh.

51661-4 Letters to and from the 6th Duke of Bedford.

51677 Letters to and from Lord John Russell.

51682 Letters to and from the Lansdowne family.

51747 Letters to and from the Comte de Flahault.

51730 Correspondence between Lord and Lady Holland.

51731-43 Correspondence between Lord Holland and Caroline Fox.

51744-7 Correspondence between Lady Holland and Caroline Fox.

51748-57 Correspondence between Lord Holland and his son Henry.

51795-6 Letters to and from the 2nd Earl and Countess of Upper Ossory.

51819 Papers relating to Jamaican affairs.

51820 Letters to and from William Wilberforce.

51867-72 Lord Holland's Political Journals.

52172-3 Correspondence between John Allen and Lord and Lady Holland.

52180-1 Correspondence between John Allen and Sydney Smith, F. Horner, J. Wishaw, the 8th Earl of Lauderdale and Lord Jeffrey.

(ii) The Fox Papers. (Add. MSS. 47559-47601) Papers and Correspondence of Charles James Fox, (1749-1806).

(iii) The Morley Papers. (Add. MSS. 48226) Papers and Correspondence of the 1st and 2nd Earls of Morley.

(iv) The Dropmore Papers. (Add. MSS. 58950-2) Correspondence between Lord Holland and Lord Grenville.

All Souls College, Oxford
Vaughan MSS. Papers and Correspondence of Sir Charles Vaughan, (1774-1849).

Bedfordshire Public Record Office
Whitbread MSS. Papers and Correspondence of Samuel Whitbread, (1758-1815).

Belfast Public Record Office
Anglesey MSS. Papers and Correspondence of Henry William Paget, 1st Marquess of Anglesey, (1768-1854).

Bodleian Library, Oxford
(i) MS.Eng.Lett. c 65, c 144, c 234, c 238, d 97, d 234, d 238, e 48, e 100.

(ii) Burdett MSS. Correspondence of Sir Francis Burdett, (1770-1844).

(iii) Wilberforce MSS. Papers and Correspondence of William Wilberforce, (1759-1833).

(iv) Heber MSS. The Correspondence of Reginald Heber, (1783-1826).

Castle Howard
Castle Howard MSS. Papers and Correspondence of Frederick Howard, 5th Earl of Carlisle, (1748-1825).

Cornell University Library
Dean MSS. Correspondence of the Marquis de Lafayette, (1757-1834).

Devon Public Record Office
Fortescue MSS. Correspondence of Hugh Fortescue, 1st Earl Fortescue, (1753-1841).

Durham University Library
Grey MSS. Correspondence and Papers of Charles, 2nd Earl Grey, (1764-1845).

Hampshire Public Record Office
Tierney MSS. Papers and Correspondence of George Tierney, (1761-1830).

Hertfordshire Public Record Office
Lytton MSS. Correspondence of the 1st Earl Lytton, (1803-1873).

Liverpool University Library
Blanco White MSS. Correspondence of Joseph Blanco White, (1775-1841).

Manchester College, Oxford
Shepherd MSS. Correspondence of William Shepherd, (1768-1847).

National Library of Scotland, Edinburgh
Ellice MSS. Correspondence of Edward Ellice, (1781-1863).

Paris
(i) *Bibliothèque Nationale*
Sébastiani MSS. Correspondence of Comte François Sébastiani, (1772-1851).

Thiers MSS. Correspondence of Adolphe Thiers, (1797-1877).
(ii) *Quai d'Orsay*
Reports and correspondence of Talleyrand, Sébastiani and Guizot while ambassadors in London, 1830-40.

Staffordshire Public Record Office
Sutherland MSS. Correspondence of George Granville Leveson Gower, 2nd Duke of Sutherland, (1786-1861).

University College, London
Brougham MSS. Papers and Correspondence of Henry, 1st Baron Brougham and Vaux, (1778-1868).

West Suffolk Public Record Office
Grafton MSS. Correspondence of Augustus Fitzroy, 3rd Duke of Grafton, (1735-1811).

(b) *PRINTED PRIMARY SOURCES*
(i) *Pamphlets*

Lord Holland, *A Dream* (London 1818).
Lord Holland, *A Letter to the Rev. Dr Shuttleworth, Warden of New College* (London 1827).
Lord Holland, *Speech of Lord Holland in the House of Lords on the Second Reading of the Bill for the Repeal of the Corporation and Test Acts* (London 1828).
Anon., *A Letter to the Right Hon. Lord Holland occasioned by the Petition from the General Body of the Dissenting Ministers of London for the relief of the Roman Catholics* (London 1829).
A Pupil of Canning, *The Irish Church. A Letter to the Rt. Hon. Lord Holland* (London 1836).
Lord Holland, *Sketch of a Constitution for the Kingdom of Naples suggested in 1815 to the Duca di Gallo by the late Lord Holland* (London 1848).

(ii) *Books*

Lord Anglesey, *Life and Letters of the 1st Marquess of Anglesey* (London 1961).
F. Bamford, *The Journal of Mrs Arbuthnot* (London 1950).
A. Aspinall, *The Correspondence of Charles Arbuthnot* (London 1941).
A. Aspinall, *Three Early Nineteenth Century Diaries* (London 1952).
A. Aspinall, *The Formation of Canning's Ministry* (London 1937).

A. Aspinall, *Lady Bessborough and her Family Circle* (London 1940).

Lord Brougham, *Statesmen of the Time of George III* (London 1843).

Lord Broughton, *Recollections of a Long Life* (London 1909).

R. Weigall, *The Correspondence of Lord Burghesh, 1808-1840* (London 1912).

L. Marchand, *Byron's Letters and Journals* (London 1973).

R. Prothero, *The Works of Lord Byron* (London 1901).

Mrs Hardcastle, *The Life of John, Lord Campbell* (London 1881).

Sir G. Leveson Gower, *The Letters of Lady Harriet Cavendish, 1796-1809* (London 1940).

A. Aspinall, *The Letters of Princess Charlotte* (London 1949).

Sir H. Maxwell, *The Life and Letters of the Earl of Clarendon* (London 1913).

Cloncurry, *Personal Recollections of the Life and Times of Lord Cloncurry* (Dublin 1849).

J. Beard, *The Letters and Journals of J. Fenimore Cooper* (Cambridge 1960).

Sir H. Maxwell, *The Creevey Papers* (London 1903).

L. Jennings, *The Correspondence and Diaries of J.W. Croker* (London 1885).

Prince Radzivill, *Memoirs of the Duchesse de Dino* (London 1909).

F. Bickley, *The Diaries of Sylvester Douglas* (London 1928).

S. Reid, *The Life and Letters of the 1st Earl of Durham, 1792-1840* (London 1906).

S. Leslie, *The Letters of Mrs Fitzherbert* (London 1944).

J. Greig, *The Farington Diary* (London 1922).

Lord J. Russell, *The Memorials and Correspondence of Charles James Fox* (London 1853-7).

C. Greville, *A Journal of the Reigns of George IV, William IV and Queen Victoria* (London 1888).

Countess of Stafford, *Leaves from the Diary of Henry Greville* (London 1905).

Lord F. Leveson Gower, *Bygone Years* (London 1905).

Lady Granville, *The Letters of Lord Granville Leveson Gower* (London 1916).

F. Leveson Gower, *The Letters of Harriet, Countess Granville* (London 1894).

Historical Manuscripts Commission, 30 *Fortescue IX and X. 76 Bathurst*

T. Taylor, *The Autobiography and Memoirs of Benjamin Haydon* (London 1926).

E. Herries, *A Memoir of J.C. Herries* (London 1880).

Lord Holland, *Some Account of the Life and Writings of Lope Felix de Vega Carpio* (London 1806).

Lord Holland, *Foreign Reminiscences* (London 1850).

Lord Holland, *Memoirs of the Whig Party during my Time* (London 1852-4).

Lord Holland, *Further Memoirs of the Whig Party* (London 1905).

Lord Ilchester, *The Spanish Journal of Elizabeth, Lady Holland* (London 1910).

Lord Ilchester, *Elizabeth, Lady Holland to her Son, 1821-1845* (London 1946).

Lord Ilchester, *The Journal of Henry Edward Fox, 4th Lord Holland* (London 1923).

J. Adeane, *The Girlhood of Maria Josepha Holroyd* (London 1896).

L. Horner, *The Memoirs and Correspondence of Francis Horner*(London 1843).

Lady Leconfield & J. Gore, *Three Howard Sisters* (London 1955).

The Autobiography of Leigh Hunt (London 1860).

L. Melville, *The Huskisson Papers* (London 1931).

S. Williams, *The Journal of Washington Irving* (Harvard 1931).

Jovellanos, *Cartas de Jovellanos y Lord Vassall Holland sobre la querra de la Independencia* (Madrid 1908-11).

Lady Caroline Lamb, *Glenarvon* (London 1816).

G. Le Strange, *Correspondence of Princess Lieven and Earl Grey* (London 1890).

L. Robinson, *Letters of Dorothea, Princess Lieven 1812-1834* (London 1902).

Lord Sudley, *The Lieven-Palmerston Correspondence, 1828-1856* (London 1943).

J. Schlumberger, *Lettres de François Guizot et de la Princesse de Lieven* (Paris 1964).

Mrs H. Wyndham, *The Correspondence of Sarah, Lady Lyttelton* (London 1912).

Earl Lytton, *The Life of Edward Bulwer, 1st Lord Lytton* (London 1913).

G.O. Trevelyan, *The Life and Letters of Lord Macaulay* (London 1959).

L. Sanders, *Lord Melbourne's Papers* (London 1889).

W. Torrens, *Memoirs of Lord Melbourne* (London 1890).

W. Dowden, *The Letters of Thomas Moore* (London 1964).

E. Ashley, *The Life and Correspondence of Lord Palmerston* (London 1879).

T. Lever, *The Letters of Lady Palmerston* (London 1957).

Parliamentary Debates.

E. Peel, *Recollections of Lady Georgiana Peel* (London 1920).

P. Clayden, *Samuel Rogers and his Contemporaries* (London 1889).
J. Hale, *The Italian Journal of Samuel Rogers* (London 1956).
D. McCarthy, *Lady John Russell, A Memoir* (London 1910).
G. Blakiston, *Lord William Russell and his Wife* (London 1972).
C. Price, *The Letters of Richard Brinsley Sheridan* (Oxford 1966).
P. Nowell Smith, *The Letters of Sydney Smith* (Oxford 1953).
Duc de Broglie, *Memoirs of the Prince de Talleyrand* (London 1891).
  The *Edinburgh Review*.
  The *Quarterly Review*.

(c) *PRINTED SECONDARY SOURCES*

A. Aspinall, *Lord Brougham and the Whig Party* (London 1972).
M. Brock, *The Great Reform Act* (London 1973).
J. Cannon, *Parliamentary Reform* (Cambridge 1972).
J. Clive, *Thomas Babington Macaulay* (London 1973).
J. Derry, *Charles James Fox* (London 1972).
W. Hinde, *George Canning* (London 1973).
Lord Ilchester, *The Chronicles of Holland House, 1820-1900* (London 1937).
W. Jones, *Prosperity Robinson* (London 1967).
S. Keppel, *Sovereign Lady* (London 1974).
E. Tangye Lean, *The Napoleonists* (Oxford 1970).
K. Miller, *Cockburn's Millennium* (London 1975).
A. Mitchell, *The Whigs in Opposition 1815-1830* (Oxford 1967).
L. Mitchell, *Charles James Fox and the Disintegration of the Whig Party* (Oxford 1971).
W. Monypenny & G. Buckle, *The Life of Benjamin Disraeli* (London 1910-20).
J. Prest, *Lord John Russell* (London 1972).
J. Ridley, *Lord Palmerston* (London 1970).
L. Sanders, *The Holland House Circle* (London 1908).
Lady Seymour, *The Pope of Holland House* (London 1906).
E. Smith, *Whig Principles and Party Politics* (Manchester 1976).
D. Stuart, *Dearest Bess* (London 1955).
E. Vincent, *Ugo Foscolo* (Cambridge 1953).
Sir C. Webster, *The Foreign Policy of Lord Palmerston* (London 1951).
P. Ziegler, *William IV* (London 1971).

Index